Who Owns Haiti?

UNIVERSITY PRESS OF FLORIDA

Florida A&M University, Tallahassee
Florida Atlantic University, Boca Raton
Florida Gulf Coast University, Ft. Myers
Florida International University, Miami
Florida State University, Tallahassee
New College of Florida, Sarasota
University of Central Florida, Orlando
University of Florida, Gainesville
University of North Florida, Jacksonville
University of South Florida, Tampa
University of West Florida, Pensacola

Who Owns Haiti?

PEOPLE, POWER, AND SOVEREIGNTY

Edited by Robert Maguire and Scott Freeman

Foreword by Amy Wilentz

UNIVERSITY PRESS OF FLORIDA

Gainesville / Tallahassee / Tampa / Boca Raton

Pensacola / Orlando / Miami / Jacksonville / Ft. Myers / Sarasota

22 21 20 19 18 17   6 5 4 3 2 1

First cloth printing, 2017
First paperback printing, 2017

Library of Congress Cataloging-in-Publication Data
Names: Maguire, Robert E. (Robert Earl), 1948– editor. | Freeman, Scott (lecturer), editor.
Title: Who owns Haiti? : people, power, and sovereignty / edited by Robert
Maguire and Scott Freeman ; foreword by Amy Wilentz.
Description: Gainesville : University Press of Florida, 2017. | Includes
bibliographical references and index.
Identifiers: LCCN 2016035948 | ISBN 9780813062266 (cloth) | ISBN 9780813064598 (pbk.)
Subjects: LCSH: Haiti—Politics and government—1986– | Self-determination,
National—Haiti. | Haiti—History.
Classification: LCC F1928.2 .W47 2017 | DDC 972.94—dc23
LC record available at https://lccn.loc.gov/2016035948

The University Press of Florida is the scholarly publishing agency for the State University
System of Florida, comprising Florida A&M University, Florida Atlantic University,
Florida Gulf Coast University, Florida International University, Florida State University,
New College of Florida, University of Central Florida, University of Florida, University
of North Florida, University of South Florida, and University of West Florida.

University Press of Florida
15 Northwest 15th Street
Gainesville, FL 32611-2079
http://upress.ufl.edu

Contents

Illustrations

Figures

Tables

Foreword

Amy Wilentz

Ever since I first began thinking about Haiti, the question this book addresses has been a focus of my investigations, no matter which book or story I was working on. Ownership is the core question at the heart of Haitian and, indeed, of all African American history. Of course the question of sovereignty is paramount for any entity that calls itself a state, but there is also an undercurrent in Haitian domestic politics and in foreign policy toward Haiti that is constantly posing the foundational question for the Haitian nation. That question is not just who owned and who owns Haiti, but who owns the Haitians themselves.

Who owns the government, who owns *le terroir*, who owns the people? Are Haitians the masters of their fates, either as citizens or as individuals? Who controls their destiny?

I arrived in Haiti for the first time at the end of January 1986 and witnessed the fall of the Duvalier dynasty that year. Since then, I've watched a variety of regime changes there, many of them including elections, some not. During almost all these relinquishings and takings of power, the manipulations and counsel of the United States (and the other "friends" of Haiti, like France, Canada, the Vatican, and especially the UN) were an extremely important (if not the most important) factor. During each regime change, the United States worked to find the candidate most acceptable to business actors in Haiti and their friends and associates abroad. These candidates were usually moderates or conservatives, often English-speaking, who had international connections and were expected to stay an economic course that would help the export-import sector as well as maquiladora owners and large landholders.

The exceptions to this rule were the elections of Jean-Bertrand Aristide and (to a lesser degree) René Préval, who slipped around the American strategy on a huge wave of popular support. Aristide's course through the sieve of U.S. policy for Haiti provided evidence of how far the Americans were willing to go to impede change in Haiti's status quo. Removed once for his impolitic behavior toward the Haitian kleptocracy, Aristide was considered to have been detoxed by the time Bill Clinton reintroduced him into the Haitian political petri dish, but he was recidivist and had to be removed again.

Of course, Haitian history did not begin with the fall of the Duvaliers. It began with the Haitian Revolution, a historic battle between property and owner and between labor and capital. At its very inception, the world's first black republic implied a battle over ownership, and Haiti's revolution a claim to self-ownership.

Recently I had an experience in Haiti that surprised me even though it shouldn't have. In 2013, I was making my belated first visit to the Citadelle Laferrière, King Henri Christophe's postrevolutionary testament to the former slaves' fear that outsiders would reimpose slavery.

I was chatting with a man who was walking a donkey next to me; he was hoping I would tire on the steep uphill walk and need paid transportation. I asked him where he was from. He said "Here." Well, I asked him, and where is your family from? Here also, he said. He said that as far back as anyone in his family had ever been able to remember, they were from here, and it came on me in a sudden wave of shock that of course he was, literally, the descendant of the people who built the Citadelle, and that all around me, walking up this steep mountainside to the fortress in the clouds, were descendants of those builders, dressed in ragged clothing today as those people had no doubt been, thin and strong, hardy survivors of history, still in place, descendants of revolution, true, but at the same time descendants of chattel. Perhaps the plantation their forefathers had worked as slaves once stood right here in the shadow of the lofty crest on which the Citadelle was built. Continuing my speculation, it's entirely possible that the land the donkey driver and his family now live on was handed to his ancestors by King Henri himself, after the revolution destroyed the sugar plantation system. The hectares of former plantations were often doled out to the families of those who had fought in the revolution.

Today, however, the guides who helped me up the mountainside were part of Haiti's slow-growing tourist industry, showing off to the descendants of slaveholders the incredible antislavery monument their Haitian forebears had built and died building.

After that initial shock, I had this same conversation with villagers in many other places in Haiti, especially in the mountains but also in the flat northern plains. Sadly, although a nice little postrevolutionary plot of land was by long tradition theirs, Haitian villagers often did not have title to it and they were always in danger of being shoved off their acreage by unscrupulous wheeler dealers. The government has always refused to consider serious land reform and by refusing has often facilitated corrupt land grabs by greedy agribusinessmen and developers. Today, in a new wave of land grabs, precious-metal mining by international companies is sweeping up vast swaths of these lands with blessings from the Haitian government, which—like so many other governments—is naturally generous, welcoming, and lenient with the rich and the connected.

But the Haitian villager never forgets that the piece of land he or she stands on—always a clearly demarcated postage stamp with beans growing and a small two-room thatched dwelling and one or two chickens wandering—has belonged to his family or hers, handed down by the ancestors from the days of the revolution. That little patch, that garden, as they call it, is beloved by them and represents a kind of freedom.

But does it?

I have argued in books and pieces on Haiti that Haiti's was the world's first purely global economy. Haiti from its inception was modern in so many ways, not good ways. It was swept clean of its indigenous population—you might call them its original owners—by the arrival of the evangelizing Spanish, who claimed the island as their own, their discovery. Now consisting of depopulated forests and meadows, mountainsides and dells, when the Spanish lost this exquisite territory to the French, the latter promptly turned it into a work camp and imported an entire labor force. Its self-styled proprietors were foreign investors who often did not even live in country but relied on local agents, also foreign, to run the works. The product created by this slave labor force was almost entirely exported.

Thus, the land itself, Haiti (or Saint-Domingue, as it was then called), was simply a free zone for the creation of the wealth of others. Europeans invented the country as a factory for producing wealth for Europe. This giant slave camp and others like it fueled the economic engine that created the great imperialist epoch. It made France; other giant slave camps like it created England, Spain, Belgium, and the Netherlands. Offspring born of encounters between owners and slaves in Haiti became, eventually, the elite of the island's new natives: these were the Eurafricans, product of the slave economy and the global trade in sugar. Along with the global-trading people of Middle Eastern descent who later came to Haiti because they sensed a place for a certain kind of money making there (trading with a markup but no added value), the descendants of the Eurafrican class have become the in-country owners of Haiti, with a lock hold on the parts of the economy and the distribution of economic perks not already controlled by outside forces.

To ring a frequently pounded bell at the opening of this book, let's recognize that the real owners of Haiti are the U.S. State Department, military, and president. Why mince words or act all coy about this avowal? The time for pretending otherwise is past. The United States created modern Haiti: that is, Haiti since the U.S. Marine occupation of 1915–1934. The political culture the occupation established there fertilized the soil in which the Duvalier kleptocracy took root. The marines accidentally created Papa Doc. And Papa and Baby Doc accidentally created Aristide. Both Papa Doc and Aristide were the nightmare offspring of those who preceded them, an inverse reflection.

Outsiders often ask: Why is Haiti like that? They add: I mean, come on. It's ridiculous. It's only, like, 600 miles from Miami.

For years I tried to explain politely about the terrible, generations-long consequences and reverberations of slavery; the unfair trade policies of the outside world; a historical revulsion toward the world's first free black nation; the crushing debt Haiti paid to the French for revolutionary reparations (about which more later).

But after a quarter of a century, I realized another thing I should have known from the start. Haiti is the way it is *because* it is 600 miles from Miami rather than in spite of that fact. In the days before the Nazis and the Soviet Union, the revolution of the slaves in Haiti, which culminated successfully (if prematurely in comparative historical terms) in 1804 and only 600 miles away from the slaveholding South, was one of the most important threats to the American way of life at the time.

The Haitian Revolution's psychological impact on Americans black and white cannot be overstated. Haiti was a beacon and ideal for people of African descent enslaved in America in the years between the revolution in Haiti and the U.S. emancipation of slaves. For white Americans, because the Haitian Revolution made explicit the equality of all men, it challenged the basis of the

U.S. economy and of U.S. morality. Our policies toward the black republic often made manifest those psychological concerns and fears, and they still do.

Postrevolutionary Haiti was a vulnerable place on the globe, susceptible to all kinds of foreign exploitation. I think the readers of this book will be able to list some of these. As Graham Greene once said, about Haiti, "It is astonishing how much money can be made out of the poorest of the poor with a little ingenuity." The earthquake of 2010 and its aftermath provided yet another set of examples of this point. Haitians often complain that their country is called "the poorest in the hemisphere" as if that were its Homeric epithet. But this is a description that, while repulsing some potential visitors, attracts another breed altogether: speculators, small-time capitalists, would-be sweatshoppers, and, of course, do-gooders, whom President Theodore Roosevelt once astutely called "sentimental humanitarians [who] form a most pernicious body, with an influence for bad hardly surpassed by that of the professional criminal class."[1]

Members of foreign aid and international nongovernmental organizations, who come by the thousands to poor Haiti to do good works such as constructing and staffing clinics and schools, building roads, and providing sanitation, have by their very presence allowed successive Haitian governments to shirk their responsibilities almost entirely. At the same time, these outsiders have worked with and enriched the French- and English-speaking Haitian elite, who for the most part have presided over and participated in the destruction of their own country's independence with great gusto, as elites everywhere have done when the propitious historical moment occurs.

"The republic of NGOs," as Haiti has often been called, is in many important ways owned by those NGOs. First Haiti was shunned by outsiders because of its revolution, creating huge initial poverty; then it was "helped" by those outsiders, who replaced its state functions; and then those outsiders asked: "Why is Haiti like that?" And they responded: "Because those people can't govern themselves."

No. Haiti is like that because it is owned and run by outsiders for their own financial and psychological benefit.

Like the industrialized work/concentration/execution camps of the Nazi era, the slave camp that was all of Haiti is not easy for its descendants to forget. The Nazi-era Jewish genocide lasted for, all told, a dozen years; the ongoing slave camp genocide in Haiti lasted for around fifteen generations.

Nor is slavery itself dead for all Haitians living today. The terrible system raises its zombified head in every generation. Here are some forms of contemporary Haitian slavery: the *restavek* system that offers orphaned or destitute children a roof over their heads in exchange for their unpaid labor until adulthood. I have met *restaveks* whose masters, in the style of prerevolutionary slaveholders, leave them purposely innumerate and illiterate in order to make them better and more trustworthy workers. Then there are the Haitian sugar cane workers in the Dominican Republic who live in *bateys*, or work camps, that are little more than slave quarters and who are kept in bondage through underpayment, lack of documents, and debt to the company. Their living and work conditions are shameful and intolerable, and the Dominican government has ensured that they and their descendants have no civil status in the Dominican Republic. Then, you could argue, there are also the masses of the Haitian people, whose pseudogovernment—having failed to provide (or having not even tried to provide) the most basic services for its people—leaves them unemployed, illiterate, sick, hungry, and poorly sheltered in unsanitary conditions with no access to clean water: slaves without work.

But the Haitians do have a job to do for the masters on a grander scale, because another way Haitians are enslaved is through the belly. After all, even this most disregarded and dismissed population must eat. Since Baby Doc fell, Haiti has become less and less able to feed itself, as outside shipments of subsidized staples like rice have flooded its markets and undercut locally sourced goods. Today half of Haiti's food is imported, as is 80 percent or more of its rice. And this behavior continues: The United States is about to dump hundreds of thousands of packets of "humanitarian" peanuts into Haitian schools, with no concern for the impact of this policy on local peanut farmers.

So although Haitians are unemployed, they do have a job: they are consumers. To eat (though not much) is their role, their work, in the global market. What they consume is the excess of the global economy in the form of subsidized overages, like that American rice, and expired goods and pharmaceuticals, used clothing, and other products and foods not easily saleable in markets where consumers have both options and protections.

Basically most Haitians are eating and consuming what would otherwise be thrown out—garbage, not to put too fine a point on it—and they're literally paying for it. Neat trick, exporters! For those who export the goods, there is profit. If the Haitians did not do their job of consuming, there would be lost product and no gain. For Haitian farmers, of course, there is loss and bankruptcy in the case of foreign rice dumps. But for American agribusinesses, it makes sense to own the Haitian economy in this way, to penetrate and control. This made sense, too, to the American president and Haitian politicians who helped the outsiders gain access to the Haitian market.

Let's look now at the debt the Haitian revolutionaries agreed to pay to France after they had freed Haiti from its French masters. Not long after Toussaint L'Ouverture and Jean-Jacques Dessalines declared independence, French warships descended into the waters outside Port-au-Prince and pressured Haiti into agreeing to pay a huge indemnity for French property lost in the revolution in exchange for recognition of Haiti's sovereignty (strange method for gaining recognition of sovereignty, that). No matter that the Haitians had won the war.

The world of race-based negotiations is topsy-turvy. The defeated white men were requiring the black victors to pay up. And the victors—or at least, their president, Jean-Pierre Boyer—agreed, committing the baby nation, only some twenty years old, to payments that would cripple the Haitian economy for the next century and that amounted to about $21 billion in today's dollars.

And what was this debt that Haiti owed to France and to the former slaveholding French planters? What exactly had the Haitians taken from the *patrie*? The planters argued that they required recompense for the property they had lost during the revolution, which included their plantations, their grand homes, their produce, and—not of least value or importance—their slaves. In other words, for more than 100 years after the revolution, generations of Haitians were paying the French for the right to call their bodies their own. They were belatedly working off their servitude, paying for their freedom after their comrades had died in great numbers gaining it.

Try to imagine this not on a national scale but on an individual basis.

You are in chains and your jailer keeps you there, feeding you, keeping you sheltered by the prison roof, forcing you to work at hard labor for his profit. He owns you. One day you break free. You leave and go set up house on a tiny piece of outlying prison property you're squatting on, in the eyes of your jailer. Sometime later, as if from the pages of *Uncle Tom's Cabin*, your Simon Legree arrives on the doorstep and tells you that you owe him, say, $200,000 for stealing yourself from him.

You're outraged. Who owns you? Surely you do. But not from your owner's point of view. He refuses to acknowledge the fact that by escaping from the jail and setting up house on your own, you've challenged his entire economic culture. He demands that you behave according to the old system. In one hand he is brandishing a gun with which he holds your whole family hostage until you agree to his terms. And eventually you do, and you end up paying him for the rest of your life while your children and grandchildren go hungry and barefoot.

That's Haiti. That's France.

Because of this debt repayment, France still essentially owned Haiti (as did the American and French banks who loaned Haiti's treasury the payment funds) until 1947, when the debt was finally paid off. By then, thanks to the U.S. Marines' occupation of Haiti, the National City Bank of New York (the final lender for reparations) had taken at least figurative ownership of valuable Haitian lands and was busily working with outside businessmen to find methods of exploiting Haiti.

All of Haitian history from revolution to earthquake invites one to believe that Haiti would have been much better off, richer, easier, less vexed, less literally denigrated had the country never experienced its unique, brilliant, world-shaking revolution. Unlike the French and the Americans, Haiti has been punished over and over for declaring the human dignity of its people and for fighting for the equality of its citizens with the citizens of all countries.

In 1804, the historical moment was not propitious for a victory of slaves over masters. With the collusion of Haitian leaders, the outside world saw to it that that victory and the liberty it implied would be confined and reduced so that only in theory and as an ideal would it be valuable. What's amazing, then, is that that theory and that ideal still embody so much of the struggle for self-sovereignty—sovereignty in its broadest interpretation. Thus, the Haitian revolution continues to this day to resonate with the unrealized implications of black power and with the unrealized overthrow of white hegemony.

I often think about Haiti and my long engagement with the country. Sometimes when I close my eyes I still see Aristide's homeless boys—ages seven through thirteen, maybe, Ti Bernard, Claude, Sonny, Ayiti, Filibert, and the rest—in the temporary home Aristide found for them in a vast peristyle of a former Vodou temple in the La Saline shantytown, a little further down Grande Rue from the church where Aristide then lived and preached.

These boys had a lot of energy. It was night. What I was doing there, I don't recall. Reporting, you could say. Let me report: Each boy had been cast off from his family or orphaned, lost somehow in the big city. They were like Fagin's abandoned boys in Dickens's London. Each had a straw mat for a bed. There was a single bulb in the center of the big empty room, fueled by electricity stolen from government lines. The floor was dirt. Some of these kids were tussling in the corners. Others were playing dominos. A card game on an overturned box was proceeding with considerable excitement, and believe me, there was money on it, even though the boys were virtually penniless. Much shouting. Much demanding of money from me that fortunately I didn't have. Many accusations of cheapness against me. Laughter. Wrestling and rolling around in the dirt. Ayiti won the game and the pot of virtually valueless Haitian gourdes, and yet there was contention about his win. Had he cheated?

I'll tell you the futures of these boys without attaching their names, because a few of them are still living. One is addicted to cheap street drugs, inhalants; I'm not even sure if he's still alive, actually. Last time I saw him, he was wandering the streets in the daytime, begging, and at night, sleeping on someone's roof for free. The roof is not a good place in a tropical city: rats and rain. He has at least two children.

Two and probably more of the boys died of AIDS in their late teens and early twenties. One boy, who was supporting his alcoholic mother and polio-stricken brother, was shot and killed in a drug-related drive-by shooting. Several of these boys died of treatable but untreated tuberculosis. I don't know of any of them who became doctors or lawyers or bakers or businessmen or priests or policemen, and that's not because they lacked talent or brilliance or charisma or ambition.

By the way, it's not a coincidence that the boys in their temporary quarters were like Fagin's band of street kids and the vast hordes of lost and starving children who roamed London's streets in the bustling era of Victoria's reign. Fagin's gang were also throwaways of a changing, more globalized economy. They were also living in a moment when an entire people's centuries-long agrarian way of life was shattered by the interests of great capitalists and corporations. There was nothing for them back in their villages across England; their families couldn't support them, so they washed up in London just the way— exactly the way—Aristide's boys washed up in Port-au-Prince. All these boys, British or Haitian, belonged to no one, not even themselves.

It's even worse now for places like Haiti, entire countries that have been left out of the global winnings. As Aristide used to say about the Haitian people,

"They're under the table, not at the table." When they grew to manhood, there was nothing for Aristide's boys in the Haitian economy because there is no real Haitian economy. What economy there is in Haiti is global, owned by others, and not really meant for Haitians—or for very few Haitians from among the elite. Even the narco-trafficking trade, where many of these boys eventually found tiny niche jobs that paid them a little and put them in mortal danger—as messengers, deliverymen, scouts, or security—even that trade is global and the profits are not for Haitians, or for very few Haitians from the elite.

Outsiders and their few Haitian associates still own Haiti and Haitians, and I suppose it is up to a new generation of leaders, thinkers, and activists—of whom there are always many in this Caribbean country of astounding genius and innovation and energy—to pull Haiti out of the churning gears of globalization. It's not for international aid organizations or interested American secretaries of state or Irish cellphone companies, or Harvard-based health care NGOs or foreign writers like me to decide what escape route Haiti will take. Along with the Haitian people, Haitian leaders are the only ones who can help their country begin to achieve the true meaning of its singular revolution: liberty and self-sufficiency. Perhaps not as ringing a series of abstracts as the trio from the French revolution, but more useful, more practical.

Note

1. Theodore Roosevelt, *Gouverneur Morris* (Boston: Houghton, Mifflin, and Company, 1888), 154.

Acknowledgments

This book derives from a symposium on sovereignty in Haiti held at the Elliott School of International Affairs at George Washington University in Washington, DC, in May 2014. The editors offer their deep thanks and appreciation to the symposium participants who have contributed chapters. Thanks are also offered to all of the other panelists and moderators who participated in the symposium. A full listing of panelists and moderators and video of all the symposium presentations and panel discussions can be viewed at http://media. elliott.gwu.edu/media/who-owns-haiti-governance-and-development.

A particular debt of gratitude is offered to Ambassador Luigi Einaudi, whose skill in moderating the final, closed-door meeting among panelists to discuss the symposium's findings greatly assisted the editors in writing the conclusion to this book. A special thank-you is also accorded, with great pleasure, to Amy Wilentz, whose participation in the symposium inspired her foreword to this volume.

The editors also wish to thank the Elliott School for supporting us. Dean Michael Brown, in particular, deserves special thanks for his support of the concept paper that resulted in the symposium and for providing the resources needed to make it happen. We also wish to tip our hats to Dr. Barbara Miller, director of the Elliott School's Institute for Global and International Studies (IGIS) for her backing of the Focus on Haiti Initiative created under the auspices of IGIS. This initiative made the organization of the symposium and the follow-up work leading to this volume possible. We offer special thanks and praise to Nic Johnson, a remarkable undergraduate student, the coordinator of the initiative, and a budding devotee of all things Haiti. Without Nic's dedication and superb organization and administrative skills, his ability to keep happy each symposium panelist who traveled from within the United States or from Haiti and beyond, and his keen appreciation of the Chicago style, we simply could not have achieved what we did.

Finally, and most important, the editors of this volume acknowledge the inspiration of the Haitians who have committed their lives to keeping themselves and their country a beacon of freedom under very trying circumstances and who have helped us understand that Haiti is truly owned by Haitians. It is to them that we dedicate this book, with honor and respect.

Abbreviations

CAED	Cadre de coordination de l'aide externe au développement d'Haïti (Framework for Coordination of External Aid for the Development of Haiti)
CARICOM	Caribbean Community
DAI	Development Alternatives, Inc.
FL	Fanmi Lavalas (Lavalas Family; Haiti)
FPC	for-profit contractor
MINUSTAH	Mission des Nations Unies pour la stabilisation en Haïti (United Nations Stabilization Mission in Haiti)
MOG	Moral Optimists for the Grand Renaissance of Bel Air (Haiti)
NGO	nongovernmental organization
OAS	Organization of American States
OPL	Òganizasyon Pèp Kap Lité (Struggling People's Organization; Haiti)
PAS	Programme D'Apaisement Social (Social Peace Program; Haiti)
PCB	Partido Comunista Brasileiro (Brazilian Communist Party; Brazil)
PT	Partido dos Trabalhadores (Workers' Party; Brazil)
UN	United Nations
UNESCO	United Nations Educational, Scientific and Cultural Organization
USAID	U.S. Agency for International Development

Introduction

Sovereignty and Ownership from the Inside and Out

Scott Freeman and Robert Maguire

The question "Who owns Haiti?" creates a stir when it is asked in public. It created such a stir when it was posed at a symposium entitled "Who 'Owns' Haiti? Sovereignty in a Fragile State, 2004–2014" held at George Washington University in the Elliott School of International Affairs. Soon after, the question was under discussion on radio airwaves in Port-au-Prince and among policy makers, analysts, scholars, Haitian Americans, and others who follow Haiti's foreign and domestic affairs. Those who posited answers ranged from the deeply reflective to the simplistic and cynical. Among the latter were those who stated that "we own nothing." Others insisted that of course Haitians own Haiti. Among the deeply reflective were those who pointed out the complexities inherent in the question that made clear and full answers difficult if not impossible. They pointed to uneven power relationships between Haiti and external forces and to the ability of Haitians throughout their history to resist and push back at the stronger powers that asserted themselves with a view toward "owning" Haiti and its people.

External assertions of Haiti's sovereignty often come wrapped in a package that presents the Caribbean land as a country in turmoil. Images of protests, burning tires, or violence perpetrated by armed groups are powerful in part because they fit into an existing narrative propagated largely by non-Haitians about "the poorest country in the Western Hemisphere." This narrative draws on Haiti as a locale that is the "odd" abomination of everything else rather than an ordinary place (Trouillot 1990b). Through a lens of poverty and violence, "black impoverished masses" are tied to the causes of their own strife. Even the moniker of "the poorest country" belies a focus on Haiti in isolation. Causes are not attached to descriptions of the country's underdevelopment and poverty, but rather this presentation of Haiti's economic, social, and political strife is seen as exclusively caused by internal factors. The truth of the matter, however, is that the Caribbean nation's travail has never been caused wholly by its own internal turmoil. In assessing "ownership" of Haiti, we are compelled to consider the overwhelming evidence that the root of the country's contemporary sovereignty dilemma is ultimately related not just to its own internal rumbling but also to roles foreign actors played.

This is not a novel analysis: Scholarship and writing on Haiti and by Haitians has in fact continually focused on the machinations of international actors in Haiti (Farmer 1994; Dupuy 2006; Schuller 2012; Gaillard 1981; Casimir 2001). From imperialism and economic extraction to the catastrophes of international aid, the roles of international actors are undeniable. While this edited volume sees Haiti as a specific and particular site, it does so while examining a larger set of international issues.

The chapters in this volume share a critical perspective of international actors but add a crucial reflection. What might we understand about Haiti by considering actions taken by the international community if we view those actions in terms of ownership? Haiti, despite its overwhelmingly negative portrayal, has always been a key target of foreign powers. From occupations to investment and tourism, Haiti is valuable, in both a material and an ideological sense. The desire to own it—in whatever forms that may take—has implications for how Haitians, particularly the majority of "non-elite" Haitians, experience the idea of a sovereign nation. Protests in the streets of Port-au-Prince illustrate the connectedness of all these players: They not only force the Haitian government to pay attention but also send ripples through the hallways of the U.S. Department of State, the White House, and Congress. Smallholding farmers and the urban poor speak through barricades and protests, peaceful demonstrations, and grassroots organizations. They are not unaware of the far-off policy makers who hamper their ability to sell crops at a competitive price, favor imported food, and hamper the electoral process.

This volume attempts to examine this convoluted set of relationships in all of its complexity. From the political meddling that sways election results to the way groups in Haiti assert alternative forms of sovereignty in daily life, this volume considers both infractions of Haiti's sovereignty and Haitians' multiple objections. Imagining Haiti's historic or contemporary lot as the exclusive result of internal turmoil not only accepts an exceedingly myopic analysis, it also denies the very reality of the Black Republic's more than 200-year history.

Given this history and in spite of an unyielding quest by Haitians to assert sovereign control over themselves and their land, ownership of that republic has continually been a matter of struggle and flux.

Since European adventurers first encountered what today is Haiti in the late 1400s, the idea of self-determination and a sovereign space has been fiercely contested. European arrival marked a set of claims about ownership that set the stage for the Haitian revolution. Hispaniola has never been truly isolated from global powers since the arrival of Christopher Columbus. After the demise of the indigenous Taino people at the hands of European conquerors and the diseases they introduced, French colonists eventually claimed ownership of the western third of the island area they called Saint-Domingue and forcibly repopulated it with enslaved Africans, whose ownership they also claimed. Eventually, in a profound act of resistance against the ownership of both land and people, those Africans and their descendants rose up to cast off their physical and colonial bondage.

Contemporary clashes over the ownership of Haiti and its political, economic, and social fabric take place against a backdrop of this most remarkable assertion of sovereignty when, over 200 years ago, Haitian independence was vociferously declared by those who made revolutionary change that was seen as "unimaginable" at the time (Trouillot 1990a). Haiti's 1804 triumph over France forced the western world to truly consider the liberal ideals of *liberté, egalité,* and *fraternité.* Adding to this were Haitians' assertions of two new sets of liberties: the humanity and freedom of previously enslaved Africans and the radical notion that self-rule by formerly enslaved people was both possible and just. The victors of that revolutionary struggle underscored these ideas when they expelled remaining Frenchmen, made foreign ownership of their land illegal, abolished the very notion of one human being owning another, and invoked a Taino name for their new nation: Ayiti. At the heart of the revolution were acts that expelled foreign influence. Similarly, Haiti's leaders asserted themselves with the creation of their flag: a blue and red banner made by the removal of the symbolically laden white stripe of the French tricolor. Such fundamental symbols of nationhood—a name and a flag—powerfully reinforced the idea of a Haiti free from foreign control.

But almost immediately in the postcolonial period, concepts of sovereignty and ownership became contentious. There is no doubt that Haitians' dominion, autonomy, authority, and self-determination over their space has been assaulted and eroded since the initial glow of revolutionary triumph. In the moments following independence, political factions in the new republic conspired to create multiple and contradictory systems of government. Despotic leaders, such as Henri Christophe, a father of Haiti's independence, invoked such titles as "emperor" and "king." Christophe reinstated forced labor and built the famous Citadelle Laferrière with the work of purportedly "free" Haitian laborers. He thus asserted his sovereignty through a monopoly of power and violence at the expense of the sovereignty and freedom of the individual.

International actors continued to impinge upon Haiti's self-dominion as they envied Haitian labor and natural resources, seeing them both as accessible and exploitable. The French intruded upon self-dominion not only in the form of merchants, diplomats, adventurers, and missionaries but also, as Amy Wilentz pointed out in her foreword to this volume, in the shape of debilitating economic retribution. Haiti's century-long payment of a post-independence indemnity to France was the path France required for recognition of the nation's sovereignty, one that robbed the country of desperately needed capital and incapacitated its future.

In the nineteenth and twentieth centuries, new external actors, most notably the United States, became dominant forces over the small republic's political, social, and economic life. Complete external ownership of an independent nation and its people is a clear marker of such struggles. The U.S. military occupation from 1915 to 1934 is the most unconcealed example of a breach of Haiti's sovereignty (Bellegarde-Smith 1990). Road building and land clearing during the U.S. occupation were done by the despised corvée chain gangs. For many Haitians, this labor form meant that the individual freedoms of the revolution had yet again receded into the past (Renda 2001). If we measure contentment by popular protests and uprisings since that occupation, it becomes evident that increasingly Haitians conclude that the postcolonial promise of freedom, autonomy, and a better life is still incomplete. Interventions in 1994 and 2004 by UN-mandated and U.S.-supported multilateral forces (which prominently included Canadian and, in 2004, French soldiers) are more recent examples of overt, militarized violations of Haiti's space.

In the ten years since its 2004 bicentennial of independence—the time frame on which this volume focuses—Haiti has witnessed a series of events that have raised further questions about its ownership. The "international community"—a term for bilateral and multilateral entities that now totes a profoundly negative connotation in Haiti—has been at the center of a series of political and economic scandals that have unfolded much like dominoes toppling upon each other. Haiti's third century of independence, for example, began with its elected president, Jean-Bertrand Aristide, forcibly flown out of the country on a U.S.-chartered aircraft after internal strife yielded a coup d'état that international powers facilitated, most prominently the United States (Dupuy 2006).

France and Canada also played crucial roles in Aristide's controversial ouster. As the 2004 coup was still unfolding, French and Canadian troops were dispatched to Haiti to join U.S. troops in what quickly became a UN multilateral force. France's support of Aristide's removal was widely attributed to French hatred of the Haitian leader, who had insisted that the indemnity Haiti had paid to the former colonizer be returned with interest, a sum of some $21 billion. The presence of Canadian troops in the 2004 multinational force was not surprising in view of the lead role Canada had taken in organizing the "Ottawa Initiative on Haiti" in early 2003. The initiative united U.S., French, and Canadian diplomats who took the lead in discussing Haiti's future, incredibly in the absence of any representatives of Haiti's government. While French involvement in the multilateral force epitomized an echo of colonialism, the presence of Canadian troops was a more recent engagement, swayed by a well-established and influential Haitian Diaspora population that lived principally in the province of Quebec.

Concurrent with the 2004 departure of Aristide, Haiti witnessed the transformation of the multilateral force into the UN Stabilization Mission for Haiti (MINUSTAH) that, while arguably maintaining a modicum of political stability, has also brought great harm to Haitians. In 2010 its soldiers introduced a deadly strain of cholera that by April 2014 had not only killed 8,562 Haitians and sickened more than 600,000 others but had also left a mark on the country into the foreseeable future as a killer lurking in its rivers and streams (Archibold and Sengupta 2014; Morrison and Charles 2015). In late 2015, the UN Security Council approved a resolution extending MINUSTAH to at least October 2016, assuring the continuity of international military presence for a total of more than a decade (United Nations Security Council 2015).

In response to the continual onslaught of international control, in the run-up to the presidential elections of 2010–2011, several candidates voiced the idea that if elected, they would seek to expand Haiti's sovereign space. Yet that election would come to be symbolic of the very foreign involvement these erstwhile national leaders argued against. By interfering with internal electoral processes, including the vote count, the U.S. government and the Organization of American States (OAS) lent their power—whether deliberately or not—to one particular candidate, Michel Martelly, setting the stage for his election in what many Haitians believe was a less-than-democratic outcome (Joseph 2014). Five years later, these same international intruders found themselves attempting to convince the ill-reputed Martelly regime to hold long-delayed local, municipal and parliamentary elections. These external impositions in Haitian affairs may be made in the spirit of upholding Haitian constitutionality, but they are widely viewed in Haiti as yet another manifestation of heavy-handed outside interference.

The primacy of international actors in Haiti over the past ten years does not stop with the presence of foreign soldiers or intrusion into elections. As the chapters of this volume demonstrate, that influence extends to the country's political process, economic policies, and development strategies. It also extends to forms of social organization and religious practice, as individuals and institutions of different stripes have steadfastly sought access to or control over the land and its people in order to own Haiti, or at least certain aspects of it. While the motives of those seeking access to Haiti's space and people are not all necessarily sinister, they continually promote a set of practices based on material or discursive ownership. These include orphanages and charities that market Haiti's poverty for their own well-being and aggrandizement (Schwartz 2008) and businessmen who use its peoples' desperation to amass profits. External religious messengers regularly descend on Haiti to compete quite literally for Haitian souls. Who flying to Haiti from the United States has not witnessed well-meaning church groups sporting matching T-shirts bearing "Hope for Haiti" slogans?

What about the motives of scholars and researchers whose subtle imposition of seemingly unending studies *on* Haiti can treat the country and its people as little more than an experimental space? This question is particularly pertinent to the authors of this volume and many who will read it. Researchers' desires to write papers that will advance careers, matched by attempts to own ideas about Haiti in English-language publications, are far too often divorced from consideration of what is owed the Haitian collaborators who facilitated the studies and data collection in the first place.

The incessant onslaught of foreign individuals and organizations and their strategies, mandates, ideas, and actions are not always enacted in isolation from Haitian counterparts. Sometimes there are willing Haitian collaborators; other times there are not. On occasion, those who are unwilling to yield enact practices of subterfuge or cooptation, commonly known in Haiti as *mawonaj*, in order to maintain a semblance of ownership and protect their sovereign rights. Externally imposed development projects that introduce unwelcome practices gain support among well-paid Haitian technicians, enlist participation through wage payments, and are abandoned as soon as the money runs out.

Always, the ebb and flow of who gets access to and control over resources and people takes place in a highly complex context. An important theme coursing through the symposium was the idea that for every case of attempted ownership of Haiti and its people, there are powerful reminders of the way Haiti cannot be owned. In the midst of diverse infractions of sovereignty, there are continual countermoves from Haitians. Foreigners who are interested in buying and owning Haitian land, for example, are countered by unique, defensive land tenure practices (see Dubois, this volume). Similarly, when international designers attempt to own or profit from the material culture of Haiti, Haitian artisans engage in continually diffuse acts of expression to ensure their ownership of uniquely Haitian art and its production. Whereas religious messengers from Europe and the United States have long attempted to expunge the perceived evils of Haitian Vodou for what they argue are the superior rewards of Christianity, the continually changing and decentralized nature of Vodou enables its devotees to maintain opportunities to serve the spirits (see Richman, this volume). Rural and urban social movements, both small and large, have long found ways of challenging, dissuading, and even co-opting foreign powers and domestic elites that aim to assert their social and cultural mores. These movements, be they peasant or labor groups, urban neighborhood organizations, or grassroots political movements, are particularly adept at creating multiple manifestations of their own sovereignty, including the aforementioned *mawonaj*, to ensure its protection and maintenance.

The general concept of sovereignty itself is in constant flux. Among scholars who ponder this on a universal scale, the concept no longer applies exclusively to the idea of fixed borders on the basis of which a state or ruler exercises sovereignty based upon a monopoly of violence, as per Max Weber's analysis (2009). As Litzinger argues, "The uncertainty and instability of the concept owes much to processes usually associated with globalization, especially those which are undermining the foundations of national sovereignty" (2006, 69). No longer are the borders of the nation-state the most important aspects of a critical examination of sovereignty. Historic representations of sovereignty have often fallen prey to simplistic representations of "western" state governments facing off against the "traditional" groups embodying notions of agency and resistance.

Conversations about sovereignty have been illuminated, and long challenged, by the critical thought in a variety of venerable and detailed ethnographic and historic accounts of life and power relationships in the Caribbean (Wolf 1982; Mintz 1985; Hansen and Stepputat 2006; Lewis 2012a). From the devastation of indigenous people through the rise of transatlantic slavery and authoritarian colonial rule, the history of the Caribbean has been one of loss and a quest to reclaim sovereignty (Lewis 2012b). Defying ideas of a sovereign and controlling nation state, planters—not states—powerfully exercised control over both space and people in the colonial Caribbean (Mintz 1985). The literal possession of people in slave-based regimes challenges assertions of supposedly sovereign state power. Philosophical examinations of the colonial Caribbean illuminate a broader conception of sovereignty that is tied to the life of the individual. Frantz Fanon ([1952] 2008; [1961] 2007), for example, considers the psychological impacts of the profound personal loss of those subjugated by a process of colonization that annihilates not only self-government but also selfhood. He argues that those who were colonized became mere objects in the eyes of those ruling over them and therefore advocates a decolonization of both self and society. Similarly focusing on the intersection of government and subject, Fanon's mentor, Aimè Césaire, examined similar impacts of colonialism (Césaire [1950] 2001), vehemently critiquing its political economy. Yet Césaire envisioned an alternative type of sovereignty in reaction to the disenfranchisement of colonial subjects when he advocated a change in the relationship of individual to the state that would transform previously colonial subjects into full citizens of the French Republic.

Within the Caribbean, Haiti in particular has illuminated much about global political economy and the nature of sovereignty. Simply considering the Caribbean nation's history shakes otherwise stable definitions of the way sovereignty is conceived. Anthropologist Michel Rolf Trouillot (1990b) famously argued that scholars should stop representing Haiti in exceptional terms. By representing the Caribbean nation as a place unlike any other, scholars relegate it to margins of analysis. Such interpretations veil the colonial and neocolonial practices that have led to Haiti's contemporary political and economic trials. In short, Trouillot argues that we should come to see Haiti not as the exception but as an "ordinary" outcome of the globalized political and economic system.

Anthropologist Yarimar Bonilla (2013) extends Trouillot's analysis to sovereignty in the broader Caribbean. Neither in the past nor in the present, she asserts, have traditional concepts of sovereignty and autonomous nation-states been characteristic of the Caribbean. Full of seeming exceptions to sovereignty—Guantánamo in Cuba, privately owned islands, the political status of Puerto Rico, the overseas French departments of Martinique and Guadeloupe—the Caribbean cases might easily be dismissed in favor of a more simplistic idea of sovereign nation-states. Yet the Caribbean, Bonilla argues, must be considered as an "ordinary" element of a global economic and political system. The region is not an exception to traditional renditions of sovereignty but rather presents realities that unmask the very instability of the concept itself. As Bonilla insists, "[Sovereignty] has not, *and has never been*, what it claims to be" (2013, 156, emphasis in original).

More recent debates on the manifestation of sovereignty have incorporated an analysis of the contemporary global economic order. As related to Haiti, this debate centers on such issues as its placement in the larger world system of economic extraction and structural violence (Farmer 1994, 1996). As Fatton notes in this volume, neoliberal actors such as nongovernmental organizations, international financial institutions, and transnational capitalists impose economic orders and challenge theories of power that rely on the neatly bounded nation-state as the primary source of control. Such analysts of the Haiti context as Farmer and Fatton surely would find themselves in accord with the assessment of aboriginal activist Bobby Sykes, who asks: "What? Post-colonialism? Have they left?" (Smith 1999).

Questions of ownership are fundamental to any examination of sovereignty. Uncertainties about who controls what and when blur the ostensibly neat lines created by diplomatic relations based on the idealized sovereign "nation-state." In their review of sovereignty, Hansen and Stepputat (2006) ask us to move away from simple ideas of legal sovereignty and toward a discussion of the daily notions of justice—a move toward a tentative and negotiated form of authority that occurs on multiple levels. Such queries and recommendations highlight the complexity of the concept that is the foundation of this volume. These provocative thoughts and definitions are at the heart, for example, of Kivland's consideration in this volume of manifestations of sovereign expression in the forms of protection and democracy in a poor Port-au-Prince neighborhood and Richman's analysis of the constant battle for religious converts that occurs throughout Haiti. They are also apparent in Freeman's chapter on the realities of international aid that beseeches us to ponder how activities previously relegated to state governments have been absorbed into the work of aid organizations.

These weighty considerations suggest that the definition of sovereignty is far from clear. Indeed, its meaning is subject to constant change that takes place over diverse landscapes. The chapters that follow consider history, political science, economics, development studies and anthropology in order to understand how the very idea of ownership of Haiti is asserted and resisted. Ranging from analyses of religion, rural labor, and urban gangs to history, political expression, and international policies, this volume provides fresh material that can advance discussions of the evolving nature of sovereignty worldwide in the twenty-first century. The authors provide a broad and profound understanding of historical and contemporary Haiti in the context of its ownership. If, as many of them contend, a multitude of externally driven infractions have impinged deeply on Haiti's sovereign space, then it is incumbent upon us to identify and analyze the diverse forces that threaten Haitian sovereign expression.

Organization of the Volume

Following this introductory chapter, Laurent Dubois, in chapter 2, takes a historical perspective, considering the question of sovereignty as rooted in the Haitian Revolution. He argues that because the French colony of Saint-Domingue was organized around the social and economic structures of slavery and the plantation, it profoundly lacked both personal and national sovereignty. During the revolution, new institutions were forged to ensure the continuity of newly gained freedoms. Most significant for Dubois are the ideas of a "counter-plantation" society: the values, procedures, and processes that were forged during the Haitian Revolution itself. As residents of postcolonial Haiti crafted institutions and practices designed to curb the return of a plantation in any form, they made it a place of remarkable and diverse sovereignties. Yet from these profound beginnings come troubling challenges and international interventions.

In chapter 3, Robert Fatton implores us to critically examine the label of "failed state" and the assumptions that go along with it. He argues that Haiti's economic structure and performance cannot be understood or explained by merely domestic factors but must be understood in relation to the impositions of neoliberal economic policy. Most important for Fatton is the fact that the disintegration of social welfare in Haiti and its economic decline are direct results of economic and political decisions imposed by l'international—the ill-reputed international community. This examination of the supposed logic of neoliberalism clarifies the uses of particular economic policies and how they benefit some groups over others. The near-imperial imposition of such policies has consistently benefited foreign institutions and actors while contributing to Haiti's marginalized position in the "outer periphery."

Chapter 4 details the complexities of U.S. pressures on Haitian domestic politics as François Pierre-Louis examines the realities of hegemonic hemispheric tactics. The relationship between domestic politics and international actors, he argues, is not simply a matter of the United States' imposition of its will on Haiti. Rather, collaborations are necessary between U.S. officials and Haitian elites who broadly share political ideologies and goals. By examining the 2010 elections and the rise of Martelly as a viable candidate for president, Pierre-Louis presents us with a case that demonstrates how political maneuvers are no longer conducted in smoky diplomatic backrooms, prodding us to think about how agreements between local elites and foreign powers attempt to dislodge members of the voting public from their ownership of decision-making power.

In chapter 5, Ricardo Seitenfus extends the analysis of international actors to focus on the role Brazil and its neighbors played in the 2004 fall of President Jean-Bertrand Aristide and the creation of the military force that would become MINUSTAH. As he examines how Latin America more broadly moved from a position of nonintervention to one aggressively supporting UN military action, Seitenfus argues that it is crucial to understand the broader political movements that precipitated both Brazil's decisions and its eventual leadership role in MINUSTAH and its preceding change of position on Aristide. As divisions in the Haitian political left created a growing distance between Latin America and Aristide, the internal politics of the São Paulo Forum became significant in determining the degree of engagement of Brazil and its Latin American neighbors. Seitenfus offers an opportunity to break out of mere discursive critiques through an understanding of the intersections of specific political movements as they pertain to Haiti.

Any examination of ideas of ownership and sovereignty would be incomplete without a rigorous critique of aid in Haiti. In chapter 6, Robert Maguire examines both the discourse and reality of U.S. foreign assistance to Haiti, which has lately become a paradigmatic case of ineffective aid and proposed reform. Many critiques of U.S.-based aid initiatives, including from within the Obama administration, focus on the top-down nature of aid initiatives and the prevalence of "beltway bandit" contractors as the real beneficiaries of aid contracts. While the U.S. government's response to the earthquake includes a framework designed to increase ownership in the receiving country, Maguire demonstrates how the Haitian government was continually kept on the margins while lucrative post-earthquake contracts were routed to U.S.-based NGOs and for-profit contractors. Even small social programs run by the Martelly administration seem to be rerouting aid benefits back to the United States through food imports. This analysis exposes the differences between a discursive shift to "Haitian ownership" and the realities of a U.S.-centric aid institution.

Chapter 7 asks the important question "Who owns Haiti's religion?" Karen Richman demonstrates how the complex interplay of Catholicism, Protestantism, and Vodou is not at all separate from international meddling. While Catholics "owned" the spiritual terrain in Haiti until the mid-twentieth century, Protestant evangelism has become an increasingly important part of Haiti's spiritual, social, and political landscape. Richman demonstrates how the opening of Haiti to American Protestantism led to new possibilities for spiritual and moral influence and created prospects for the erosion of the Haitian state when such typical state responsibilities as education were ceded to missionaries. Richman demonstrates that even in the realm of religion, Haiti's sovereignty is constantly in question as it becomes the domain of international involvement. Despite Catholic and Protestant efforts to marginalize and eliminate Vodou, the indigenous spiritual beliefs and practices have not been stymied. Adaptive ways for Haitians to serve the spirits demonstrate that even state-sanctioned efforts to stamp out such practices are likely to fall short of their goal.

In chapter 8, Scott Freeman discusses aspects of sovereignty and solidarity as practiced by rural labor groups. He notes how the histories of environmental aid have often been based on the insertion of foreign funds at the discretion of foreign "experts." Since the arrival of development institutions in Haiti in the mid-twentieth century, soil conservation has been part of many environmental conservation projects. Often ignoring larger systemic causes of degradation, experts have continually recommended a set of practices that attempt to pay wages to Haitian rural labor groups when they implement soil conservation measures. Despite these incentives, farmers rarely if ever do the specific interventions of their own accord. Freeman argues that in this context, smallholding farmers do not choose not to adopt externally imposed practices because they do not understand them but rather because of a conceptual distinction between the individualized work that aid interventions sponsor and the collective agriculture groups practice in the countryside. Rural localities thus become a setting for indigenous labor groups' engagement with (and often rejection of) imposed external aid designs.

Chapter 9 introduces the idea of sovereignty as contemplated in neighborhoods of Port-au-Prince. Chelsey Kivland argues that the concept of respect is paramount in Haitian conceptions of sovereignty, using informal street organizations known as *baz* to illustrate how sovereign space is maintained in urban settings. Often marginalized or dismissed as merely "gangs," *baz* are brokers of development between NGOs and the neighborhoods that they control. As such, they are fundamentally a part of the larger issues of sovereignty contemplated in this volume. Kivland demonstrates how these neighborhood groups became key players in the distribution of aid as development projects entered their neighborhoods in the post-earthquake context. Unlikely intermediaries, these groups simultaneously play the roles of the state, grassroots organizations, and pseudo-military power brokers. As such, they provide insights into Haiti's "fragile" circumstance, suggesting that we must look to more localized notions of sovereign organization if we are to understand not only contemporary urban challenges but also possible ways of strengthening sovereignty at the national scale.

Chapter 10, the volume's conclusion, emanates from a post-symposium discussion among panelists and moderators as they sought to synthesize and expand the gathering's emergent themes with a view toward achieving three goals: better analyzing issues pertaining to Haitian sovereignty, identifying obstacles to and opportunities for reforming relationships with international actors in order to achieve an expansion of the country's sovereign space, and identifying recommendations for action.

Throughout Haiti's history, foreign forces, institutions, and individuals have attempted time and again to exert some form of possession over Haiti and its people. They have also sought to undercut a fundamental idea of Haiti's historic sovereignty: the universal embrace of freedom and human dignity and the accordance of honor and respect to its land and all those who occupy it. An array of foreign actors, including missionaries, aid workers, diplomats, and contractors harbor the arrogant conceit that they know what Haitians need and what is best for their country. This attitude seems to fit neatly into the antiquated ideologies of colonialism cast off in that land more than 200 years ago. Yet infractions on Haiti's sovereignty—both large and small—continue unabated.

Intrusions by armed soldiers and pushy diplomats are easy, clear targets for a critique of sovereignty and ownership. More difficult is an analysis of sovereignty and infringements upon it as measured by the less clear notion of how the "idea" of Haiti is used. Within these pages are considerations of the ownership of Haiti as seen through an array of issues, domains, and magnitudes of both infractions and assertions. Those considerations reflect the limits of sovereignty and ownership and as how Haitians experience and respond to infractions of them. All of this is part of the complex response to "Who owns Haiti?" a question that inevitably appears unanswerable.

References

Archibold, Randal C., and Somini Sengupta. 2014. "U.N. Struggles to Stem Haiti Cholera Epidemic." *New York Times*, April 19. Accessed April 20, 2016. http://www.nytimes.com/2014/04/20/world/americas/un-struggles-to-stem-haiti-cholera-epidemic.html.

Bellegarde-Smith, Patrick. 1990. *The Breached Citadel*. Boulder, CO: Westview Press.

Bonilla, Yarimar. 2013. "Ordinary Sovereignty." *Small Axe* 17 (3 42): 152–65.

Casimir, Jean. 2001. *La Culture Opprimée*. Port-au-Prince: Imprimerie Lakay.

Césaire, Aimé. (1950) 2001. *Discourse on Colonialism*. New York: New York University Press.

Dupuy, Alex. 2006. *The Prophet and Power: Jean-Bertrand Aristide, the International Community, and Haiti*. Lanham, MD: Rowman & Littlefield Publishers.

Fanon, Frantz. (1952) 2008. *Black Skin, White Masks*. Grove Press.

———. (1961) 2007. *The Wretched of the Earth*. Grove Press.

Farmer, Paul. 1994. *The Uses of Haiti*. Monroe, ME: Common Courage Press.

———. 1996. "On Suffering and Structural Violence: A View from Below." *Daedalus* 125 (1): 261–83.

Gaillard, Roger. 1981. *Les blancs débarquent: Premier écrasement du cacoïsme*. Vol. 3. Port-au-Prince: Roger Gaillard.

Hansen, Thomas Blom, and Finn Stepputat. 2006. "Sovereignty Revisited." *Annual Review of Anthropology* 35: 295–315.

Joseph, Raymond A. 2014. *For Whom the Dogs Spy: Haiti: From the Duvalier Dictatorships to the Earthquake, Four Presidents, and Beyond*. New York: Arcade Publishing.

Lewis, Linden, ed. 2012a. *Caribbean Sovereignty, Development and Democracy in an Age of Globalization*. Routledge.

———. 2012b. "Introduction: Sovereignty, Heterodoxy and the Last Desperate Shibboleth of Caribbean Nationalism." In *Caribbean Sovereignty, Development and Democracy in an Age of Globalization*, edited by Linden Lewis, 1–16. New York: Routledge.

Litzinger, Ralph A. 2006. "Contested Sovereignties and the Critical Ecosystem Partnership Fund." *PoLAR: Political and Legal Anthropology Review* 29 (1): 66–87.

Mintz, Sidney. 1985. *Sweetness and Power: The Place of Sugar in World History*. New York: Viking Penguin.

Morrison, Arron, and Jacqueline Charles. 2015. "Haiti PM: United Nations Has Moral Responsibility in Haiti Cholera Outbreak." Haitian-Truth.org, September 27. Accessed June 15. http://www.haitian-truth.org/haiti-pm-united-nations-has-moral-responsibility-in-haiti-cholera-outbreak/.

Renda, Mary A. 2001. *Taking Haiti: Military Occupation & the Culture of U.S. Imperialism, 1915–1940*. Chapel Hill: University of North Carolina Press.

Schuller, Mark. 2012. *Killing with Kindness: Haiti, International Aid, and NGOs*. New Brunswick, NJ: Rutgers University Press.

Schwartz, Timothy T. 2008. *Travesty in Haiti: A True Account of Christian Missions, Orphanages, Food Aid, Fraud, and Drug Trafficking*. Charleston, SC: Booksurge.

Smith, Linda Tuhiwai. 1999. *Decolonizing Methodologies: Research and Indigenous Peoples*. London: Zed Books.

Trouillot, Michel Rolph. 1990a. *Haiti, State against Nation: The Origins and Legacy of Duvalierism*. New York: Monthly Review Press.

———. 1990b. "The Odd and the Ordinary: Haiti, the Caribbean, and the World." *Cimarron* 2 (3): 11.

United Nations Security Council. 2015. UN Security Council Resolution 2243 (2015). (Resolution Extending the Mandate of MINUSTAH for One Year While Maintaining Its Authorised Troop Strength at 2,370 Military Personnel and 2,601 Police.) 15 October. Accessed April 20, 2016. http://www.securitycouncilreport.org/atf/cf/%7B65BFCF9B-6D27-4E9C-8CD3-CF6E4FF96FF9%7D/s_res_2243.pdf.

Weber, Max. 2009. *From Max Weber: Essays in Sociology*. New York: Routledge.

Wolf, Eric R. 1982. *Europe and the People without History*. Berkeley: University of California Press.

2

Haitian Sovereignty

A Brief History

Laurent Dubois

The question this volume poses, Who owns Haiti?, is, of course, a provocative one. In this chapter, I approach the question by drawing on my book *Haiti: The Aftershocks of History* in order to offer some ideas about how we might think about the long-term history of Haitian sovereignty. I'm interested in particular in some of the ways that Haitian history allows us to encounter the present and possibly rewrite the future. Only through a sustained engagement with Haiti's history will we be able to develop approaches suited to the present and nourish different directions for Haiti. Engaging with Haiti historically is key to understanding the layered practices, structures, and discourses that shape its realities. That is true for any society, of course. But it is particularly urgent and necessary in Haiti because of how it is constantly misrepresented and misunderstood (Dubois 2012).

Retracing the history of Haiti's contested sovereignty invites us to think about some deep and disturbing ironies of history. How is it that a country that so importantly pioneered and developed ideas of sovereignty has seen its sovereignty so persistently undermined both by conflicts within and by pressures from outside? How is it that this particular nation has seen its sovereignty and the self-sovereignty of its people undermined and refused?

Part of the answer to this question is that there is of course a fundamental relationship between Haiti's powerful demand for sovereignty through its revolution and the consistent refusal of recognition and respect for that sovereignty. As Michel Rolph Trouillot (1995) argued in his classic work *Silencing the Past,* Haiti's revolution and Haiti's mere existence profoundly challenged not only the reigning political order of the day but also the very structures of thought that dominated—and in many ways still dominate—understandings of world history. Trouillot's intervention in that work was driven by a strong sense that there were serious and immediate consequences to the fact that many actors found it nearly impossible to think about and with Haiti in a productive way. "Haiti disturbs," my colleague Jean Casimir (2001) likes to say, and that is because a real engagement with its history as global history forces us to reconsider and challenge many of the commonplace thoughts—I might even say ruts—in which we find ourselves embedded. Really finding a different way of thinking about Haitian sovereignty requires us to look at the broader order from a perspective rooted in the country's history and use the ideological and cultural resources that history has produced for thinking about the world.

Haiti's long-term political history has been studied in rich detail, notably in the magisterial work of Claude Moïse (1988). Approaching this history means understanding not only particular events but also the long-term sedimentation of structures of perception, thought, and action. Our means of access to history must be multiple and open: A history of Haiti told only through traditional written sources inevitably limits and even distorts that history. And we also have to think about the many ways history can and should be told. In this sense, this chapter outlines the central role humanistic and cultural knowledge must play in all discussions about policy toward Haiti.

My goal is to offer some ways of using a broad understanding of Haitian history as a way to better understand the present and nourish different kinds of futures. I'll try and show that the fundamental political problems that have shaped Haiti's history since 1804 are rooted in the remarkable events of the Haitian Revolution of 1791 to 1804. That revolution was both a local and a global event, a true world-historical moment in ways that are increasingly acknowledged today. One useful way for us to think about the Haitian Revolution is as perhaps the most radical (and therefore one of the most important) assertions of a right to sovereignty in modern history. Even more so than the American and French Revolutions with which it was intertwined, the Haitian Revolution posed a set of absolutely central political questions. It did so in a way that was illegible to many and forcibly repressed by others. But any true analysis of modern political history, not only of Haiti but of the world, has to grapple with the implications of this revolution for core concepts surrounding sovereignty.

The French colony of Saint-Domingue, the pinnacle of the Atlantic slave system and the richest of the plantation colonies of the Americas, was based on a radical refusal of sovereignty to the majority. Ninety percent of the population of the colony was enslaved—more than half of them African born, many of them recent arrivals in the colony at the beginning of the revolution in 1791—and were not considered legal or political subjects in any sense. They were chattel—property, in other words—and were refused any possibility for self-sovereignty. This order was based on a complex but powerful set of racial ideologies that emerged out of and were buttressed by the Atlantic slave system. At the core of these ideologies was a kind of dialectic that enabled the simultaneous celebration of a capacity for free action and sovereignty on the part of certain groups while simultaneously denying that same capacity to others. The colony's system of racial thinking was based on a set of arguments about the fundamental incapacity of a group that was defined by its skin color to successfully exercise sovereignty over itself. The story here is certainly complicated, and the Haitian Revolution played a central role in the transformation and solidification of racial ideologies during the late eighteenth and nineteenth centuries. But the key point is that the slave plantation system out of which Haiti emerged was one of the most extreme (and for a time one of the most successful) mechanisms for the mass denial of sovereignty in the history of the modern world.

It is thus not surprising that those who set about courageously, brilliantly, and systematically destroying this system starting with the 1791 slave insurrection crafted particularly strong and powerful assertions of the right to self-sovereignty and, in time, to national sovereignty. Building on the work of Trouillot (1995), I have argued (Dubois 2004a, 2004b) that in the Haitian Revolution we can find the true origins of modern discourses of human rights, that Haiti was the place where the assertion of true universal values reached its defining climax during the Age of Revolution. Enslaved people who were considered chattel rather than human beings successfully insisted first that they had the right to be free and then that they had the right to govern themselves according to a new set of principles. Their actions were a signal and a transformative moment in the political history of the world. The Haitian revolutionaries propelled the Enlightenment principles of universalism forward in unexpected ways by insisting on the self-evident—but then largely denied—principle that no one should be a slave. They did so at the very heart of the world's economic system, turning the most profitable colony in the world into an independent nation founded on the refusal of the system of slavery that dominated all the societies that surrounded it in the Americas (Dubois 2004a).

These events were the foundation upon which all of Haiti's subsequent history was built. The conflicts and aspirations born of revolution have shaped and defined the political history of the country. There has never been stasis, of course, and each generation in Haiti has remade history in changing economic, environmental, and global political contexts up to the present day. Yet the basic problems the Haitian Revolution posed are still there in all these struggles. The Haitian Revolution has haunted and spurred forward different generations as an event whose conflicts and contradictions have been replayed, though never in precisely the same way, during the past 200 years.

Let me try to offer a few tentative answers to the larger question of this book by breaking down the question of sovereignty into a few smaller, perhaps more manageable parts: 1) Who owns the idea of Haiti? 2) Who owns the Haitian state? and 3) What insights do *longue-durée* Haitian social and cultural structures have to offer about these questions?

I'll offer some answers to the first question by thinking through the long-term impact and legacies of the reaction to the Haitian Revolution outside the country's borders. I'll then turn to question two by offering some thoughts about the central issues at work in the long-term history of the country's political institutions. I'll offer some thoughts about the third question by focusing on what Jean Casimir has called the counter-plantation system that emerged in Haiti through and after the revolution. Understanding this system, I'll suggest, is really the key to understanding the foundations and future of Haitian sovereignty. Within each of these main currents and critical countercurrents, I'll be calling attention to the aspects of the latter legacies that seem to me to be the most valuable. These are worth comprehending and nourishing in constructing new Haitian futures.

Reaction

The Haitian Revolution posed a profound threat to the world order as it was. Though the history of revolt against slavery was as old as slavery itself and though maroon communities in several Caribbean islands had secured their freedom, the scale of the success in Haiti was stunning and transformative. Jean Casimir (2001) sometimes describes Haiti as an entire nation of maroons, and in a way this best captures the radical threat the country posed. It changed the terms of the debate about slavery everywhere, and it changed the terms of the imagination of what was possible. It was an inspiration and example to the enslaved and was carried throughout the Atlantic world in news, song, and performance. It was also a powerful example in part because it was based in important ways on alliances between the enslaved and radical whites who embraced the revolution. That aspect of the period is often overlooked in favor of easier, racial readings, but in fact understanding the Haitian Revolution chiefly through the lens of race limits and circumscribes its true political and ideological meaning.

The reaction among power holders in the world, who at the time were deeply invested in maintaining the slavery system, was, not surprisingly, hostile. Jefferson was only one among many who clearly articulated a desire to contain what he called the "cannibals of the terrible republic" (Matthewson 2003, 97–101). He put in place a policy of diplomatic nonrecognition that lasted until 1862. And as is well known, France only acknowledged Haiti's independence in 1825 in exchange for the payment of a large indemnity. The payment of this indemnity and the interest on the loans taken out to service it sapped the Haitian treasure for nearly a century (Matthewson 2003; Brière 2008).

As important, though, are the intellectual and discursive reactions, which began a long history of condescending and willfully distorted portrayals of Haiti. There is, I would argue, no country on earth that has been burdened with the same kind of obsessive critique and negation as has been directed at Haiti for the last two centuries. This discourse is a kind of labyrinth, taking many forms, some of them easy to identify and undo, others much more insidious. Racism and racialist readings of Haitian history—which have often shaped historical narratives produced in the country—are a part of this legacy. Such representations of course were reconfigured and reactivated at different moments, particularly during the U.S. occupation of Haiti from 1915 to 1934. Scholars have studied and confronted these representations in increasingly rich and careful ways (see notably Ramsey 2011). This work is critical, for the only way to begin to emancipate ourselves from these visions is to study the enemy carefully—a difficult task, since often these racialized representations infuse even the most well-meaning depictions of the country.

There were, however, always countercurrents to this hostility, notably in African American thought and practice in the United States. Intellectuals, antislavery activists, and artists persistently offered an alternative vision of Haiti. Indeed, large groups of African Americans immigrated to the country in the 1820s and again in 1861. Among the latter group was James Theodore Holly, founder of Haiti's Episcopal Church. One trace of the important place the country of Haiti played in the African American imagination is the presence of a neighborhood called Hayti in Durham, North Carolina. Founded in the decades after the Civil War, this community of African Americans likely took on this name as a way to express pride in its autonomy and independence (Dean 1979).

Political Structures

The second of the legacy of the Haitian Revolution is the country's political institutions and practices. Their early history was deeply shaped by the broader context of hostility. Haiti's early leaders were paranoid, but they had many good reasons to be given the international reaction to their very existence. The new nation's political culture was deeply shaped by the idea that freedom was fragile and that both old and new enemies might well attempt to reestablish slavery. The refusal of both France and the United States to recognize Haiti diplomatically and the widespread racist representations of the country and its revolution were constant reminders of this threat. The question was how to best protect the country and solidify its autonomy.

Toussaint L'Ouverture first confronted the problem during the revolution. The solutions he developed were maintained by post-independence Haitian leaders including Jean-Jacques Dessalines, Henry Christophe, and Jean-Pierre Boyer. Their strategy was to establish a secure foundation for self-defense and economic autonomy by maintaining the plantation economy. Only through the production and sale of plantation commodities, these leaders insisted, could they maintain an army, build forts, and foster alliances with foreign powers that would keep Haiti safe.

To the Haitian people, their leaders offered this deal: In order to be preserved, freedom had to be circumscribed. What that meant was that these leaders insisted that most of the population continue working on plantations. Though working conditions were clearly an improvement from those of slavery, they fell far short of the kind of freedom and autonomy most of the formerly enslaved envisioned for themselves. Leaders beginning with L'Ouverture responded to this resistance with various forms of coercion, often violent, and developed a militarized and autocratic set of institutions that they justified as necessary for the protection and preservation of Haiti's independence.

The most famous symbol of this approach is the Citadelle Laferrière built by Henry Christophe: a vast fortress, visible from miles away, meant to withstand a new invasion by the French and just as much to stand as a forceful symbol of the determination of Haitians to remain free. Some of the stones used to build this fortress were literally carried from old plantations and sugar works from the plain below by former slaves rounded up to do the work under conditions many contemporaries described as brutal, even a new kind of slavery.

As Robert Fatton Jr. has argued, these early styles of governance laid the foundations for a long-term tendency in Haiti toward regimes constructed around militarism (almost all nineteenth-century presidents were generals first), and political authoritarianism (Fatton 2007). But though it was always under pressure and circumscribed, there is also a long tradition of Haitian parliamentarianism going back to the Pétion regime. Even Christophe's regime, which is often lampooned because of his construction of a local Haitian aristocracy, can more usefully be seen as a creative attempt to forge a kind of coalition government out of an extremely diverse and fragmented leadership class in the North. At certain moments in Haiti's history, the parliaments were in fact sites of intense and vivid opposition. One clear case of this is during the 1840s, when a liberal opposition to Boyer—who was hated, among other things, for his private and nonconsultative signing of the 1825 indemnity with France—found voice in the Parliament and in Haiti's burgeoning press. The African-born Félix Darfour wrote passionately and brilliantly against Haiti's colorist political order, and a 24-year-old named James Blackhurst, inspired by the ideas of Saint-Simon, created a cooperative farm. In 1843, the liberal opposition began a mass uprising, one that a British observer described as being "unparalleled in history" because of the startlingly peaceful way it was carried out. "Democracy," another observer wrote, "flowed full to the brim. And what democracy!"(Dubois 2012, 123).

This 1843 Parliament-infused revolution was followed by an even more remarkable mobilization among peasants in the South, led by Acaau, which showcased inventive forms of political discourse and symbolism that grew from grassroots organizing among small farmers. These two revolutionary groups from north and south came into conflict, and ultimately the reformist hopes of a younger generation were dashed. But the democratic forms of mobilization that would repeatedly be used in Haiti's political history were clearly present during this period. The same could be said of the period of the 1880s, when the intellectual and statesman Anténor Firmin pursued an ultimately failed bid for president.

This tradition of resistance and opposition continued when the United States occupied Haiti in 1915. Opposition came first from members of Parliament who resisted the rewriting of the Haitian constitution, prompting the U.S. Marines to shut down and muzzle the Haitian Congress. And then it came from the Caco uprising, which was led by rural elites, including Charlemagne Péralte. The movement was highly democratic in character and held large meetings in the countryside to develop strategy. The Cacos saw themselves as inheritors of the traditions of the Haitian Revolution, and indeed they organized themselves both in military and political ways that drew on the traditions of those ancestors. Just as they had shut down Congress, the U.S. Marines shot Péralte and ultimately crushed his movement. The marines exposed and photographed his dead body and then distributed the photograph among the population as a message to stop resisting. But even the story of that image—which was rapidly reappropriated and ultimately became a symbol of remembrance and resistance—hints at the powerful ways a politics of hope for democracy and autonomy persisted in Haitian communities (Schmidt 1995; Gaillard 1982).

This is all critical to remember so that we can better understand something that Jean Dominique articulated in a beautiful essay called "La fin du marronage haïtien" (1985). Dominique argued that the grassroots democratic organizing that led to the overthrow of Jean-Claude Duvalier in 1986 in fact tapped into a very long and deep tradition of political imagination and practice. When we forget that history, we also let go of a set of powerful precedents and intellectual resources through which we can imagine the future of Haitian democracy not as something that has to be invented or imported but instead as something that simply needs to be cultivated from within the country's own diverse traditions (Smith 2009).

The Counter-Plantation System

These oppositional and alternative forms of politics were rooted in a larger cultural and social system. This system is, in fact, the most significant and most radical product of the Haitian Revolution. While understanding the other legacies of the revolution that I have described here is critical to understanding the many constraints and pressures placed on Haiti's people both from the inside and outside, understanding the counter-plantation system in its full complexity—a task Jean Casimir undertook in 2001—is ultimately, I would argue, the most critical analytical task before us. It is out of an engagement with this system that we can best think collectively today about what Haiti is and should be.

The counter-plantation system that was built by the formerly enslaved began during the Haitian Revolution. This group was—we must remember—majority African born, and many of them had in fact been in the colony just a few years by the time the revolution began. In the years before the revolution, about 40,000 enslaved were brought to the colony each year, so in 1791 there may have been as many as 100,000 people or more for whom enslavement was just a very brief part of longer lives of freedom in Africa followed by freedom in Saint-Domingue and then Haiti. In creating the counter-plantation system, they drew on multiple sources: African forms of agricultural organization, family structure, and spirituality; the example of maroon communities; and the spaces of autonomy built within the plantation world. Many of these individuals were at the forefront of the military and social struggles of the revolutionary period, including as leaders. Macaya and Sans-Souci were both African born, for instance. They made use of the interstices the independence conflict opened up to craft a new way of life on the plantations where they had once been slaves (Dubois 2004a).

The system, one that of course has parallels in all other post-emancipation societies in the Americas, was based on not simply dismantling the plantation but also setting up structures that were organized to avoid its return in any form. From the perspective of this majority, a plantation was still a plantation whether its profits were meant to fend off the French or not. So they turned their backs on the plantation-based projects of their early political leaders, taking control of the land and putting it to their own uses. The counter-plantation system was the most radical production of the Haitian Revolution, since it insisted that only through a complete transformation of the social and economic order could real freedom actually be attained. Its creators refused the idea state leaders advanced that they had to accept serious limits on their liberty in order to preserve it. They built their own kind of Citadelle through a set of social institutions rooted in individual land ownership anchored in a set of broader family and community institutions.

On that land, they did all the things that had been denied them under slavery: They built families, freely practiced their religion, and worked for themselves. They grew food for themselves and for local and regional markets, but they also found that coffee, once a plantation crop, could also be successfully grown on small family farms and could bring in money they could use to buy other goods from the towns. That combination guaranteed rural Haitians a better life, materially and socially, than that available to most other people of African descent in the Americas throughout the early nineteenth century. Over time, despite opposition from certain leaders and the institution of laws meant to save the plantation, rural Haiti was largely transformed into a space divided into small landholdings, a space of striking social and political autonomy. And despite many attempts—including those made during the 20-year U.S. occupation of Haiti—efforts to rebuild plantations in Haiti have largely met with failure.

Along with Casimir, the greatest analyst of this "counter-plantation" system was Georges Anglade, the noted Haitian geographer who was lost in the earthquake of 2010 and whose work brilliantly explores all the layers and complexities of this system (Anglade 1982). What he and others have shown is that the counter-plantation system was actually economically viable, producing the coffee exports that sustained the Haitian economy in the nineteenth century while also providing all the food needed for the country's population. The relative success of this system can perhaps be summarized by one crucial fact: During the nineteenth and early twentieth century, few people left Haiti. The country was instead a significant magnet for immigration. People came from as close as other parts of the Caribbean, including Guadeloupe and Martinique, and as far away as Europe and the Middle East. Thousands of African Americans also made the journey to Haiti in the 1820s and early 1860s. Many of these migrants become part of Haiti's rural communities (Dubois 2012, 93–94, 153–156; Dean 1979).

Writing the history of the counter-plantation system is a complicated challenge. Hostile outsiders and Haitian political leaders have left behind ample archives for us to grapple with. The rural population of ex-enslaved people, the majority of them African born, who created a new Haiti in the early nineteenth century left far fewer written traces. In fact, it is in many ways easier to write the history of the involvement of the enslaved in the Haitian Revolution than it is to write the history of the post-independence rural Haitians. If we limit ourselves to written texts, we end up depending essentially on the laws and pronouncements such as the Code Henry or Boyer's Code Rural that were meant to contain and reverse the counter-plantation system.

But we do have a series of archives that we can delve into to understand these systems: land tenure practices; family structures; Haitian Vodou songs, which often refer to and reflect on the cultural construction of this system; and other cultural and social practices. The Haitian Creole language, in its forms of address, its proverbs, its ways of condensing ideas of morality, and its analysis of power, also offers up a rich archive of ways of seeing and being. So too does Haitian art. All of these cultural forms offer up resources for confronting Haiti's current challenges. We need to engage with them, because if we are to create a participatory future in Haiti we need a fully participatory analytical and methodological framework.

Both outsiders and many Haitian thinkers have long misunderstood the counter-plantation system as an atavistic form of retreat, as subsistence or worse. In fact, though, it is nothing of the sort. Rather, it is a historically crafted response to a very particular historical experience: that of having successfully destroyed slavery and the plantation and having systematically set about making sure it never returned. It is not a system of escape, but rather a system of engagement that is based on an absolute commitment to maintaining autonomy and dignity as the basis for an engagement without the broader world. It is nourished by the vivid and realistic memory that for a long time many in the world saw Haitians only as victims or potential laborers at the bottom of the global economic order. It is a consistent refutation of that vision and a cultivation of something else: another political imagination, one that continues to deeply challenge the world as it is, reminding us that it is not the world as it must be.

Conclusion

Let me conclude with a painting that I think crystallizes the themes I have explored here. It is from 1994, done by an artist named Dominique Fontus, and represents the arrival of U.S. troops into the town of Jacmel. The central actor of the painting, or so it seems at first, is the U.S. soldier who is disarming a local army officer. The U.S. soldier shows with his hand what is to happen: Time to put your gun down. The Haitian soldier is acquiescing, putting his gun down, and—strikingly—his hat is midair, seemingly propelled off his head by some unknowable force, symbolizing the end of his power.

But who is really acting here? The painter suggests that the U.S. soldier is in fact just a refraction of a bigger political battle: In front of him the Lavalas rooster is decisively defeating a bloodied Duvalierist *pintade*, or guinea fowl. The bigger political battle is also depicted in the painting by the arriving demonstration, which is effectively backing up—or perhaps forcing the hand of—the U.S. soldier. Though this, too, is ambiguous, since behind the demonstration is a U.S. army jeep. Is it just following the demonstration, watching it, or encouraging it? None of this is particularly clear: Who is really acting? Visible actions are being driven by less visible ones, and power articulated openly depends on other forms of power. The painting captures all the ambiguity of this moment when Haitian sovereignty is being expressed through the actions of a foreign soldier. But what makes the painting truly remarkable is that in the midst of this scene is placed an interlocutor for us as the viewers: the woman to the left. We don't know who she is, why she is there, how she is involved. Related to the soldier who is being disarmed? Part of the demonstration or just standing by? Is she, perhaps, the painter Dominique Fontus? Whoever she is, she is standing and thinking, asking a question of her own, it seems, and asking a question of us. And we can perhaps imagine her asking: Who owns Haiti?

Figure 2.1. Painting by Dominique Fontus, 1994.

References

Anglade, Georges. 1982. *Atlas critique d'Haïti*. Montréal, Québec: Groupe d'études et de recherches critiques d'espace, UQAM.

Brière, Jean-François. 2008. *Haïti et la France, 1804–1848: Le rêve brisé*. Paris: Kharthala.

Casimir, Jean. 2001. *La culture opprimée*. Delmas, Haïti: Impr. Lakay.

Dean, David M. 1979. *Defender of the Race: James Theodore Holly, Black Nationalist and Bishop*. Newton Center, MA: Lambeth Press.

Dominique, Jean. 1985. "La fin du marronage haïtien: Éléments pour une étude des mouvements de contestation populaire en Haïti." *Collectif Paroles* 32: 39–46.

Dubois, Laurent. 2004a. *Avengers of the New World: The Story of the Haitian Revolution*. Cambridge, MA: Belknap Press of Harvard University Press.

———. 2004b. *A Colony of Citizens: Revolution & Slave Emancipation in the French Caribbean, 1787–1804*. Chapel Hill: Published for the Omohundro Institute of Early American History and Culture by the University of North Carolina Press.

———. 2012. *Haiti: The Aftershocks of History*. New York: Metropolitan Books.

Fatton, Robert, Jr. 2007. *The Roots of Haitian Despotism*. Boulder, CO: Lynne Rienner Publishers.

Gaillard, Roger. 1982. *Charlemagne Péralte Le caco*. Port-au-Prince: Roger Gaillard.

Matthewson, Tim. 2003. *A Proslavery Foreign Policy: Haitian-American Relations during the Early Republic*. Westport, CT: Praeger.

Moïse, Claude. 1988. *Constitutions et luttes de pouvoir en Haïti, 1804–1987*. Montréal: Editions du CIDHICA.

Ramsey, Kate. 2011. *The Spirits and the Law: Vodou and Power in Haiti*. Chicago: University of Chicago Press.

Schmidt, Hans. 1995. *The United States Occupation of Haiti, 1915–1934*. New Brunswick, NJ: Rutgers University Press.

Smith, Matthew J. 2009. *Red & Black in Haiti: Radicalism, Conflict, and Political Change, 1934–1957*. Chapel Hill: University of North Carolina Press.

Trouillot, Michel Rolph. 1995. *Silencing the Past: Power and the Production of History*. Boston: Beacon Press.

3

Haiti and the Limits of Sovereignty

Trapped in the Outer Periphery

Robert Fatton Jr.

The neoliberal regime that has governed the world system for the past four de-cades has created a new zone of catastrophe, a zone of generalized inequities and ultra-cheap wages whose politics offers a simulacrum of electoral "democracy" under the tutelage of a self-appointed international community. I have called this zone the outer periphery (Fatton 2014). It differs from the three other ar-eas of the world economy—the core, the semi-periphery, and the periphery (Wallerstein 1979). The dramatic accentuation of global inequalities that has marked the past twenty-five years (Piketty 2014) has provoked the division of the periphery into two strata: the traditional lower stratum of peripheral states and the newer lowest stratum of the outer periphery (Fatton 2014). The outer periphery is a zone of extreme poverty often besieged by wars, natural disasters, regime change, and foreign occupation. It is characterized by the evisceration of state capacity, zero-sum politics, deeply unequal life chances, and virtually nonexistent sovereignty. This zone is comprised of the states that conventional wisdom defines as "fragile" or "failed" states (Torres and Anderson 2004; Brock et al. 2012; Rotberg 2004; Englebert 2009; Caplan, 2007). I prefer to call them instead the states of the outer periphery.

I have coined this label because failed-state theorists tend to argue that failed states are the product of their own traditional culture, one that resists in dys-functional ways the liberalizing, progressive, and rational impact of globaliza-tion. These theorists contend that failed societies can be "fixed" only if they abandon their "backward-looking" norms and embrace "modernity" and its triad: rule of law, liberal democracy, and entrepreneurial behavior. In turn, as theorists would have it, this transformation is impossible without the full cultural, economic, and often military intervention of a western-led international community.

For instance, Paul Collier, a well-known economist, World Bank consultant, and author of an influential report on Haiti (2009), has argued that countries such as Haiti are failing because they are stuck in "the conflict trap, the natural resource trap, the trap of being landlocked with bad neighbors, and the trap of bad governance in a small country" (Collier 2007, 5). While these traps may impede economic growth, they ignore the utterly subordinate position of the outer periphery in the world system. Because they ignore the destructive interferences of the hegemonic powers of the core in the outer periphery, failed-state theorists are blind to the realities of imperial politics and the devastating effects of past and future interventions.

This interventionism, in Collier's view, "has to do much more to strengthen the hand" of local "reformers" who are chosen by a self-appointed international community to implement the neoliberal policies that have paradoxically caused the current crisis. Collier argues self-righteously that the international community "has to learn to be comfortable with infringing upon sovereignty" (Collier 2007, 178).

In a similar vein, Stephen Krasner, the former director of the policy planning staff at the U.S. Department of State under the George W. Bush administration and a professor of political science at Stanford University, has argued:

> Left to their own devices, collapsed and badly governed states will not fix themselves because they have limited administrative capacity, not least with regard to maintaining internal security. Occupying powers cannot escape choices about what new governance structures will be created and sustained. To reduce international threats and improve the prospects for individuals in such polities, alternative institutional arrangements supported by external actors, such as de facto trusteeships and shared sovereignty, should be added to the list of policy options. (Krasner 2004, 86, 119)

A new version of the white man's burden is thus in vogue that calls for the imposition of de facto trusteeships on failed states. It is infused with militaristic impulses hidden by humanitarian and cosmopolitan gestures (Keohane 2003, 275–298; Duffield 2007; Rawls 1999; Hobson 2012; Fearon and Laitin 2004; Mallaby 2002; Krasner and Pascual 2005). The element that is new is neoliberalism, which has deepened local and global inequalities (Piketty 2014; Therborn 2013) and contributed to the disintegration of already-weak states. Neoliberalism is the global system that maximizes market transactions, privatizes public companies, lifts tariffs and trade barriers, and removes governmental responsibility for social obligations. While this system has not undermined states in core capitalist nations, it has eviscerated nations in the periphery and especially in the outer periphery. In fact, neoliberal institutions such as the World Bank and the International Monetary Fund have inflicted waves of economic austerity and deregulation on the poorest and most dependent nations to the point that their states can no longer perform vital functions and are increasingly supplanted by nongovernmental organizations (NGOs) (Bourdieu 1998; Harvey 2005; Kaplinsky 2005; Klein 2007; Panitch and Gindin 2012; Sassen 2014; Therborn 2013). Bypassed by foreign aid that privileges NGOs in funding decisions, such states have become empty shells incapable of providing minimal services to their citizenry. The decomposition of the state has generated political decay, increased levels of insecurity, and narco-trafficking, not to mention the complete erosion of the sense of civic obligation.

Under the weight of an externally imposed neoliberal regime, a quasi-permanent crisis of governance, and the devastating earthquake of January 2010, Haiti has tumbled into the outer periphery. While domestic social forces have played a fundamental role in Haiti's collapse, the nation's fall cannot be comprehended accurately without an understanding of how it was precipitated by the world system. The patterns of imperial interventions Haiti has endured over the years, especially in the aftermath of the fall of the Duvalier regime and the quake, have transformed the country into a virtual trusteeship.

Incursions at the Outer Periphery

The Interim Haiti Recovery Commission, which was responsible for coordinating reconstruction after the earthquake, symbolized this reality. The now-defunct entity was created in Washington by key figures in the State Department in consultation with private consultants and lawyers in the United States. The commission was parachuted into the Haitian government with little warning (Johnston 2014).[1] While it eventually underwent some changes at the behest of the Préval administration and some other major international players, this foreign control of reconstruction efforts clearly demonstrated the limits of Haitian sovereignty.

Integrated into the margins of the margin of the global economy, starved of direct foreign investments, and compelled to engage in ultra-cheap labor activities for exports (Worker Rights Consortium 2013), Haiti is at the farthest end of the global production process. Trapped in the outer periphery, it has come under the control of international financial institutions, NGOs, and what Robert Maguire refers to as for-profit contractors (FPCs) (Maguire 2014). FPCs work symbiotically with powerful states to advance the neoliberal agenda in peripheral and mostly outer peripheral regions. They seek to capture the bulk of foreign assistance extended to poor nations and tend to undermine local state capacity and privatize developmental projects. For instance, Chemonics, a paradigmatic FPC, was the top recipient of U.S. government funding for earthquake relief in Haiti for 2010–2011 (Ramachandran and Walz 2012, 12). Not surprisingly, FPCs and NGOs "have risen to play a prominent role in Haiti . . . becoming the main thoroughfare for foreign assistance" (Ramachandran and Walz 2012, 14). They symbolize the deliberate privatization of the public domain that has resulted in the incapacity of the Haitian state to execute the policies and laws it promulgates and provide basic services to its citizens. As Ramachandran and Walz contend, "The available evidence suggests that NGOs and private contractors provide almost four-fifths of social services in Haiti. One study conducted before the January 2010 earthquake found that NGOs provided 70 percent of healthcare while private schools, mostly run by NGOs, accounted for 85 percent of education" (Ramachandran and Walz 2012, 19). The earthquake exacerbated already dire conditions and pushed Haiti into a social impasse.

In fact, U.S. military and humanitarian intervention in the aftermath of the quake demonstrated the complete helplessness of the Haitian state under the Préval administration. The state had neither the institutional capacity nor the resources to deal with the catastrophe. Once more the country was turned into a laboratory for humanitarian assistance and worldwide charity. The resulting experiments are rooted in a pattern of decades-long interventionism by major world powers and organizations. In fact, the most significant moments in the last thirty years of Haiti's history would not have occurred had it not been for some form of imperial *ingérence* (meddling) in its internal affairs.

This interventionism has ranged from covert support for coups to foreign imposition of economic sanctions and embargoes to outright military occupation and heavy-handed humanitarianism (Dupuy 2007; Farmer, Gardner, and van der Hoof Holstein 2011; Fatton 2002; Jean and Maesschalck 1999; Hallward 2007; Robinson 2007; Vorbe 2010). The orchestration and funding of elections have also deeply reflected imperial decisions and interests, as have their final outcomes. For instance, President Aristide's return to power in 1994 and his forced departure into exile ten years later would have been impossible without the massive intrusion of the United States, France, and Canada (Dupuy 2007; Fatton 2002; Jean and Maesschalck 1999; Hallward 2007; Robinson 2007). More recently, the election of Michel Martelly as president in 2010 would have been unthinkable had it not been for the controversial involvement of *l'international*,[2] the word Haitians use to describe the major powers and organizations of the foreign community. Haitian rulers are the product of their own idiosyncratic milieu, but both their ascendancy to and downfall from positions of power are dependent on external and internal forces (Johnston and Weisbrot 2011).

The confluence of continuous imperial interferences and domestic forces in the making of Haiti's predicament explains why treating the country as a failed state is so erroneous. The Fund for Peace, which has placed Haiti seventh among the worst ten failed states on the planet (Fund for Peace 2012, 14–17),[3] measures failure using indicators that are primarily derived from the internal political economy of a society. In other words, these measures trace state evisceration, economic decline, social conflicts, and political instability back to local mismanagement, corruption, and culture. In such portrayals of Haiti's situation, it is as if the unbroken pattern of imperial interventions in Haiti had nothing to do with the country's massive failures. In reality, it is only by analyzing the opportunistic convergence of interests between reactionary domestic social forces and imperial powers that we can begin to understand what is wrong with Haiti. Dependence, agricultural collapse, military coups, and state disintegration are intelligible only through the prism of this convergence of interests, which has ultimately set Haiti in the outer periphery. The country's dire condition is the product of the hierarchical interconnections between local and global political economies that continuously reproduce the massive disparities of power and influence of our current global system.

As a state of the outer periphery, Haiti is at the extreme lower end of the production process. Wages barely assure the biological reproduction of the individual worker, let alone of his or her household (Worker Rights Consortium 2013). Not only is Haiti afflicted by ultra-cheap wages and abysmal social inequities, it is also dominated by unusually high rates of unemployment and a vast informal sector. In addition, its political system is but a simulacrum of representative democracy; the elections that are held more or less regularly are largely fraudulent. Outside powers not only finance these elections but (along with "pro-democracy" organizations with little knowledge of the local terrain) certify them as "free and fair." The Haitian state's extreme reliance on foreign institutions and sources of funding for its own electoral process symbolizes its incapacity to exercise any effective national sovereignty.

Given this context of acute dependence, it is not surprising that Haiti has an increasingly subservient economic relation with its relatively better-off neighbor, the Dominican Republic. In fact, the Dominican Republic's altruistic reaction to Goudougoudou (the Haitian Creole term for the 2010 earthquake) should not mask the reality that Haiti has become its periphery. Moreover, it is clear that like many "disaster capitalists," powerful Dominican economic agents have been eager to be part of what former U.S. ambassador Kenneth Merten called the "gold rush" Goudougoudou precipitated (Merten 2010).[4] The earthquake had positive effects on the Dominican Republic because its territory was used as a major conduit for providing assistance to Haiti, and several major Dominican firms have been directly engaged in the reconstruction effort. In fact, it is estimated that in 2010, 2 percent of the 7.7 percent increase in the Dominican Republic's gross domestic product was attributable to its role in the relief operation (Antonini 2012, 6).

The Dominican Republic's extensive economic involvement in Haiti predates the earthquake. It took off in the early 1990s at the time of the economic embargo the international community imposed on Haiti as a result of the military dictatorship of General Raoul Cédras. Since then, the Dominican Republic's involvement in Haitian affairs has become significant. Trade between the two countries is "nearly unidirectional"; Dominican Republic exports to Haiti were estimated at a total of $2 billion in 2012 (Antonini 2012; Agence Presse Média Caraibes 2013). Haiti depends on the Dominican Republic for 30 percent of its imports and 10 percent of its gross national product. Clearly, the Dominican Republic and Haiti have relations that are looking increasingly like those characterizing core and peripheral countries.

Moreover, the Dominican Republic is now bent on exploiting ultra-cheap Haitian labor in Haiti or near the frontier. This new Dominican strategy seeks to limit the political costs of massive inflows of poor Haitians into its heartland. Indeed, the Dominican Republic has exploited Haitian migrant workers as a socially invisible and humiliated people for the past seventy years. For generations, Dominican Republic rulers and cultural entrepreneurs have articulated an *antihaitianismo* (Sagás 2000)—an anti-Haitian credo—that rejects blackness as a sign of primitiveness and espouses a Hispanic and white identity. This racist and xenophobic state ideology has left a legacy of seeing Haitians as the permanent outsiders, the polluting others. This context helps explain why in September 2013 the Constitutional Court of the Dominican Republic invalidated the citizenship of unauthorized migrants born in the country from 1929 to 2010 (Abiu Lopez and Coto 2013, Agence France Presse 2013). The ruling affected some 200,000 Dominicans, mainly Dominicans of Haitian descent who were born in the Dominican Republic and had never set foot in Haiti. These individuals became "undocumented" and "stateless."

Not surprisingly, the ruling generated international condemnation and the furious protests of Haitian politicians and intellectuals (Bell 2013; Groupe d'Appui aux Rapatriés et Réfugiés 2014). Responding to such condemnation, the Dominican Republic announced a Naturalization Law that would allegedly "solve" the problem of statelessness. While it reestablished the Dominican nationality to those who had been born in the country between 1929 and 2007 and were officially registered with the government, it left out some 180,000 undocumented people, who continued to face bureaucratic and legal hurdles to establish their citizenship (Groupe d'Appui aux Rapatriés et Réfugiés 2014). With its rejection of the ruling of the Inter-American Court of Human Rights that nullified the Naturalization Law as "out of season, biased and inappropriate," the Dominican government clearly indicated that it would not contemplate any further changes in the law and that the matter had been settled (Robert F. Kennedy Center for Justice & Human Rights 2014).

Haiti's increasing dependence on the Dominican Republic is only one aspect of its outer peripheral status. A more critical symptom is the evisceration of governance. This evisceration is not only the product of the venality of the Haitian political class, it is also the direct product of neoliberal policies that have consistently undermined state capacity. For the past thirty years, the major financial institutions and organs of foreign assistance have deliberately bypassed the state and have instead funded nongovernmental organizations. Such policies have weakened government institutions to the point that at the time of the tragic earthquake of January 12, 2010, the Haitian state was utterly incapable of responding to the catastrophe. It was a powerless shell at the mercy of the international community. And yet in the aftermath of the earthquake, the pattern of foreign assistance has continued to bypass the government and has reinforced state incapacity. As Paul Farmer pointed out in the foreword to the report of the special envoy for Haiti, "With over 99 percent of relief funding circumventing Haitian public institutions, the already challenging task of moving from relief to recovery—which requires government leadership, above all—becomes almost impossible" (Office of the Special Envoy for Haiti 2011, 2).[5]

Of the $2.43 billion committed or disbursed in humanitarian funding, only $25 million was provided to the government of Haiti. Moreover, Haitian NGOs were virtually excluded from relief or recovery funds. Only two—Perspectives pour la Santé et le Développement (Prospects for Health and Development) and Adventist Development and Relief Agency Haiti—received funding, and that amounted to only an embarrassing $800,000 (Office of the Special Envoy for Haiti 2011, 15–16). In fact, a significant portion of both relief and recovery assistance funded organizations located in the donor countries. For instance, more than "75 percent of USAID funds went to private contractors inside the Washington, DC 'Beltway'" (Ramachandran and Walz 2012, 13).

The Haitian state's incapacity to become an effective vehicle for the resolution of the most pressing problems confronting the country is thus not just a reflection of an enduring domestic political crisis; it is also the direct result of the type of foreign intrusions and interferences that have marked the country's history. In this perspective, if Haiti is a "failed state," it is so because the world economy is a failed world economy. This failure is vividly demonstrated by the Martelly government's post-earthquake economic slogan: "Haiti is open for business." The cruel irony is that the slogan is nothing but a repackaging of the ineffective policies of the 1970s and 1980s. Not surprisingly, not even capitalists believe in the slogan. In reality, the country's political instability and lack of infrastructure, characteristics of its outer peripheral nature, have discouraged foreign investors. For instance, although direct foreign investments increased to a record high in 2011, they amounted to only $181 million (Economic Commission for Latin America and the Caribbean 2012, 30). In comparison, the Dominican Republic received $2.371 billion that same year (Economic Commission for Latin America and the Caribbean 2011, 10). Moreover, in the 2012–2013 Global Competitiveness Index of the World Economic Forum, Haiti ranked a miserable 142nd out of 144 nations (Schwab 2012, 13). Similarly, in the World Bank's Ease of Doing Business Index, Haiti ranks 174 out of 183 (World Bank 2011).

Subordination to the World Economy

The continued absence of productive capital investments in an outer periphery such as Haiti is no accident. It reflects the preferred movement of capital on a world scale. What James Ferguson writes about Africa applies even more trenchantly to the realities of Haiti: "Capital does not 'flow' from New York to Angola's oil fields, or from London to Ghana's gold mines; it hops, neatly skipping over most of what lies in between. . . . Capital is *globe-hopping*, not *globe-covering*" (Ferguson 2006, 38, Ferguson's italics).

Capital has thus largely "hopped over" and bypassed Haiti. The logic of privatization, state withdrawal, and market "rationality" neoliberalism unleashed on the country has further debilitated its already fragile governmental capacity, national infrastructure, and tenuous sovereignty. Paradoxically, capital creates zones that are so devastated that it no longer seeks to penetrate them. In fact, Haiti is a geographical space occupied and managed by "peacekeepers," FPCs, and NGOs of a self-appointed international community. NGOs, which international financial institutions promote as substitutes for corrupt and "failed" states, have unwittingly become part of the neoliberal "assemblage of occupation" (Duffield 2007, 27) in postdisaster and post–regime change nations.

Trapped in this "assemblage of occupation," Haiti's domestic economic policies are largely framed in the headquarters of the major international financial institutions and bilateral donor agencies. Similarly, Haiti's electoral process is heavily funded by foreign powers and under the surveillance of *l'international*'s apparatus of democratic legitimation, which imposes strict limits on political choice. In turn, these limits are protected and enforced by the presence of "6,270 troops . . . and a police component of up to 2,601 personnel" (United Nations 2015) from the United Nations—the so-called Mission des Nations Unies pour la Stabilisation en Haïti (MINUSTAH).

While Haiti owes much of its problems to its own domestic social forces and processes, it is also the product of the history of its incorporation into the world economy in a subordinate position (Amin 1974; Frank 1967; Wallerstein 1979; Fatton 2014). The interaction between imperial actors and Haitian rulers has created the country's massive dependence on *l'international*. This dependence, however, does not entail the absolute subservience of the latter to the desires and objectives of the former. In fact, Haiti's internal politics, class structure, material environment, and cultural matrix mediate the imperial reach of *l'international*.

In other words, while the major players of *l'international* seek to maximize their control and minimize the cost of their domination over the country, Haitian rulers maneuver to keep a degree of autonomy and extract badly needed scarce resources from *l'international*. There is thus a space for negotiating the extent of domination and dependence. This space varies, depending on statecraft, chance, and geopolitical realities. What is clear, however, is that Haiti must conform to what Alasdair Roberts has referred to as the logic of discipline (Roberts 2010), a logic that has compelled virtually all nations to devise policies and institutions that protect and insulate the interests of global capital from democratic practice. This logic is rooted in a "deep skepticism about the merits of conventional methods of democratic governance" (4) because these methods undermine the freedom of capital and slow the spread of globalized markets. Neoliberal globalization required the transfer of authority to "technocrat guardians" whose mission was to depoliticize "certain subjects from the realm of everyday politics" and impose new legal and contractual constraints "on the exercise of discretion by elected officials and voters" (5–9). The rule of the market had to be unquestioned and state intervention in the "commanding heights" of the economy was a "forbidden territory" (12). Neoliberalism demanded a "distinctive program of state renovation. This program was not aimed simply at dismantling or shrinking the state but also at rebuilding government so that it would complement a liberalized and globalized economy" (12).

This rebuilding of government has had deleterious consequences for rulers of outer peripheral nations such as Haiti. Their already limited capacity to make autonomous policies was further restricted by the exigencies of the globalized economy. These rulers, however, are not helpless. They can manipulate their domestic political environment and strategic choices to achieve certain objectives. The recent history of Haiti's relations with Cuba and Venezuela demonstrates well the manipulative and creative capacity of Haitian rulers in crafting their diplomacy. It is well known that the United States strongly opposed the further development of Haitian relations with Havana and Caracas. From 2006 to 2008, the United States sought to block, and then undermine, the Petro-Caribe agreement that President Préval signed with Venezuela,[6] even though the U.S. embassy acknowledged that it "would save [Haiti] USD 100 million per year" (Coughlin and Ives 2011). U.S. ambassador Janet Sanderson warned Préval and his senior advisors that "a deal with Chavez [sic] would cause problems with us." She cautioned them against "the larger negative message that [the PetroCaribe deal] would send to the international community at a time when the GOH [Government of Haiti] is trying to increase foreign investment" (ibid.). Ultimately, the Préval administration defied the United States and implemented the PetroCaribe plan.

Moreover, to the dismay of Ambassador Sanderson, Préval decided to attend as a "special observer" the summit of the Bolivarian Alternative for the Americas in Venezuela for the express purpose of finalizing a trilateral assistance agreement between Haiti, Venezuela, and Cuba (ibid.). Not surprisingly, Préval's determination to defend Haiti's national interest contributed to the deterioration of his relations with the United States. Ambassador Sanderson noted sharply that Haitian officials did not understand that the United States was not willing to tolerate a greater regional role for Venezuela and Cuba (ibid.).

In spite of continued misgivings among U.S. officials, Haiti under President

Martelly seems determined to follow Préval's friendly foreign policy toward Havana and Caracas. This policy is more than a matter of establishing some independence from Washington; it is a response to the simple reality that unlike other foreign donors, Venezuela is willing to provide foreign assistance to the Haitian state instead of privileging NGO-led development. Whatever their ideological differences may be, Haitians have realized that the results of some forty years of NGO- and FPC-led development have been at best meagre. They have come to understand that it is time to change trajectory. They agree with the analysis of Ricardo Seitenfus, the former special representative of the Organization of American States in Haiti, who denounced donors and NGOs for corruption and lack of transparency. As he put it:

> We have hundreds of millions of dollars in the hands of the NGOs without any sort of social control, without any transparency, or government management. And we are accusing the government of Haiti of being corrupt when the government of Haiti doesn't even have money in their hands to be corrupt with! We cannot demand from Haiti what we do not demand for ourselves . . . All projects that come in to Haiti that weaken even more the weak Haitian state, should be discarded . . . We cannot make of Haiti a "Disneyland" of the NGOs. (Seitenfus quoted in Elizondo 2011)

It is clear, however, that local institutions remain extremely fragile. At this point it would be difficult for them to function without the largesse of external donors, which control the country's development agenda. In truth, what passes for Haiti's "civil society" is largely made up of foreign organizations funded by foreign sources and controlled by foreign agents. Most so-called local NGOs are subcontractors of transnational entities that are not accountable to the local population. Moreover, NGOs and FPCs have created powerful networks that can challenge and/or supplant governmental policies. The parallel and mostly internationalized space NGOs and FPCs have created in Haiti undermine Haitian sovereignty and crowd out local grassroots civil society.

With little control over their economy and territory, Haiti's politicians are compelled to rely on foreign sources of power for their continued hold on office. In the post-Duvalier era, rulers of such different political persuasions as Jean-Bertrand Aristide, Raoul Cédras, Gérard Latortue, René Préval, and Michel Martelly rose to, remained in, and fell from positions of power depending on their respective relations with France, Canada, and the United States. There is little doubt, for instance, that Michel Martelly became president because of the massive interference of *l'international* in organizing, funding, and counting the votes of the 2010–2011 elections (Katz 2013, 268–272; Chérubin 2012, 252–324; Seitenfus 2015).

In October 2012, Martelly acknowledged that his presidency was in essence "coup proof" precisely because he is the man of the international community. In an interview on the French cable television station France 24, Martelly declared, "Today, there is this peacekeeping unit maintaining order, this force of the United Nations, the international community that watches over Haiti. . . . Even if there were a coup d'état against my government, I think it would not be tolerated" (Martelly quoted in Perelman 2012; my translation).

While the presence of MINUSTAH may well protect Martelly from being overthrown, it will not ease the crisis of governance that has besieged Haiti's unending transition to democracy. Haitians perceive the UN troops as an unwelcome occupation force that has caused a deadly cholera epidemic, been guilty of sexual abuses, and failed to create the security it promised (Higgins 2012; Katz 2013, 224–231). MINUSTAH is thus contributing to the growing popular discontent with the status quo. This discontent is stoked by a sense that reconstruction is nothing but a long trail of unfulfilled promises, that the political system is paralyzed in futile opportunistic battles, and that the cost of living, which has spiked with the massive influx of foreign NGO staff and humanitarian aid workers, is prohibitively high for the average Haitian.

Seeking another Paradigm

What can be done? While I have little to offer in terms of remedies for Haiti's failures, it is clear that the post-earthquake strategies of reconstruction should be abandoned because they differ little from past development efforts and will lead to the same impasse. Although these strategies pay lip service to building state capacity, agricultural renewal, and economic decentralization, in reality, they are "old wine in new bottles" (Government of the Republic of Haiti 2010). These programs continue to privilege the development of the assembly industry sector and of agricultural exports, principally mangoes and coffee. They follow Paul Collier's 2009 economic report on Haiti to the secretary-general of the United Nations. For Collier, export processing is the heart of Haiti's economic revival. This is especially the case for garments: "In garments the largest single component of costs is labour. Due to its poverty and relatively unregulated labour market, Haiti has labour costs that are fully competitive with China, which is the global benchmark. Haitian labour is not only cheap[,] it is of good quality" (Collier 2009, 6). While garments, mangoes, and coffee should not be

neglected, they cannot be the priority in a balanced strategy of poverty alleviation and self-sustaining economic growth.

In fact, Collier's neoliberal export-processing recommendations, which have
guided Haiti's post-earthquake economic strategy, echo the Duvalier policies
of the late 1970s and early 1980s and favor the continued bypassing of the state.
This strategy will merely create more dependence, more food insecurity, and
more inequalities. In addition, it is likely to intensify rural migrations to urban
areas, which will not provide the employment and wages required to avoid the
further expansion of slums.

However, the key foreign powers and financial institutions that fund Haiti's
neoliberal developmental project reject anything that departs from the neoliberal model as unrealistic and misguided. Mats Lundahl, a Swedish development specialist at the Stockholm School of Economics and a leading scholar on
Haiti, offers a forceful defense of the neoliberal mode of industrialization these
powers advocate. He contends that Haiti must submit to the discipline of world
market prices and take advantage of its cheap labor if it is to engage in production for export, which at this time implies the apparel industry. Lundahl views
this strategy as the only viable option (Lundahl 2013, xxiv, 284, 341). He rejects
as "utopian" any plan that would privilege the development of agriculture and
food sovereignty.

Moreover, in Lundahl's view, giving priority to agriculture not only leads to
poor economic outcomes, it is also impractical given extreme soil erosion, a
high person-land ratio, and the absence of an effective titling system. In fact,
Lundahl contends that feeding Haitians through Haitian agriculture is not feasible: "Increasing food production simply contributes to soil destruction, to
'mining' the soil. . . . For the process to be reversed, the man-land ratio must
decrease, not increase" (277). Not surprisingly, he argues that reducing the rural
population can be achieved only by creating employment "elsewhere, in the
context of an open economy, and then there is only one viable alternative: the
manufacturing sector, apparel production, where Haiti has a comparative advantage in terms of wages and privileged access to the American market" (xxiv).

The problem with Lundahl's argument is that the neoliberal strategy he espouses was adopted by Jean-Claude Duvalier's dictatorship in the mid-1970s
and early 1980s to create the "Taiwan of the Caribbean." It had devastating
consequences. It failed to industrialize the nation and instead led to massive
corruption, utter neglect of agriculture, and the creation of vast slums in the
vicinity of the so-called industrial zones. Lundahl offers no reason to believe
that following the same path at this time will lead to a different outcome. In fact,

while he applauds the recently inaugurated free-trade area of Caracol in the northeast of Haiti, he acknowledges that things could go very wrong: "Unless social services, housing, urbanized villages, etc. are prepared[,] what you will get is simply a new Cité Soleil or Martissant, with an impatient and disorderly labor pool" (292).

It is hard to believe that the neoliberal industrialization Lundahl advocates is more realistic than a plan that gives priority to the development of agriculture. In fact, an explicit anti-rural bias runs through the policies the international community favors. For instance, in a report for the influential Rand Corporation, Keith Crane unambiguously claimed:

> Some of Haiti's best prospects for growth are to attract foreign and domestic investment to the garment industry. Haiti has too many people engaged in agriculture. The country is heavily populated, and more land is cultivated than is ecologically sustainable. In contrast, labor-intensive industries, such as garment manufacturing, provide an attractive source of jobs and income, especially given Haiti's competitive, low-cost labor force. (Crane et al. 2010, 84)

Not surprisingly, Marc Cohen, a senior researcher at Oxfam America, reported that between "2000 and 2005, aid to agriculture and rural development accounted for just 2.5 percent of all official development assistance to Haiti" (Cohen 2013, 3). This neglect of agriculture is also reflected in the fact that "the Ministry of Agriculture and Rural Development accounted for only 3.3 percent of the recurrent budget over 2002–2004 and 4.4 percent over 2005–2007, and only some 4 percent of the investment budget. This was less than 10 percent of what the Ministry had requested." Moreover, "donor allocations show commitments to agriculture averaged around 7 percent of total since 1995 to 2006 but [were] down to 2 percent in 2007 with $10 million out of $624 [million]" (Fukuda-Parr 2009, 11). As Sakiko Fukuda-Parr explains, such meager funding "leads to very little investment in agricultural support infrastructure such as roads, research and extension which are essential in any country" (ibid.).

While privileging the existing structures of rural production or a return to some idyllic nineteenth-century *lakou* agriculture (Dubois 2012, 107–112; Lundahl 2013, 19–21) would lead to an impasse, there is no convincing reason to assume that the modernization of the countryside need be naively utopian.[7] In fact, launching a coherent agrarian reform, transitioning to higher tariffs, and implementing a public plan of reforestation would do more to employ, feed, and equalize life chances of Haitians than any neoliberal industrialization based on cheap labor and uncertain foreign demands for apparels. In fact, the utopian belief is that after investing the bulk of scarce resources in the apparel industry for more than three decades, it can now miraculously generate the virtuous cycle of development that it has consistently failed to deliver.

This is not to say that export-oriented production should not be part of a development plan, but it should not be its central driving force. The agricultural sector, particularly food production for the domestic market, should have priority. As Fukuda-Parr explains, "In Haiti, with approximately 55 percent of the population in rural areas, and two thirds of them relying on agriculture as the main source of income, this sector is still the predominant economic base for the population. Agricultural development can play a central role in poverty reduction because it is the source of direct and indirect livelihood of the majority of the poor" (Fukuda-Parr 2009, 10). Moreover, she correctly points out that

the experience in countries such as Thailand, Malaysia, Korea and India, who have achieved rapid poverty reduction with fast growth in recent years shows [that] labour intensive export-oriented manufacturing needs to be complemented with deliberate investments in agriculture. These countries invested heavily in a supportive institutional and physical infrastructure such as feeder roads, agricultural credit, [and] agricultural research and extension to upgrade technology. . . . Conditions in these countries are not so different from those in Haiti[,] as they are based on small scale family holdings that were oriented to subsistence production, rather than large scale plantation agriculture characteristic of South America, or large mechanized farms of North America. (ibid.)

Prioritizing agriculture does not amount to a form of peasant triumphalism, nor is it a call for a return to an idyllic pastoral life. It entails using agriculture to build a modern infrastructure of roads, irrigation canals, and electrical plants. Labor-intensive methods should be privileged in order to reduce the high levels of unemployment and the exodus from rural areas. To implement this plan, the Haitian government must first engineer a transition period that would impose certain protectionist measures. The country simply cannot afford to continue to have an open-door policy that destroys its domestic economy. This plan is neither radical, nor backward looking, but it does conflict with the dogma of the international financial institutions and the interests of powerful domestic and foreign forces. Unless Haitians decide to take matters into their own hands and challenge these forces, any plan of this kind is unlikely to see the light of day.

While taking matters into their own hands is no easy task for Haitians, it is a challenge they must meet lest the country fall into further economic and political decay. Let me end, however, with a disclaimer, because it is easy to proclaim from afar in the comfort of well-paid American academia in the heart of the capitalist world economy. While it is possible to "feel" Haitian in the Diaspora, it is quite another thing to face the vicissitudes, uncertainties, and insecurities of daily life in Haiti itself.

I have no right to claim any moral high ground in my condemnation of those responsible for Haiti's predicament. In fact, consciously or unconsciously, an intellectual such as me partakes in some of the privileges generated by this warped global system that is monopolized by a mere fraction of humanity. As a member of the Haitian elite and of the Diaspora that has opted to adopt the American nationality, I must acknowledge that I am a privileged individual living in a cocoon of fundamental contradictions. I have the luxury of distance; I can afford to look at Haiti's present and future with a deeply critical eye and a certain sense of despair. The vast majority of Haitians simply cannot. To go on facing the daily struggle for food and shelter, they must ultimately believe that things will change and that they cannot simply fall apart continuously. People must believe that the struggle continues not just for themselves, but also for future generations. It is this belief that inspires hope.

Notes

1. Jake Johnston (2014) contends that

> the Commission was presented as a response to the devastation of the earthquake. But its basic tenets—and its slogan, "Build Back Better"—were actually agreed upon by the U.S. and U.N. in the year prior. The commission's formation was handled not by the Haitian government, but by the staff of the Clintons, mainly Cheryl Mills and Laura Graham, as well as a team of U.S.-based private consultants. The commission's bylaws were drafted by a team from Hogan Lovells, a global law firm headquartered in Washington, D.C. A team from McKinsey and Company, a New York based consultancy firm, handled the "mission, mandate, structure and operations" of the commission. Eric Braverman, part of the McKinsey team, later went on to become the CEO of the Clinton Foundation.

2. The term *"l'international"* (the "international community") alludes mainly to the United States, France, and Canada. More recently, Brazil, Argentina, and Venezuela have been included in the group.

3. According to the Fund for Peace (2012, 14), Haiti's index of failures have improved since the earthquake, though the improvement has made little difference for most Haitians:

The third most improved country, Haiti, continues to languish at seventh place. However, this is a significant improvement over its fifth place finish in 2011 as a result of the catastrophic January 2010 earthquake. Though Haiti improved by a solid 3.1 points in 2012, this should be interpreted merely as a partial return to pre-earthquake levels and a recognition of the harsh conditions Haitians experience even when there is not the added calamity of natural disasters. Though Haiti did improve in 2012, we should not forget that Haiti was the most worsened country in 2011.

4. Kenneth Merten, "TFHA01: Embassy Port Au Prince Earthquake Sitrep as of 1800," telegram, February 1, 2010, http://wikileaks.org/cable/2010/02/10PORTAUPRINCE110.html#, accessed February 2, 2014.

5. According to the Office of the Special Envoy for Haiti (2011, 15), of the $2.43 billion committed or disbursed in humanitarian funding,

- 34 percent ($824.7 million) was provided to donors' own civil and military entities for disaster response
- 28 percent ($674.9 million) was provided to UN agencies and international NGOs for projects listed in the UN appeal
- 26 percent ($632.5 million) was provided to other international NGOs and private contractors
- 6 percent ($151.1 million) was provided (in kind) to unspecified recipients
- 5 percent ($119.9 million) was provided to the International Federation of the Red Cross and national Red Cross societies
- 1 percent ($25.0 million) was provided to the government of Haiti

6. The PetroCaribe agreement served the interests of Haiti well, as Dan Coughlin and Kim Ives (2011) explain: "Under the terms of the deal, Haiti would buy oil from Venezuela, paying only 60 percent up front with the remainder payable over twenty-five years at 1 percent interest."

7. In the nineteenth century, peasants resisted the predatory reach of the state by developing the *lakou* system. As Laurent Dubois explains:

In its most basic sense, a *lakou* (from the French *la cour*, or courtyard) refers to a group of houses—sometimes including a dozen or more structures, and usually owned by an extended family—gathered around a common yard. But the *lakou* also came to represent specific social conventions meant to guarantee each person equal access to dignity and individual freedom. . . . Unable to transform the national political system, rural residents found another solution: they created ". . . an egalitarian system without a state." Profoundly innovative, this system was predicated on the "auto-regulation" of local communities. These communities took on many of the tasks of social organization that might otherwise have been supervised or legislated by the authorities, such as the regulation of inheritance, land ownership, and family relationships. (Dubois 2012, 108)

References

Abiu Lopez, Ezequiel, and Danica Coto. 2013. "Dominican Ruling Strips Many of Citizenship." Associated Press, September 26.

Agence France Presse. 2013. "La République dominicaine "dénationalise" des milliers d'Haïtiens." Accessed October 3, 2013. http://www.france24.com/fr/20131003-haiti-republique-dominicaine-nationalite-dechenace-transit-immigrants.

Agence Presse Média Caraibes. 2013. "La balance commerciale reste encore trop déséquilibrée entre Haïti et la République dominicaine." Accessed February 8, 2013. http://www.maximini.com/fr/news/haiti/economie/-la-balance-commerciale-reste-encore-trop-desequilibree-entre-haiti-et-la-republique-dominicaine-21005.html.

Amin, Samir. 1974. *Accumulation on a World Scale*. 2 vols. New York: Monthly Review Press.

Antonini, Blanca. 2012. *Relations between Haiti and the Dominican Republic*. Oslo: Norwegian Peacebuilding Resource Centre.

Bell, Lis. 2013. "Rép. Dominicaine: La "dénationalisation" des Dominicains d'origine haïtienne planifiée par le PLD et la FNP depuis 2008." *AlterPresse*, December 3. Accessed December 13, 2013. http://www.alterpresse.org/spip.php?article15624#.Uv2Xgv2_20s.

Bourdieu, Pierre. 1998. *Acts of Resistance*. New York: The New Press.

Brock, Lothar, Hans-Henrik Holm, Georg Sørensen, and Michael Stohl. 2012. *Fragile States: War and Conflict in the Modern World*. Cambridge: Polity Press.

Caplan, Richard. 2007. "From Collapsing States to Neotrusteeship: The Limits to Solving the Problem of Precarious Statehood in the 21st Century." *Third World Quarterly* 28 (2): 231–244.

Chérubin, Ginette. 2012. *Le ventre Pourri de la bête*. Port-au-Prince: Éditions de l'Université d'État d'Haiti.

Cohen, Marc J. 2013. "Diri nasyonal ou diri Miami? Food, Agriculture and US-Haiti Relations." *Food Security* 5 (4): 597–606.

Collier, Paul. 2007. *The Bottom Billion*. Oxford: Oxford University Press.

———. 2009. *Haiti: From Natural Catastrophe to Economic Security. A Report for the Secretary-General of the United Nations*. Oxford.

Coughlin, Dan, and Kim Ives. 2011. "WikiLeaks Haiti: The PetroCaribe Files." *The Nation*, June 1. Accessed June 3, 2011. http://www.thenation.com/article/161056/wikileaks-haiti-petrocaribe-files?page=0,0.

Crane, Keith, Laurel E. Miller, Charles P. Ries, Christopher S. Chivvis, Marla C. Haims, Marco Overhaus, Heather Lee Schwartz, Elizabeth Wilke. 2010. *Building a More Resilient Haitian State*. Santa Monica, CA: Rand Corporation. http://www.rand.org/pubs/monographs/2010/RAND_MG1039.pdf.

Dubois, Laurent. 2012. *Haiti: The Aftershocks of History*. New York: Metropolitan Books.

Duffield, Mark. 2007. *Development, Security and Unending War*. Cambridge: Polity Press.

Dupuy, Alex. 2007. *The Prophet and Power*. Lanham, MD: Rowman and Littlefield Publishers.

Economic Commission for Latin America and the Caribbean (ECLAC). 2012. *Foreign Direct Investment in Latin America and the Caribbean, 2011.* Santiago, Chile: United Nations Publications.

Elizondo, Gabriel. 2011. "An Insider's Critique of What Went Wrong in Haiti." *Al Jazeera,* January 8. Accessed January 8, 2011. http://blogs.aljazeera.com/blog/americas/insiders-critique-what-went-wrong-haiti.

Englebert, Pierre. 2009. *Africa: Unity, Sovereignty, and Sorrow.* Boulder, CO: Lynne Rienner.

Farmer, Paul, Abby Gardner, and Cassia van der Hoof Holstein. 2011. *Haiti after the Earthquake.* New York: Public Affairs.

Fatton, Robert, Jr. 2002. *Haiti's Predatory Republic.* Boulder, CO: Lynne Rienner Publishers.

———. 2014. *Haiti: Trapped in the Outer Periphery.* Boulder, CO: Lynne Rienner Publishers.

Fearon, James D., and David D. Laitin. 2004. "Neotrusteeship and the Problem of Weak States." *International Security* 28 (4): 5–43.

Ferguson, James. 2006. *Global Shadows.* Durham, NC: Duke University Press.

Frank, Andre Gunder. 1967. *Capitalism and Underdevelopment in Latin America.* New York: Monthly Review Press.

Fukuda-Parr, Sakiko. 2009. "Empowering People: Human Rights Review of Haiti's Poverty Reduction and Growth Strategies." Issue paper, The New School, New York. Accessed May 15, 2015. http://sakikofukudaparr.net/wp-content/uploads/2013/01/EmpoweringPeopleHaitiPRSPReview2009.pdf.

Fund for Peace. 2012. *Failed States Index: 2012.* Washington, DC: The Fund for Peace. Accessed November 4, 2012. http://www.fundforpeace.org/global/library/cfsir1210-failedstatesindex2012-06p.pdf.

Government of the Republic of Haiti. 2010. *Action Plan for National Recovery and Development of Haiti.* Accessed May 24, 2016. whc.unesco.org/document/106244.

Groupe d'Appui aux Rapatriés et Réfugiés. 2014. "Position de la plateforme GARR autour du dossier de la dénationalisation des Dominicains/Dominicaines d'ascendance haïtienne." Accessed January 31, 2014. http://reliefweb.int/report/dominican-republic/position-de-la-plateforme-garr-autour-du-dossier-de-la-d-nationalisation.

Hallward, Peter. 2007. *Damming the Flood: Haiti, Aristide, and the Politics of Containment.* London: Verso.

Harvey, David. 2005. *A Brief History of Neoliberalism.* Oxford: Oxford University Press.

Higgins, Michael. 2012. "UN Peacekeepers to Blame for 7,500 Cholera Deaths in Devastated Haiti: Public Health Expert." *National Post,* October 24. Accessed October 24, 2012. http://news.nationalpost.com/2012/10/24/haiti-cholera-that-has-killed-7500-blamed-on-un-troops-from-nepal/.

Hobson, John M. 2012. *The Eurocentric Conception of World Politics.* Cambridge: Cambridge University Press.

Jean, Jean-Claude, and Marc Maesschalck. 1999. *Transition politique en Haiti*. Paris: L'Harmattan.

Johnston, Jake. 2014. "Outsourcing Haiti: How Disaster Relief Became a Disaster of Its Own." *Boston Review*, January 17. Accessed January 17, 2014. https://www.bostonreview.net/world/jake-johnston-haiti-earthquake-aid-caracol.

Johnston, Jake, and Mark Weisbrot. 2011. "Haiti's Fatally Flawed Election." Center for Economic Policy Research. Accessed March 2, 2011. http://www.cepr.net/documents/publications/haiti-2011-01.pdf.

Kaplinsky, Raphael. 2005. *Globalization, Poverty and Inequality*. Cambridge: Polity Press.

Katz, Jonathan. 2013. *The Big Truck That Went By*. New York: Palgrave Macmillan.

Keohane, Robert. 2003. "Political Authority after Intervention: Gradation in Sovereignty." In *Humanitarian Intervention: Ethical, Legal, and Political Dilemmas*, edited by J. L. Holzgrefe and Robert Keohane, 275–298. Cambridge: Cambridge University Press.

Klein, Naomi. 2007. *The Shock Doctrine*. New York: Metropolitan Books.

Krasner, Stephen D. 2004. "Sharing Sovereignty: New Institutions for Collapsed and Failing States." *International Security* 29 (2): 85–120.

Krasner, Stephen D., and Carlos Pascual. 2005. "Addressing State Failure." *Foreign Affairs* 84 (4): 153–163.

Lundahl, Mats. 2013. *The Political Economy of Disaster*. London: Routledge.

Maguire, Robert. 2014. "Priorities, Alignment & Leadership: Improving United States' Aid Effectiveness in Haiti." *Cahiers des Amériques Latines* 1 (75): 59–78.

Mallaby, Sebastian. 2002. "The Reluctant Imperialist: Terrorism, Failed States, and the Case for American Empire." *Foreign Affairs* 81 (2): 2–7.

Merten, Kenneth. 2010. "TFHA01: Embassy Port Au Prince Earthquake Sitrep as of 1800." Telegram. WikiLeaks. Accessed February 1, 2010. http://wikileaks.org/cable/2010/02/10PORTAUPRINCE110.html#.

Office of the Special Envoy for Haiti. 2011. *Has Aid Changed? Channelling Assistance to Haiti before and after the Quake*. New York: Office of the Special Envoy for Haiti.

Panitch, Leo, and Sam Gindin. 2012. *The Making of Global Capitalism*. New York: Verso.

Perelman, Marc. 2012. "Michel Martelly, président haïtien." *France 24*, October 29. Accessed October 29, 2012. http://www.france24.com/fr/20121027-2012-lentretien-michel-martelly-president-haiti-seisme-crise-alimentaire-economique.

Piketty, Thomas. 2014. *Capital in the Twenty-First Century*. Cambridge, MA: Harvard University Press.

Ramachandran, Vijaya, and Julie Walz. 2012. "Haiti: Where Has All the Money Gone?" CGD Policy Paper 004. Washington, DC: Center for Global Development. Accessed May 21, 2012. http://www.cgdev.org/content/publications/detail/1426185.

Rawls, John. 1999. *The Law of Peoples*. Cambridge, MA: Harvard University Press.

Robert F. Kennedy Center for Justice & Human Rights. 2014. "RFK Center Welcomes Landmark Ruling on Dominican Nationality in Inter-American Court." Accessed

October 24, 2014. http://rfkcenter.org/rfk-center-welcomes-landmark-ruling-in-inter-american-court.

Roberts, Alasdair. 2010. *The Logic of Discipline*. Oxford: Oxford University Press.

Robinson, Randall. 2007. *An Unbroken Agony. Haiti, from Revolution to the Kidnapping of a President*. New York: Basic Civitas Books.

Rotberg, Robert. 2004. *When States Fail: Causes and Consequences*. Princeton, NJ: Princeton University Press.

Sagás, Ernesto. 2000. *Race and Politics in the Dominican Republic*. Gainesville: University of Florida Press.

Sassen, Saskia. 2014. *Expulsions: Brutality and Complexity in the Global Economy*. Cambridge, MA: Harvard University Press.

Schwab, Klaus, ed. 2012. *The Global Competitiveness Report 2012–2013*. Geneva: World Economic Forum.

Seitenfus, Ricardo. 2015. *Haiti: Dilemmes et échecs internationaux*. Port-au-Prince: Éditions de l'Université d'État d'Haiti.

Therborn, Goran. 2013. *The Killing Fields of Inequality*. Cambridge, MA: Polity Press.

Torres, Magui Moreno, and Michael Anderson. 2004. *Fragile States: Defining Difficult Environments for Poverty Reduction*. London: Poverty Reduction in Difficult Environments.

United Nations. 2015. "MINUSTAH: United Nations Stabilization Mission in Haiti." Accessed May 17, 2015. http://www.un.org/en/peacekeeping/missions/minustah/background.sht.

Vorbe, Charles. 2010. "Earthquake, Humanitarianism and Intervention in Haiti." *Latin American Studies Association Forum* 41 (3): 16–18.

Wallerstein, Immanuel. 1979. *The Capitalist World-Economy*. Cambridge: Cambridge University Press.

Worker Rights Consortium. 2013. *Stealing from the Poor: Wage Theft in the Haitian Apparel Industry*. Accessed October 15, 2014. http://www.workersrights.org/freports/WRC%20Haiti%20Minimum%20Wage%20Report%2010%2015%2013.pdf.

World Bank. 2011. "Doing Business in a More Transparent World." Doing Business 2012. World Bank Group. Accessed October 20, 2011. http://www.doingbusiness.org/rankings.

4

New Wine in Old Bottles

The Failure of the Democratic Transition in Haiti

Francois Pierre-Louis Jr.

On January 30, 2011, U.S. Secretary of State Hillary Clinton landed in Haiti to meet with the three finalists in Haiti's presidential election, which was tainted by accusations of fraud at the hand of the ruling Inite (Unity) Party. Clinton's trip was the final attempt by the U.S. government to salvage an election that had already cost it and the international community over $29 million (Alterpresse 2010). Despite the presence of the Organization of American States (OAS), the United Nations Stabilization Mission for Haiti (MINUSTAH), and hundreds of foreign observers, the first round of the 2010 general election for presidential and parliamentary offices was far from democratic and fair. This was the sixth general election Haiti had held since the overthrow of the Duvalier regime in 1986. Only one of these elections, in 1990, went uncontested.

One might believe that the answer to the question "Who owns Haiti?" was evident when Secretary of State Hillary Clinton pressured Inite candidate Jude Célestin, who finished second in the first round of voting according to the official tally in Haiti, to withdraw his candidacy. Following Clinton's visit, Célestin, the Préval government's official candidate, was replaced on the runoff ballot by Michel Martelly, who was widely viewed within Haiti as the candidate the United States favored. The fact that a foreign political figure such as the U.S. secretary of state flew to Haiti to settle a national electoral issue raises several fundamental issues about sovereignty, the limits of the nation-state as we know it, and the interventionist role of foreign powers as a last resort, especially when the local elite is unable to find the common ground required for it to effectively manage Haiti's political space. In this chapter, I argue that Clinton's intervention would not have happened if the Haitian elite and the Haitian Parliament had not pursued the politics of self-interest that worked to the detriment of the country and population.

Because of complex issues related to interdependence, access to resources, and power, the idea of sovereignty has often been a contested one. When Max Weber (1974) wrote his classic definition of a sovereign state as having a fixed border, a legitimate government, and a monopoly on force, he was basically recognizing an established truth for the European powers that had gained control of their sovereign space mostly through war and other acts of aggression. For a nation-state to be sovereign, however, it also has to be recognized as such by the community of states, especially those that are its neighbors. This recognition supposes nonintervention in its internal affairs, the right for the population to choose its own leaders, and respect for the sovereign state's laws, culture, and history.

To understand how Haiti, which was once a proud independent nation, ended up so susceptible to external infringements such as Clinton's, one has to understand the character and role of its economic and political elite. An argument can be made that during the period from 2004 to 2014, the international community was no longer working behind the scenes in Haiti to impose a government but rather worked overtly to impose its will. This work, however, was facilitated by a dysfunctional and self-interested elite. In this chapter, I discuss the history and composition of the Haitian elite and their questionable relationship with both representative democracy and fair elections. Specifically, I examine the informal association of individuals and organizations called the Group of 184 that was active in the early years of this time frame in order to understand how the Haitian elite have played a significant role in political developments in Haiti.

Transitions, Elections, and Elites

The transition from authoritarian rule to elected governments that took place in Latin America in the 1980s has provided a significant understanding of liberal democratic regimes and how they evolve. Such concepts were further developed when the Soviet Union collapsed and countries from Eastern Europe chose liberal democracy as a model for rebuilding their societies and economies. Munck notes that as these countries adopted democratic values and principles, scholars disaggregated the post-authoritarian transition toward democracy into two distinct questions: "What are the conditions for a transition from some form of authoritarianism to democracy?" and "What are the factors that account for the durability or endurance of democracy?" (2011, 5).

After the fall of the Duvalier dictatorship in 1986, many projected that Haiti would pursue a path similar to that of other countries that had recently experienced regime change. Both the international community, which felt that over time Haiti would develop and strengthen democratic policies, institutions, and practices, and exiled leaders of the Haitian Diaspora who hastily returned to their country of birth when Duvalier departed encouraged this path. Yet thirty years after the fall of Duvalier, there is a general consensus that Haiti has failed to adopt democratic norms that would have successfully transitioned it to a stable and prosperous society (Fatton 2014, 2002; Dupuy 1997).

Pivotal to the success of the democratic model that surged in Latin America, Asia, and Eastern Europe in the 1980s is navigation of the fine line between a transition to democracy and the establishment of a democratic society. O'Donnell, Schmitter, and Whitehead (1991) note that the transition to democracy often takes place when the authoritarian regime is forced to open up the political process to the opposition by extending civil and political rights to individuals and groups and liberalizing the media. As these actions begin, internal discipline within an authoritarian regime breaks down, thereby strengthening the democratic opposition. This process usually leads to the resignation of authoritarian leaders and a subsequent transition to a democratic government that is established through elections. Individuals and nascent organizations that fundamentally believe in the process and are willing to create all the necessary conditions for it to succeed usually spearhead this process.

The fundamental flaw that exists with regard to Haiti's application of this model has been the tendency of foreign powers to abrogate Haitian sovereignty by intervening to support national leaders who are far from democratic. In the contemporary period, this began with international intervention to support the military regime that replaced Duvalier after he left in 1986 and has continued since. Fearing the rise of leftist and radical groups, the United States and Haitian elites have coalesced to keep control of the political process by limiting participation and maintaining the status quo—what some call Duvalierism after Duvalier. This has meant preventing leaders of the nascent popular movement, which is made up of poor peasants, residents of slum areas, and the working class and their allies, from taking control of the post-Duvalier transition from authoritarianism to democratic governance. A fear of a democratic and inclusive government continues to haunt Haiti's elite and their international supporters, as demonstrated by the latter's unwavering support of individuals who consistently oppose popular movements.

Another obstacle to Haiti's envisaged democratic transition is the fact that its elite are not a singular entity. Rather, it is composed of two distinct groups: mulatto businessmen, or the "possessing elite," and black politicians, or the political class that has historically competed for political and economic power. According to Mosca (1939), an elite is an organized minority that controls public power. Unlike other countries in Latin America and the Caribbean, where unified elites do not have major contradictory objectives, Haiti's two sets of elite can diametrically oppose each other largely because their power comes from different sources.

The possessing elite depends heavily on foreign sources that support its agenda. Robert Fatton describes the possessing elite as "a class that has accumulated wealth through private ventures and independently of direct state predations" (2002, 36). In Haiti, this group is composed primarily of people of mixed European and African ancestry, but it also includes descendants of early-twentieth-century Levantine immigrants. Most of them are involved in the import-export economy and hold dual citizenship to protect their investments and family interests (Nicholls 1996). Fatton notes that "both the possessing and ruling classes in Haiti have no social project, except the day-to-day struggle of keeping themselves in positions of power, wealth, and prestige" (2002, 37). Possessing elites have rarely sought political office because Haiti's overwhelming African-descendant population is very suspicious of white and light-skinned Haitians.

In contrast, Haiti's political elite, which is comprised of descendants of revolutionary leaders who have formed an intellectual and middle class over time, has been deeply engaged in vying for office. While this group—which is sometimes described as *la classe politique*—holds political power, its independent grasp on economic power is limited. Hence, a political system described as *la politique de doublure* (politics by understudy) has evolved in Haiti in which those who hold political power depend on those who hold economic power to implement desired policies and programs (Trouillot 1990).

This dynamic has not changed since the demise of the Duvalier dictatorship in 1986. Instead of building a unified national identity to manage the state in the aftermath of that pivotal moment, the two branches of Haiti's elite have continued their rivalry. In so doing, they have continued the dictatorship's practice of relinquishing to international entities the responsibility of developing a nation and providing services for citizens. As a result, multitudes of international nongovernmental organizations (NGOs) are present in Haiti, taking on functions that should be the responsibility of the state (Etienne 1997; Pierre-Louis 2011; Schuller 2012).

Unlike such Latin American countries as Brazil and Chile, where important institutional changes have taken place to assure a democratic transition after the fall of authoritarian regimes, Haiti has struggled to introduce major reforms. Its 1987 constitution, which was structured to support democratic changes, has fallen short because key agencies required for its implementation have failed to materialize. One of these agencies is an independent permanent electoral council. Almost three decades after the constitution was ratified, this important agency that is necessary for creating a degree of certainty in the political process still does not exist. None of the governments that followed the ratification of the constitution have made a serious effort to create it. This has led to scenarios where elections usually take place after their constitutionally determined date and are managed by provisional electoral councils that disband as soon as elected officials take power. In her evaluation of the electoral council and the runoff election of 2011, Ginette Cherubin, a member of the 2007 provisional electoral council that disbanded following that election, reinforced this fact:

> From my installation in December 2007 to my departure in 2011, none of the scheduled elections took place according to the constitutional calendar. Those that were supposed to take place in November 2007 took place in April 2009. Those that were scheduled for November 2009 took place in November [sic] 2011. The business of postponing scheduled elections seems to be inscribed in the exercise of Haitian democracy. (2013, 62)

The condition Cherubin described has created a state of permanent distrust of the electoral process among the populace. Provisional electoral councils are widely viewed as tools that governments in power use to rig elections in favor of their own candidates. Since 1987, there have been fourteen electoral councils. Members of these councils are often accused of committing fraud. The combination of this lack of trust in the political process and the systematic delay of elections over the years has created the perfect conditions for unending political instability. In the rare instances when members of the councils have endeavored to organize honest elections, they have had to flee into exile to escape arrest and jail time. Such was the case of Leon Manus, a respected lawyer and president of the 2000 election commission who refused to validate the highly disputed parliamentary elections of mid-2000 and then had to flee the country due to threats. After its rise to office in May 2011, Michel Martelly's government attempted to arrest the president of the 2010 Provisional Electoral Council, Gaillot Dorsinvil, on what many believe were trumped-up corruption charges. Because Dorsinvil was tipped off about his imminent arrest, however, he, too, managed to flee the country (Radio Caraibes 2011).

The Group of 184

Jean-Bertrand Aristide is the only president in the history of Haiti to be overthrown by a military coup d'etat and then reinstated in office with the support of the United States. He is also the only president who has been elected twice (1990 and 2000) and has gone into exile twice (1991 and 2004). Most Haitians saw Aristide's return in 1994 after three years of exile as a triumph for the rule of law and for Haiti's democratic process. The elected president's triumphant return was not celebrated by everyone, however. Elites who had collaborated with the army to overthrow him continued their opposition. Although Aristide disbanded the army in 1995, most soldiers took their weapons home with them. The toxic mix of continuing resentment toward Aristide, his allies, and their populist policies on the part of certain elites and former soldiers and the widespread presence within the country of weapons fueled the violence that plagued Haiti through 2004, when Aristide once again was sent into exile. By that time, opposition to Aristide in Washington among Republicans in the U.S. Congress had grown to the extent that the conditions they had attached to aid disbursements in the mid-1990s had expanded to the suspension of most U.S. and multilateral aid after controversial parliamentary elections in mid-2000.

In Haiti, opposition groups emboldened by increased international disapproval of Aristide by late 2003 vehemently protested against his government, and in some cases they openly rebelled. Leading the protests was an organization that called itself the Group of 184, a coalition of opposition political parties and grassroots organizations of diverse ideological backgrounds, led by individuals associated with Haiti's economic elite. Shortly after Aristide was forced into exile in late February 2004, the coalition disbanded, replicating a classic Haitian pattern of temporary alliances of opposing groups that are forged to overthrow a common enemy and then falter once that common goal is achieved.[1]

After Aristide's departure, a Council of Wise Men that some leaders of the Group of 184 and the key international players of the United States, Canada, and France supported named a new government. It chose Gérard Latortue, a former UN official, as interim prime minister, and Boniface Alexandre, the head of Haiti's Supreme Court, as interim president. This government's mission was to hold national elections as rapidly as possible. Realizing that it could not govern the country without international support, Latortue's government invited the UN Security Council to authorize a military mission to stabilize Haiti and assist in preparations for the elections. Opposition to Latortue quickly emerged as Aristide supporters mobilized en masse to challenge his authority. Large and angry protests against his government and the Group of 184 erupted throughout the country, especially in the slums of Port-au-Prince. In the months after Aristide's departure, interim government officials, Haitian police, and UN forces were unable to penetrate such neighborhoods in the capital as Cité Soleil, Bel Air, and Carrefour Feuilles, where Aristide's Fanmi Lavalas (FL) party was strong.

Although the United Nations Stabilization Mission in Haiti (MINUSTAH) came to Haiti to facilitate a democratic transition, it found itself caught between conflict promulgated by supporters of the Group of 184, on one hand, and Aristide partisans, on the other. Talk of "witch-hunts" perpetrated by the former against the latter abounded. Realizing that it could not tamp down the FL protests by force alone, MINUSTAH undertook social and economic programs in the slums in an effort to win back the sympathy of the population.[2] When MINUSTAH took this initiative, violence in the capital decreased and the Latortue government organized general elections. René Préval, who had been elected president under the banner of the Lavalas platform in 1996, was elected from a field of thirty-three candidates to a new five-year term (Alterpresse 2005). According to international agencies and election observers, Préval's second-term victory "represent[ed] a major victory for the popular democratic sector because he was seen as the only candidate in a field of thirty-three presidential aspirants to represent the interests of the poor majority" (Dupuy 2007, 21).

Préval's campaign platform called for decentralizing the state apparatus. Just a month after he assumed office, he named Jacques-Édouard Alexis as his prime minister.[3] In his confirmation address to Parliament on June 7, 2006, Alexis reiterated the campaign's platform of decentralizing the state and declared that "the Haitian Constitution has placed local governments at the center of the new constitution" (Alexis 2006).

Préval and Alexis promised that their administration would create a decentralized partnership between the central government and local governments in order to promote investments and reinforce local institutional capacity to govern. Préval also launched a strategy of creating presidential commissions composed of elite members of Haitian society from various sectors and political tendencies to advise him on key issues and sectors with a view toward building consensus over long-term planning and program implementation.

Alexis invited opposition members to join his government, acting on the belief he shared with Préval that it would be impossible to achieve stability as long as certain political sectors or tendencies were left out of the government. Given the high level of violence that took place before the 2006 elections and the dire economic conditions that Préval and Alexis encountered when they took office, the decision to include opposition figures in the new government was well received by foreign governments and the business community, including the Haitian Chamber of Commerce and the Economic Forum, a convention of import businesses, manufacturers, and banking interests.

As part of the effort to bring political stability to the country and attract foreign investment, Alexis also proposed a stopgap program called Programme D'Apaisement Social (PAS; Social Peace Program) to alleviate poverty by infusing cash into the Haitian economy through job creation, feeding programs, and agricultural development. The program was the first government attempt to address the immediate needs of the population since Aristide's ouster in February 2004.

PAS also called for community restaurants, leisure and sports programs, renovation of public parks, and agricultural projects to increase domestic production of food staples, along with job creation for the population in the slum areas. Another component of the program called for the restoration of basic services that were destroyed during the 2004–2006 years of post-coup violence, when the capital and its surrounding areas were shut down because of neighborhood protests. The program, which the Haitian government budgeted at U.S. $50 million, received a vote of international support at a donors' conference held in Haiti in July 2006. The International Monetary Fund, for example, stated that it "has been encouraged by the President's commitment to entrench recent reforms, focus on the needs of Haiti's poor, and improve the country's prospects for sustainable higher living standards over time" (Alterpresse 2006b). Because Préval and Alexis took over a government that was practically bankrupt, the leaders counted heavily on the international community to support the PAS program and sought direct budgetary support from the IMF, the United States, the European Union, and others (Alterpresse 2004).

Despite the international community's stated support for the PAS program, very few donors actually contributed to it.[4] Alexis reported to a Caribbean Community (CARICOM) delegation visiting Haiti in 2007 that the program was stalled due to the "slow disbursement of the pledged financial support" (Alterpresse 2007). The fact that PAS did not receive the resources it required to get off the ground reflected badly on the Alexis government and citizens began to question his capacity to deliver on promises. As a result, the government's popularity sagged in public opinion polls. The lack of international support for the program was the beginning of the unraveling of the Alexis government, ushering in a return to public prominence of many who had opposed Aristide, including some members of the Group of 184 who subsequently played an important role in undermining the Préval-Alexis administration's efforts to create greater social and economic consensus and to breach the gap between rich and poor through presidential commissions and PAS.

Unable to implement PAS, Préval was powerless to pursue his key objective of bringing social peace by reining in urban gangs, whose violent behavior had plagued neighborhoods for years. As kidnappings and random violence surged, fear ran rampant in Port-au-Prince. In mid-December 2006, kidnappings targeting schoolchildren forced the schools to close. On the morning of December 13, twenty-three schoolchildren in La Plaine, a suburb of the capital, were kidnapped while they were on a school bus (Alterpresse 2006a).

Weak and inconsistent support from Haiti's political class threw fuel on the fire. In spite of the fact that Prime Minister Alexis received near-unanimous support when he presented his governing plan to Parliament in 2006, parliamentarians failed to move on legislation that would reinforce his government's capability to address the dire economic conditions of the population. The failure of the prime minister to secure required legislation even though his governing coalition held a majority in Parliament's two bodies can be attributed in large part to the individualistic mentality of elected officials who were concerned more about their own well-being than that of their constituents. In addition, political opposition galvanized around resentment of the idea that if he succeeded, Alexis would be a shoo-in for president in Haiti's 2010 elections.[5]

Préval and Alexis took steps to include diverse social and economic actors in envisaging a future Haiti and created a government that included diverse political actors because they wanted to address traditional rivalries and heal the wounds that the coup against Aristide and the years of violence that followed had created. Their political strategy backfired, however, when individuals Alexis selected from opposition parties to serve as cabinet ministers chose to pursue patronage politics conducive to their own interests, not those of the country. Hiring their own supporters to key positions in their ministries might have helped them prepare for upcoming general elections, but it did not strengthen the capacity of those ministries to enact PAS programs. One minister even refused to provide reports at cabinet meetings as a way of keeping his activities secret from the prime minister's office when he went on a hiring binge as a way to undermine the government. A few years after this incident, at a meeting in Gonaïves, in the central valley of the country, President Préval accused that former minister of being irresponsible by hiring over 13,000 new teachers with no budget allocation for them (Radio Metropole 2009).

Government ministers situated in the executive branch were not the only officials who behaved in this manner. Members of Parliament also practiced "me first" politics by delaying the ideas and actions the prime minister initiated. Their favorite tactic was to invite Alexis or a cabinet member to testify before their committee while circulating rumors that the prime minister or testifying ministers would be given a vote of no confidence at the hearing, thus taking him or her out of office. Once such a rumor spread, work on important policy issues stopped. Accompanying rumors of no-confidence votes was a corollary that if the minister or prime minister did not "negotiate" with members of that particular parliamentary committee (that is, pay bribes), they would be more likely to be voted out of office.[6] Another delaying tactic was for parliamentarians to call for a hearing and then refuse to appear at it themselves. The vulnerability of the prime minister and his cabinet to these parliamentary maneuvers eroded public confidence in the government's ability to address its needs. Very little legislation was enacted in support of Préval and Alexis's programs.

Parliamentarians had more interest in taking action when that action was accompanied by a bribe. On January 25, 2007, for example, a private bank reportedly paid members of Parliament between $15,000 and $30,000 not to indict a high-level official who was accused of mismanaging the bank's assets, thereby preventing a government investigation of the senior managers and partners involved in the scandal. The Soca Bank Affair made headlines for weeks as parliamentarians accused each other of taking bribes to protect bank officials (Le Nouvelliste 2007).

By January of 2008, the inability of the government to address the population's misery, high-profile corruption scandals, self-serving and deceitful ministers, and the absence of coherent government policies to confront Haiti's chronic problems began to take their toll. As the price of food escalated because of global production and trade issues and the government was powerless to offer any solution in response to the rising anger of the population, Alexis decided to change the cabinet, asking Préval for his blessing for that move. In effect, Alexis gave up on the idea that the opposition could play a constructive role in governance. Alexis's conclusion came too late. The corruption scandals and the difficulty in obtaining international support for the PAS program had already sparked protests that reminded the president and his prime minister of the days when the Group of 184 took to the streets. Only this time, the protests were engineered more by the political class than the possessing class, with the probable exception of a powerful group of food importers. In early 2009, protests over the high cost of basic staples such as rice and wheat began in the southern city of Les Cayes and spread to Port-au-Prince, where slum residents took to the streets. Alexis was blamed for the government's slow response to the rising prices the importers had set.

After a protest on April 7, 2008 in Port-au-Prince that turned violent, a majority of senators, some of whom were already opposed to Alexis, gave him an ultimatum: resign or suffer a vote of no confidence. After a week of intense negotiations between Alexis and opposing senators, the Senate gave the prime minister a no-confidence vote that was spearheaded by senators who blamed him for the high cost of rice in markets.[7] Although the food riots appeared to have been the immediate cause for the downfall of Alexis, they were only the symptoms of a larger ailment: a deeply engrained political culture that encourages politicians to look out for themselves to the detriment of the common good. The demise of Alexis and his PAS program only underscored the inability of Haiti's elite—especially its political class in this instance—to effectively manage a post-autocratic transition to democracy, reinforcing the belief among foreigners that in a Haiti fraught by division and self-aggrandizement, its leaders were unable to govern their country.

Hillary Clinton, the United States, and the rise of Michel Martelly

We now return to Hillary Clinton and U.S. intervention in Haiti's electoral process. Eighteen months after the fall of Alexis, on January 12, 2010, Haiti experienced one of the worst natural catastrophes of modern times when a major earthquake destroyed most of the country's capital, killed more than 230,000 people, injured a similar number, and left some 1.5 million homeless in an instant. Although the magnitude of the disaster would have created difficulties for any government, it was amplified in Haiti because the quake killed thousands of civil servants, striking a weak government that was already vulnerable to all forms of crisis.

The disaster exposed the flaws of President Préval's low-key leadership; he did not address the shocked population until a day and a half after the disaster. It also uncovered Préval's penchant for less-than-transparent deal making in order to achieve economic and political goals. In the quake's aftermath, the Haitian president relied on his network of close friends and families, members of the possessing class, giving them government contracts for such activities as buying tents, water, and food for the displaced population, instead of forming a broad coalition of political and institutional leaders to respond to the crisis (Thompson and Lacey 2010; Cave 2010). The resultant corruption among distributors of food and housing materials compounded widespread frustration with Préval's faulty postdisaster leadership. One outcome of this frustration was the fact that political parties and donor institutions that were thinking of postponing elections that were scheduled for that year subsequently reversed their position, arguing that elections were needed and could be organized in spite of the devastation.

Parliamentary and presidential elections took place in November 2010. Among the more than forty-three candidates seeking the presidency was Michel Martelly, a popular musician and supporter of prior autocratic and military regimes. The first round of voting took place on November 29th. Given the administration's control of state resources, observers assumed that Jude Célestin, the candidate representing Préval's Inite Party, would win outright. As votes were being cast, all candidates except Célestin joined forces at a news conference to announce that they were withdrawing from the election in protest of what they said were massive irregularities. This created a grave political crisis that was compounded by the fact that at the end of the day, only 23 percent of eligible voters had cast their ballots (Beeton and Nienaber 2014). Despite the disruption of the ballot and low voter turnout, both the UN, which oversaw election logistics, and the Provisional Electoral Council moved forward to tally the vote, insisting that there were no rules regulating what percentage of participation would lead to annulment of a vote.

Two weeks after the November election, the council announced preliminary results, acknowledging that no candidate had won an outright majority of the votes and declaring Préval's candidate in a run-off with first-place winner, Mirlande Manigat of the Rasanbleman Demokrat Nasyonal Pwogresis Yo (Rally of Progressive Democrats Party). Even though the Provisional Electoral Council's determination is final, the results were thrown into doubt when the U.S. embassy issued a statement rejecting them. In response to the embassy's statement, Martelly's supporters took to the streets with violent demonstrations in Port-au-Prince and Les Cayes in order to force the Provisional Electoral

Council and the Préval government to reinstate their candidate as a finalist in the second round of voting. This set the stage for the appearance of the U.S. secretary of state in January 2011.

The international position on how to resolve the dispute about the vote count quickly became controversial. For example, Ricardo Seitenfus, then the representative of the OAS in Haiti, reported that Edmond Mullet, the UN secretary general's special representative in Haiti, had applied strong pressure on Préval to resign and leave the country—an action that nearly amounted to a coup d'etat against a duly elected president. Was this going to be February 2004 all over again, wondered Haitian political insiders? Préval's prime minister, Jean-Max Bellerive, avoided that scenario, however, by refusing to acquiesce to the UN representative's demand. Préval also resisted by responding that he would rather "die like Salvador Allende than leave the country."[8] Although Préval successfully resisted this intrusion by international actors, under the continuing and severe pressure that included Secretary Clinton's visit, he eventually accepted the proposal that the OAS and the U.S. State Department recount the ballots. That recount resulted in the removal of Jude Célestin from the second round, when Michel Martelly was elevated to second place. In March 2011, Michel Martelly was declared the winner of the runoff election, and in May 2011 he was inaugurated as Haiti's president.

Although the majority of the political leaders protested Martelly's election as one imposed through force, the United States, the OAS and the UN stood by the results. Martelly, with his conservative background and malleable demeanor, immediately enjoyed the backing of the U.S. and other governments as a breath of fresh air in Haitian politics after a year of Préval's halting acquiescence to international postdisaster plans and his attempt to manipulate Haiti's electoral process (Archibold 2011). Martelly's association with individuals who had orchestrated the 1991 and 2004 ousters of Aristide did not deter the United States and others from supporting him, demonstrating again that the United States and the so-called Friends of Haiti will not hesitate to intervene in Haiti's political affairs or to support individuals they perceive as best for their interests, if not for the Haitian democratic process, especially when Haitian political actors provide them with an opening through their mismanagement of the political process.[9]

Despite high hopes for Martelly, his political honeymoon in Haiti was short lived. He created numerous crises with opponents in Parliament and within established political parties. Shortly after his inauguration, for example, he ordered the arrest of Arnel Belizaire, a member of Parliament and a Martelly critic, on charges that he had insulted the president. The action was clearly in violation of Haiti's constitution, which gives parliamentarians immunity from political persecution. A parliamentary commission rapidly concluded that Martelly had abused his power (Alterpresse 2011). The lack of cooperation between the president and Parliament delayed parliamentary and municipal elections that were due to take place in 2012, creating a governance crisis when offices were left vacant. Subsequently, Martelly named persons loyal to him as "interim executive agents" in order to fill vacant mayoral posts (Alterpresse 2012). Martelly's inability to organize elections continued into early 2015, by which time the terms of all elected officials in Haiti with the exception of one-third of the Senate had expired. As a result, the Haitian president began to rule by decree.

Conclusion

In this chapter I have argued that although Haitians own Haiti, that ownership is fraught with dysfunction that invites international actors to impinge upon it. As competing elites have hindered the country's post-authoritarian democratic transition and as inept, scheming, and self-centered politicians have failed to address issues of utmost importance to the country's ordinary citizens, they have left the door open to proxy organizations such as the UN, the U.S. Department of State, and NGOs to assume ownership of Haiti, or at least a piece of it.

It is very easy to argue that the international community has contributed to Haiti's predicaments since its independence in 1804. It is harder, however—but of utmost importance—for Haitian economic and political elites to look in the mirror and see how, by virtue of their pursuit of narrowly defined interests, they have been willing partners to this predicament by failing to develop a common vision and then work unselfishly to govern the country in the interests of and to the benefit of all. Too often, politicians have prioritized narrow personal agendas over national interests, betraying Haitian ownership of Haiti.

Haiti's people have demonstrated time and again by virtue of their participation in electoral processes (albeit often delayed and usually flawed) how eager they are to have a normal-functioning state that can address their dire economic and social conditions. Again and again, elected officials have failed them by encouraging the politics of impunity and by using state power and resources as their own private domain. Will Haiti's elites learn from the past to set aside these tendencies and focus, with all devotion and sincerity, on helping all Haitians strengthen their ownership over their country? This remains to be seen, but certainly the vast majority of ordinary Haitians are hoping that the political debacles of the past ten years will not repeat themselves over the next ten.

Notes

1. This type of temporary alliance for the purpose of overthrowing an existing government is legendary in Haiti. Examples include the overthrows of President Élie Lescot in 1946, Dumarsais Estimé in 1950, Paul Eugène Magloire in 1956, and Daniel Fignolé in 1957 and the myriad coups d'etat after the fall of Jean-Claude Duvalier in 1986. See Smith (2009).

2. In 2004, a banner on Bourdon Road in the wealthy section of the capital that leads to Pétionville, Haiti's wealthy suburb, thanked MINUSTAH for saving Haiti. This was put up by members of the Group of 184 who wanted UN forces to "eradicate" the Lavalas partisans. See WikiLeaks cable on Haiti (Ives and Herz 2011).

3. I was a member of Jacques-Édouard Alexis's senior staff from 2007 to 2009.

4. One exception was the U.S. government, however, which quickly supported PAS by agreeing to fund a program called KATA (Konbit Ak Tet Ansanm) that would create 40,000 jobs throughout Haiti (Alterpresse 2006c).

5. Jacques-Édouard Alexis was seen as the official presidential candidate who would replace René Préval in the 2010 elections. Politicians from Alexis's inner circle and from the opposition who wanted to run for the presidency thought that they should undermine his tenure as prime minister in order to decrease the chance that Préval would select him.

6. During the Préval administration, Parliament ousted the minister of culture because he did not give each member enough funding to organize the annual carnival in his or her district even though these representatives knew quite well that he had a limited budget.

7. It should be noted that the high price of staples in 2008 was a worldwide phenomenon and that many other governments in other countries suffered the same fate.

8. See Préval's interview in Raoul Peck's 2012 documentary *Assistance mortelle* (*Fatal Assistance*).

9. The Friends of Haiti is composed of the United States, Canada, France, Brazil and other South American countries that have expressed interest in ending Haiti's political instability through dialogue and elections.

References

Alexis, Jacques-Édouard. 2006. "Declaration de Politique Generale du Premier Ministre Jacques-Édouard Alexis." Policy Statement. Port-au-Prince, Haiti. May 24. Document in author's possession.

Alterpresse. 2004. "Haïti: Nouveau gouvernement face à des défis de taille." *Al-*

terpresse, March 17. Accessed April 26, 2016, http://www.alterpresse.org/spip. php?article1261#.Vxjb6vkrKwU.

———. 2005. "Haïti-Elections: Une quarantaine de candidats dans la course au fauteuil présidential." *Alterpresse*, September 15. Accessed April 26, 2016, http://www.alterpresse.org/spip.php?article3253#.VxjcIvkrKwU.

———. 2006a. "Haiti: Cri d'alarme de Justice et Paix à propos du climat d'insécurité." *Alterpresse*, December 14. Accessed April 26, 2016, http://www.alterpresse.org/spip. php?article5477#.VxjcYPkrKwU.

———. 2006b. "Haiti-Coopération: L'ONU satisfaite des résultats de la conférence des bailleurs." *Alterpresse*, July 26. Accessed April 26, 2016, http://www.alterpresse.org/ spip.php?article4970#.VxjcmfkrKwU.

———. 2006c. "Haïti: Les Etats-Unis financent un programme de création d'emplois de 81 millions de dollars sur quatre ans." *Alterpresse*, December 30. Accessed April 26, 2016, http://reliefweb.int/report/haiti/ha%C3%AFti-les-etats-unis-financent-un-programme-de-cr%C3%A9ation-demplois-de-81-millions-de.

———. 2007. "Haiti Support Group Calls on Donors to Honour Pledges to Support the Government's Rapid Impact Social and Economic Programme." *Alterpresse*, March 29. Accessed April 26, 2016, http://www.alterpresse.org/spip.php?article5833#.Vxj-MofkrKwU.

———. 2010. "Haiti-Elections: Pourquoi le scrutin du 28 novembre 2010 ne peut pas etre annule par le CEP?" *Alterpresse*, November 30.

———. 2011. "Haiti: L'épisode de l'arrestation du député Arnel Bélizaire tel qu'établi par la commission d'enquête du Sénat." *Alterpresse*, November 22. Accessed April 26, 2016, http://www.alterpresse.org/spip.php?article11934#.VxjMyvkrKwU.

———. 2012. "Haïti-Politique: Martelly affirme avoir l'autorité pour renvoyer les commissions communales élues." *Alterpresse*, March 6. Accessed April 26, 2016, http:// www.alterpresse.org/spip.php?article12479#.VxjdU_krKwU.

Archibold, Randal C. 2011. "With Subtraction and Addition, Haiti Sets Its Presidential Runoff." *New York Times*, February 3. Accessed April 26, 2016, http://www.alterpresse. org/spip.php?article10346#.V=cBmIWcfUK.

Beeton, Dan, and Georgianne Nienaber. 2014. "Haiti's Doctored Elections, Seen from the Inside: An Interview with Ricardo Seitenfus." *Dissent*, February 24. Accessed June 19, 2016. https://www.dissentmagazine.org/online_articles/haitis-doctored-elections-seen-from-the-inside-an-interview-with-ricardo-seitenfus.

Cave, Damien. 2010. "Rubble of a Broken City Strains Haitians' Patience." *New York Times.* May 29.

Cherubin, Ginette. 2013. *Le ventre Pourri de la bete.* Port-au-Prince: Editions de l'Universite d'Etat d'Haiti.

Dupuy, Alex. 1997. *Haiti in the New World Order: The Limits of the Democratic Revolution.* Boulder, CO: Westview Press.

———. 2007. *The Prophet and Power: Jean Bertrand Aristide, the International Community, and Haiti.* Lanham, MD: Rowman and Littlefield.

Etienne, S. E. 1997. *Haiti: L'Invasion des ONG*. Montreal: CIDIHCA.

Fatton, Robert. 2002. *Haiti's Predatory Republic: The Unending Transition to Democracy*. Boulder, CO: Lynne Rienner.

———. 2014. *Haiti: Trapped in the Outer Periphery*. Boulder, CO: Lynne Rienner.

Ives, Kim, and Ansel Herz. 2011. "Wikileaks Haiti: The Aristide Files." *The Nation*, August 5.

Le Nouvelliste. 2007. "Affaire BRH/Socabank: encore des revelations." *Le Nouvelliste*, February 2.

Mosca, Gaetano. 1939. *The Ruling Class*. New York: McGraw-Hill.

Munck, Gerarddo L. 2011. "Democratic Theory after Transitions from Authoritarian Rule." Paper presented at the 107th annual meeting of the American Political Science Association, Seattle, Washington, September 14.

Nicholls, David. 1996. *From Dessalines to Duvalier*. New Brunswick, NJ: Rutgers University Press.

O'Donnell, Guillermo, Philippe C. Schmitter, and Laurence Whitehead, eds. 1991. *Transitions from Authoritarian Rules: Comparative Perspectives*. Baltimore, MD: Johns Hopkins University Press.

Pierre-Louis, Francois. 2011. "Earthquakes, Nongovernmental Organizations, and Governance in Haiti." *Journal of Black Studies* 42 (2): 186–202.

Radio Metropole. 2009. "Polemique autour du recrutement de 13,000 enseignants." *Radio Metropole*, aired May 14. Port-au-Prince, Haiti.

Radio Caraibes. 2011. "Moïse Jean Charles nie toute participation à la fuite de Gaillot Dorsinville." June 6. Accessed April 26, 2016, http://www.radiotelevisioncaraibes. com/nouvelles/haiti/4216.html.

Schuller, Mark. 2012. *Killing with Kindness: Haiti, International Aid and NGOs*. New Brunswick, NJ: Rutgers University Press.

Smith, Matthew. 2009. *Red and Black in Haiti: Radicalism, Conflict, and Political Change, 1934–1957*. Chapel Hill: University of North Carolina Press.

Thompson, Ginger, and Marc Lacey. 2010. "In Quake's Wake, Haiti Faces Leadership Void." *New York Times*, January 31.

Trouillot, Michel-Rolph. 1990. *Haiti: State against Nation: Origins and Legacy of Duvalierism*. New York: Monthly Review Press.

Weber, Max. 1974. *On Universities: The Power of the State and the Dignity of the Academic Calling in Imperial Germany*. Translated, edited, and with an introductory note by Edward Shils. Chicago: University of Chicago Press.

5

Brazilian and South American Political and Military Engagement in Haiti

Ricardo Seitenfus

MINUSTAH is the best example of a mismatch between needs
on the ground and the tools the Security Council uses to address them.

*Mark Lyall Grant, representative of the United Kingdom, at the meeting
of the United Nations Security Council on October 10, 2013*

In early 2004, as armed gangs composed of drug dealers, former soldiers, and political opportunists overran police stations in northern Haiti and moved toward Port-au-Prince with the intention of overthrowing the government of President Jean-Bertrand Aristide, the Rio Group of Latin American and Caribbean countries made public its intention to halt the overthrow of Aristide.[1] The action of the group, which was formed in 1986 to seek a coordinated response to issues of shared interest, departed from the French and U.S. decision to abandon Haiti's embattled president. It issued a communiqué stating its support for the activities of the Organization of American States (OAS) and the Caribbean Community that sought a peaceful solution to the situation in Haiti and for the UN's offer of humanitarian assistance to Haiti. Further, the Rio Group urged the parties involved to endorse the Prior Action Plan that CARICOM had proposed that called for Aristide to complete his term in office and forcefully condemned the acts of violence taking place in Haiti.

Despite this broad Latin American and Caribbean support of Haiti's constitutionally elected president and opposition to his removal, in the predawn hours of February 29, 2004, Aristide was forced into exile. On March 4, Brazil's president Luiz Inácio Lula da Silva spoke about Haiti by telephone with U.S.

president George W. Bush and French president Jacques Chirac. Following that conversation, Lula's spokesperson, André Singer, announced:

> President Chirac said that during the second stage of international peace-keeping operations in Haiti, when the United Nations multilateral force will be formed by decision of the Security Council, the participation of Brazilian troops will be fundamental. He added that it will also be extremely important for Brazil to assume the command of that force, to be made up of Canadian, French, U.S., and Argentine contingents in addition to the Brazilian ones. The President of France stated that this was the opinion of UN Secretary General Kofi Annan. President Lula said that Brazil is honored by that proposal, and that it is at the disposal of the United Nations both to send troops and to assume the command. He also informed President Chirac that a contingent of 1,100 members of the Brazilian military specially trained for such missions is about to be sent to Haiti.[2]

In just over a week, Brazil had radically changed its position, taking several of its Rio Group neighbors along with it. From an intransigent defense of the principle of nonintervention, Brazil made an about-face and took command of the military segment of the future United Nations Stabilization Mission in Haiti (MINUSTAH). This chapter explores the evolution of this surprising and unthinkable turnabout among South American nations, with a special emphasis on Brazil's leadership in MINUSTAH.

Lula's decision was a broad departure from Brazil's historical position of nonintervention in the internal affairs of states. Despite the fact that Brazil's intervention in Haiti occurred within a context of long-standing collaboration with the UN system for the prevention and solution of disputes, in many ways the South American nation's participation in this peacekeeping operation was both unique and novel. In effect, even though MINUSTAH was formed following the general rules of the UN's Department of Peacekeeping Operations, the stabilization mission had a strong regional bias. Its military command was entrusted to Brazilian leadership and the vast majority of its soldiers were drawn from Latin American armed forces.[3] Of the 6,589 soldiers from Latin American military forces serving in UN peacekeeping operations worldwide in late 2014, no fewer than 4,621 were in Haiti. Latin American soldiers represented an average of 72 percent of MINUSTAH soldiers. In other words, of every ten Latin American soldiers available to the UN, seven were sent to Haiti.

Why this outpouring of Latin American military support? Latin American soldiers were present in Haiti for two primary reasons. The first was to pave the way for a new insertion of Latin America in global affairs. The second was related to Latin American leaders' strong aversion after 2000 to the Lavalas movement of Jean-Bertrand Aristide. This position was evidenced by debates and policy statements that the São Paulo Forum, a group of leftist political parties and movements in the Latin American region, had issued over the previous two decades. This chapter explores and analyzes this factor and how it resulted in intensive South American engagement in Haiti.

The Reinsertion of South America in International Relations

South American governments that participated in MINUSTAH viewed their insertion in Haiti's affairs as a way to reengage internationally following their broad refusal to participate in the U.S.-led (but not UN-sanctioned) "Coalition of the Willing" that invaded Iraq in 2003. These governments also portrayed their engagement as an expression of a desire to participate more actively in dispute prevention and conflict resolution. If, the thinking went, South American states were not capable of offering an alternative to a low-intensity domestic conflict in Haiti, how could their governments aspire to influence international matters of peace and security?

Latin Americans typically share a vision of solidarity with Haiti, drawing from the historical significance of the Haitian revolution and its dramatic and positive impact on liberation movements across the continent. Latin America's interest in Haiti was rekindled following the end of the Duvalier dictatorship in 1986 and the subsequent election in 1990 of Jean-Bertrand Aristide to his first term as president. When Aristide was ousted in a coup d'état in 1991, Latin American nations, including Brazil and Argentina, intensified their focus on Haiti, a shift that led to their participation in the UN-led intervention in Haiti in 1994. Given this engagement and prior knowledge, Latin Americans tended to view Haiti's early-twenty-first-century political crisis as a multifaceted one that had roots that went far deeper than its security aspects. Among South American governments, it was thought that peacekeeping strategies should take into account the causes and origins of instability, not just the results and consequences. With this approach, South Americans increased the complexity of the rationale of UN peacekeeping operations. From this perspective, one of the greatest challenges in international relations has to do with the ineffectiveness of the international system for preventing and resolving conflicts. Many South Americans view the instinctive use of militaries to resolve disputes that characterizes post-1945 intervention strategies as ineffective because of its detrimental impacts on the economic and social development of developing countries.

This shared concern among South American nations has given rise to the concept and practice of solidarity diplomacy. In essence, this concept is about international collective action that is carried out under the auspices of the UN Security Council third-party states that intervene in internal or international conflict for reasons that do not include their own national interest. Often these states are motivated solely by a duty of conscience. Material or strategic disinterest is the trademark of this approach. In order to avoid accusations of self-interest, it is also necessary that no previous special relationship exist between the intervening state and the state that is the object of the intervention.

When does a state—an entity devoid of feelings—make the decision to intervene in the affairs of another state? There are two primary sets of factors. First is the supposed existence of national interests to defend, be they financial, military, strategic, political, diplomatic, or linked to national prestige. Second, a state will act in the event of natural and humanitarian disasters or civil and international wars that eclipse other interests. In the latter case, an active and influential public opinion arises to demand a response designed to bring an end to the suffering of a defenseless civilian population. Was solidarity diplomacy at work among South American actors in the Haiti case? Neither of these two decision-influencing factors appears to have pressured South American states to act. Brazil, for instance, acted on its own, without any pressure from public opinion or explicit expression of interests. Other South American states, including Chile, Argentina, and Uruguay, seem to have taken a similar approach. Thus, neither national interests nor humanitarian concerns impelled Brazilian and other South American states to intervene in Haiti's affairs.

At the time of Brazil's initial intervention in Haiti in 2004, its foreign minister, Celso Amorim, provided a valuable and original contribution to the theory of solidarity diplomacy when he declared that Brazil is "profoundly committed to Haiti, politically and emotionally, in the long run" (Seitenfus 2006, 8). In doing so, he indicated that Brazil's decision to intervene should be understood in light of criteria other than those stemming from cold calculations of national interests. Implicit in Amorim's statement was a belief that Brazil's intervention was related to Haiti's security and the need to foster political dialogue among factions and parties. Above all, the engagement would be part of a plan meant to reinforce Haiti's economic development and ameliorate its serious social problems.

Further, Brazil's government hoped that its active participation on the military side of MINUSTAH would bolster the nation's credentials for becoming a permanent member of the UN Security Council, though government officials did not verbalize this hope publicly. In 2004, many Brazilian leaders believed that the path to a seat on the Security Council would pass through Port-au-Prince.

MINUSTAH was not Brazil's first experience with a UN peacekeeping mission. Nevertheless, this experience includes three factors that make its action in Haiti both special and emblematic:

(1) Brazil's MINUSTAH military contingent is the largest it has deployed outside its national borders since the end of World War II.

(2) For the first time, Brazilian military commanders were at the head of a mission from the time of its creation.

(3) Brazil's engagement goes beyond the objectives of ensuring the establishment of safe conditions to include the pursuit of a process that guarantees freedom of expression for the Haitian people when choosing their leaders.

Brazil's intervention in Haiti was not just militaristic. Socioeconomic conditions in Haiti, aggravated both by decades-long political crises and by repeated natural disasters, influenced Brazil to engage in social, technical, and civic initiatives such as Viva Rio, a Brazilian NGO that operates in several low-income neighborhoods in Port-au-Prince. These initiatives were meant to assist the Haitian population, express solidarity with them, and draw the attention of the international community to the country's plight.

From the outset, President Lula expressed a strong humanist attitude toward Haiti that recognized the importance of the values of solidarity and cooperation.[4] In September 2005, for example, he declared, "We do not accept an unjust international order as a consummated fact. . . . Our diplomatic action is based on the defense of principles, but also on the search for results. It has a utopian dimension without ceasing to be pragmatic" (Seitenfus 2014b, 5). Later, Brazil's president mentioned the idea of nonindifference as a principle that guided his government's actions in Haiti: "In a globalized and interdependent world, our contribution to peace and democracy is determined by the Principle of Non-Indifference. That is why we are engaged in the efforts to stabilize Haiti" (ibid.).

Lula's discourse on Haiti paralleled his government's involvement in other arenas of international action. These included the growing intensification of Brazil's relations with African countries and its stepped-up presence in South-

South dialogue. As his government moved forward on these fronts, Lula emphasized the importance of the principle of nonindifference. He argued that Brazil would engage "because we will not be wealthy if we have impoverished countries behind us where hunger, unemployment, and misery persist." Hence, the philosophical underpinnings of Lula's diplomacy were defined prior to Brazil's engagement with Haiti. According to Amorim, Brazil's diplomatic principles and actions were based on a desire to assume new responsibilities in the international scene. Brazil sought to be proactive and lofty, without forgetting that such an approach to international affairs would be "steeped in a humanist perspective such that it would be, at one and the same time, a tool for national development and a defender of universal values" (Amorim 2005).

In 2005, the humanist perspective of Brazil's international activity was reinforced when Amorim insisted that it could not be used as a pretext for refusing to act in solidarity when a situation required that response:

> Brazilian diplomacy is guided by the principle of non-intervention in internal matters, enshrined in our Constitution. The government of President Lula considers that associated with this basic principle is an attitude that we describe as non-indifference. We have provided our support and active solidarity in crisis situations, so long as we are requested [to do so] and consider that we have a positive role to play. (Amorim 2005)

Brazil would not define its role as simply that of standing by. The concept of nonindifference was put into practice through the concept of solidarity diplomacy. Through their solidarity diplomacy in Haiti, a number of Latin American countries provided an example of how diplomacy might go beyond cold calculations of national interest.

In prevailing Latin American political thought, nonindifference appeared to give legitimacy to a belief that international action had to be reconceived so it could better respond to the demands of a region in crisis. This process required sustained engagement if it was to mature and consolidate. It also demanded dialogue beyond the state level, for it is a political action that responds more broadly to the human condition. Although Table 5.1 summarizes the characteristics of implementation of the nonindifference principle that currently exist, it is a nascent concept and lacks a theoretical foundation and a practice that would make it general and constant, allowing it to be transformed into law. While the concept and legality of nonintervention are well established, a long road must be traveled if the principle of nonindifference is to be consolidated as a legal concept in international law.

The Latin American presence in Haiti must also be understood in the context of contemporary debates about the role of the armed forces in a democratic society. Throughout the region, the movement toward forming a South American security and defense body, such as that outlined in an envisaged Union of South American Nations, remains timid and subtle. However, the experience in Haiti, as viewed in Table 5.2, represents a military rapprochement in the South

Table 5.1. Characteristics of the principle of nonindifference

Origin	Lula's foreign policy of solidarity with countries of the South
Basic concept	International solidarity and shared responsibility
Institutionalization	In the absence of any institutionalization, it is recorded in the speeches and practices of public figures
Action	Such actions as pardoning debts and not exercising power in negotiations with weak countries
Antecedents	It draws inspiration from the South-South cooperation ideas and models, the philosophy of the New International Economic Order (NIEO), and elements of solidarity diplomacy

Table 5.2. Latin American composition of MINUSTAH by country

Country	Soldiers	Police	Totals
Brazil	1,670	5	1,675
Uruguay	936	5	941
Argentina	569	20	589
Chile	464	12	476
Peru	373	0	373
Bolivia	206	0	206
Paraguay	164	0	164
Ecuador	68	0	68
Guatemala	137	0	137
El Salvador	34	7	41
Colombia	0	25	25
Totals	4,621	74	4,695

Source: United Nations Department of Public Information, Peace and Security Section. United Nations Peace Operations, Year in Review, April 2013.

American region, particularly among nations of the Southern Cone: Argentina, Brazil, Chile, Paraguay, and Uruguay. Brazil's essential role in the UN mission goes beyond its provision of the largest contingent of soldiers. It has maintained its command of the UN mission since its inception in 2004, in contrast to its role in other UN peacekeeping operations.

It is important to note that explanations for the troop commitments Brazil made to MINUSTAH were given after commitments had been made. In other words, first there was a decision to participate in the proposed UN mission, then explanations and supposed motivations followed some months later. In addition, it should be noted that in 1994, when a UN force was being assembled to intervene in Haiti in order to remove a military junta and restore Aristide's elected government, Brazil opposed the joint military action the United States proposed. Even though he was the head of the Ministry of Foreign Affairs in both 1994 and 2004, Celso Amorim adopted diametrically opposed positions in those years.

Examining the path to Latin America and Brazil's historic involvement in MINUSTAH illuminates the intersection of novel diplomacy and a broader set of international goals within the region. Yet this does not sufficiently explain the extent to which Brazil and Latin America went from a position of nonintervention to leading a militarized peacekeeping force in Haiti.

The South American Left: Creating Distance from the Lavalas Movement

In addition to military intervention, political maneuvering played a key role in the region's stance and actions toward Haiti. In 2000, governments throughout Latin America broke with Jean-Bertrand Aristide and his ruling Fanmi Lavalas (FL) party. Four years later, following the controversial February 2004 coup that forced Aristide from Haiti, the South American left unanimously condemned Aristide with unusual legal, political, and ideological contortionism, again distancing itself from Lavalas and supported foreign military intervention. In doing so, the South American left helped give legitimacy to the coup and became associated with the positions of the United States, France, and Canada, providing them with ideological support and opening the door for the inclusion of major South American states in the composition of the UN peacekeeping force (Seitenfus 2006).

It was soon clear that the region would have a new and significant role in Haiti's security. While it was not the result of a Security Council resolution, the invitation for Brazil to command what became MINUSTAH made it clear that Washington and Paris had already negotiated the matter informally with the other permanent member states of the UN Security Council and with the UN secretary-general. In a matter of months, Brazil took command of the mission. Forces from Canada, France, and the United States were notably absent from MINUSTAH. The military side of the peacekeeping force was composed principally of troops from Latin America and Asia.

The apparently radical shift away from Aristide in Latin America was fundamentally influenced by an irreconcilable dispute within the Haitian left that blew up in 1999 as a struggle between Aristide and Gérard Pierre-Charles, a noted scholar and a venerable leader of Haiti's institutionalized socialist movement. In order to understand why leftist social movements and political parties in Latin America distanced themselves from Aristide's Lavalas movement and declared their solidarity with Pierre-Charles, it is crucial to understand the nature of this division within the Haitian left during this period.

The foundation of this shift of support toward Pierre-Charles was laid earlier in the decade. By 1990, dozens of leftist social movements and political parties in Latin America and the Caribbean had created a forum for dialogue and coordination. The first meeting, which the Workers' Party (Partido dos Trahalbodores; PT) of Brazil called, was held that year in São Paulo under the heading of "Meeting of Parties and Political Organizations of the Left of Latin America and the Caribbean." The movement became known as the São Paulo Forum. Its first executive secretary, Marco Aurélio Garcia, was also in charge of foreign relations for the PT. It was the PT, under the leadership of Luiz Inácio Lula da Silva and the Communist Party of Cuba, that took the lead in establishing the forum. Its emergence flowed from a strategy of breaking the isolation of the left after the fall of the Berlin Wall. At the time, José Ramón Balaguer, head of the Cuban Communist Party's Department of International Relations, remembered:

> The situation was quite complicated for the leftist and revolutionary forces in Latin America and the Caribbean. The word "imperialism" was no longer heard, and one no longer spoke of socialism. Some parties changed [their] name. Indeed, some considered that there was no longer any need to make a revolution. (Balaguer 2013)

The forum held nineteen meetings in the period 1990 to 2013. According to the official documentation presented at the May 2011 meeting in Managua, the São Paulo Forum went through three major evolutionary stages. The first was marked by "resistance to neoliberalism" (1990–1998); the second by the victories that brought the left to power in national governments (1998–2009); and the third and current one "began with the crisis of capitalism and the counterattack of the right." The major challenges forum members faced included "maintaining the spaces won, especially the national governments, and continuing to struggle to defeat the right where it is in power" (Balaguer 2013). Individuals who identified themselves as representing the Haitian left have participated in the São Paulo Forum since its founding. Principal among them, until his death in October 2004, was Gérard Pierre-Charles.

In the mid-1990s, Pierre-Charles was designated as coordinator of Aristide's Organisation Politique Lavalas (OPL). Pierre-Charles took an active role in the forum, serving as a member of the editorial board of its magazine, *América Libre*. Through Pierre-Charles's engagement, Haiti was an active member of the forum, and the forum as a whole was concerned with Haiti's well-being. At its eighth meeting in Mexico City in November 1998, which took place during a period of political turmoil in Haiti, forum members adopted a resolution on Haiti that stated: "Having taken note of the political blockade that is aggravating the economic crisis and also the danger of instability in the institutional life [of Haiti] . . . [the São Paulo Forum] proclaims its solidarity with the Haitian people and decides to organize an informational mission to Haiti in order to propose mediation among the parties in conflict" (Balaguer 2013).

Yet at its next meeting in Managua, in February 2000, as turbulence accompanied the approach of Haiti's May 2000 parliamentary elections, the political crisis in Haiti was not even mentioned. This situation changed rapidly in subsequent months. Haiti's controversial parliamentary elections occurred in May 2000 and Aristide was viewed as manipulating vote tallies in favor of his FL candidates. This resulted in a divorce between Aristide's Fanmi Lavalas and Pierre-Charles's Òganizasyon Pèp Kap Litè (OPL) platform.[5] Pierre-Charles loudly condemned Aristide and formed a new political coalition, the Democratic Convergence, in opposition to Aristide and the FL. Subsequently, in late 2001, Pierre-Charles and members of the Democratic Convergence were targets of reprisals at the hands of militant Aristide supporters after an alleged coup attempt against Aristide in mid-December.

The forum's close relationship with Pierre-Charles, its only Haitian member, explains its support of his political position and its condemnation of Aristide. Thus, when the tenth meeting was held in Havana in December 2001, the resolution adopted on Haiti espoused the political viewpoints of Pierre-Charles rather than a perspective of solidarity with Haiti. The text reads:

The Tenth Meeting of the São Paulo Forum, held December 4 to 7, 2001, in Havana, Cuba, calls attention to the consequences of the fraudulent elections of the year 2000 in Haiti, which exacerbated a prolonged institutional crisis, evidencing the inability of the populist and corrupt government of Aristide to address the grave problems of the nation. Poverty and discontent are on the rise, while repression and human rights violations feed a growing instability and political polarization. The repeated missions for reconciliation undertaken by the OAS and CARICOM have not yet been able to facilitate a negotiated solution between Lavalas and the Democratic Convergence which, with the support of broad sectors of the population, is the alternative to this personalist regime that thwarted popular expectations.[6]

With its statement that used terms such as "populist," "corrupt," and "personalist," the forum defended the idea that Haiti should do without elections and simply remove Aristide from power and replace him with Pierre-Charles.[7]

At its eleventh meeting, which took place in Antigua, Guatemala, in December 2002, the forum, proclaimed that it was profoundly concerned about the violence and repression that had taken place in Haiti in recent months and adopted a resolution on the Haitian crisis that denounced the anti-democratic policy of the government of Jean-Bertrand Aristide in Haiti as destroying the hopes of the people and subjecting Haiti to a regime that violated political rights and individual liberties.

On February 17, 2004, just days before the coup against Aristide, the Working Group of the forum meeting in São Paulo, issued a special resolution on Haiti. The resolution, whose wording was confusing as the result of its hasty translation to Portuguese from Spanish or French, was nonetheless clear in its support of the removal of Aristide from power. For the first time, the forum gave support to a specific party and a specific politician in an official document on the Haitian crisis:

> The political crisis the Haitian nation is experiencing arose from the flagrant repudiation of the democratic institutions by the government of Jean-Bertrand Aristide and the constant violation of human rights in recent years. . . .
>
> The Working Group of the São Paulo Forum expresses its solidarity with the struggle of the Haitian people and of the Democratic Platform in particular, [and] states its broadest political backing for the Organization of the People in Struggle, headed up by Gérard Pierre-Charles, a sister party that is a member of the São Paulo Forum.[8]

What would have been unthinkable before became a reality. The Latin American left not only gave its unqualified backing to the coup, it also called for it to happen. Bolstered by the apparent full support of the São Paulo Forum, Pierre-Charles's Democratic Convergence and the OPL continued to pursue a strategy in Haiti of avoiding a negotiated solution to the country's exploding crisis. France, the United States, and Canada soon annulled this zero-sum strategy, however, when they supported Aristide's ouster but did not include Pierre-Charles and his allies in the interim government.

Even after Aristide was removed from office, the Latin American left continued to condemn him. In 2005, President Lula's diplomatic emissary, Marco Aurélio Garcia, went on a mission to Haiti and confirmed what he expected to find. He reported that he received "from many sectors very serious information in relation to Aristide. First, human rights violations, on which I had direct information, because I had met many people previously. Second, that he was involved in drug trafficking and that he was also responsible for problems of corruption" (quoted in Seitenfus 2014a, 136). Garcia declared that he did not have a basis for giving this opinion and had merely "taken note." He further suggested that the interim Haitian government should commence a judicial proceeding that "they said they were going to do and they didn't do" (ibid.). Such accusations were not objective recordings of the 2005 political situation. Rather, Garcia acted as a megaphone for those in the opposition and the foreign sectors who were behind the coup. However, the Lula administration and numerous governments in Latin America assimilated these biased perspectives as unquestionable and objective truths.

Brazil's position on Haiti in 2005 was not entirely monolithic. A single fissure in the forum's position on Haiti emerged during its twelfth meeting, which took place in São Paulo in that year, when the Brazilian Communist Party (Partido Comunista Brasiliero; PCB) opposed a draft resolution on Haiti and urged a review of the forum's Haiti analysis. The draft resolution stated:

> Considering that the São Paulo Forum respects and applies as a general principle of international law the right to self-determination of peoples, we state our wishes for the swift sovereign reinsertion of the Caribbean nation to the international community.
>
> With this aim in mind we ask that the entire foreign debt of Haiti be pardoned as a contribution to overcoming the situation of extreme poverty that affects its people.

We demand that donor countries committed to the United Nations to finance the plan for the reconstruction of Haiti carry out this commitment immediately.[9]

The PCB was uncomfortable with several aspects of this draft. Although the document mentions the principle of self-determination, the PCB took issue with the timid language "state our wishes," arguing that the resolution should call for the withdrawal of MINUSTAH. Further, it pointed out that the document used the words "ask" and "demand" only in reference to the donor countries and those that held a share of Haiti's external debt. In other words, the draft referred to developed states but did not include Latin American governments. Subsequently, the forum backed away from its draft resolution and sent a mission to Haiti with the objective of taking a more in-depth look at the situation and discussing common actions for the political, economic, social, and environmental reconstruction of Haiti.

In spite of the PCB's objections in 2005, it was not until 2012 that strong public criticism of the forum's position toward Haiti appeared. At that time, Atilio Boron, the well-known Argentine communist and pro-Chávez intellectual, after taking stock of the final declaration of the forum's eighteenth meeting, which was held in Caracas, noted that it

condemns coup attempts against Evo Morales, Mel Zelaya, Rafael Correa, and more recently against Fernando Lugo. It forgets to note, unfortunately, the coup perpetrated against Jean-Bertrand Aristide, in Haiti, in 2004. It is a serious error because one cannot dissociate that oversight from the unfortunate presence of troops from several Latin American countries—Brazil, Chile, and Argentina, among others—in Haiti, when in reality what is lacking in that long-suffering country are doctors, nurses, teachers. But Cuba takes charge of that; its generous internationalism is one of the most honorable signals of its revolution.[10]

On responding to Boron's criticism, PT member Valter Pomar, executive secretary of the São Paulo Forum, stated that "perhaps Boron didn't know, but the final declarations are arrived at by consensus in the meetings of the Working Group, which included the participation in this 18th Meeting of Haitian leaders, who presented a resolution, approved in the plenary, on the situation in Haiti."[11]

This exchange presents three revealing lessons. The first is that the forum did not consider the removal of Aristide to have happened as the result of a coup d'état. Despite the active and decisive foreign intervention—with troops—Aristide's removal was a simple "overthrow" as far as the forum was concerned. Yet it is futile to make use of such semantics when the facts are crystal clear. The second lesson reveals the forum's frivolous treatment of Haiti.

Practically all the countries in the region have several leftist parties and social movements that participate in the forum and transmit detailed, at times contradictory, perceptions regarding their national reality. This was not the case for Haiti. In his remarks about the participation of Haitian leaders, Pomar did not make clear—for obvious reasons—that they referred exclusively to political leaders of the OPL. In other words, a party deeply at odds with Aristide, one that claimed to be representative of Haiti's left but in fact was hardly a major political force in Haiti, was Haiti's only representative in the forum. The OPL's candidate in the 2006 presidential elections received only 2.5 percent of the vote and the party did not even participate in the 2010 presidential elections.

During Haiti's 2010 elections, more than thirty political parties and coalitions ran candidates who espoused a wide array of ideologies. Many are on the left or the center left. But because the OPL has a monopoly as Haiti's forum representative, none of those organizations or their candidates have been affiliated with or heard within the forum. By way of comparison, the Dominican Republic, which has a similar number of political parties, is represented by six different groups in the São Paulo Forum.

The third lesson is that any forum discussion on the presence of Latin American military forces in Haiti appears to be taboo. How can one reconcile the discourse on self-determination and respect for the principle of nonintervention in the internal affairs of states with the massive Latin American intervention in Haiti? Such contradictory actions mean that any mention of the situation might lead to a criticism of the policies of constituent governments. Given this, the forum prefers to say nothing. Furthering the position it had expressed in 2005 and noting that the forum had continued to remain silent on the issue of South American troop presence in Haiti, the Brazilian Communist Party issued a pointed note at the forum's August 2010 gathering that proposed a hemispheric and worldwide campaign for the withdrawal of all foreign troops in Haiti today, urging that they be replaced by engineers, doctors, and other professionals who could help the country recover from its misery, which was aggravated by hurricanes in 2008 and the earthquake in 2010.

It is apparent that the PCB's criticism struck a nerve, as the Basic Document statement that emanated from the 2010 gathering referred to the matter in the following terms:

From the outset, the 13th Meeting addresses the parties that form part of governments that have troops in the MINUSTAH, to convey that in our opinion it is necessary to create the conditions for replacing the presence of troops of MINUSTAH by exclusively humanitarian support, as soon as possible.[12]

The forum's subsequent failure to act on this position reveals the lack of consensus among its members on this delicate issue. Haiti returned to the agenda of the forum at the seventeenth meeting, which was held in Managua in 2011, when the Basic Document simply mentioned the need to take concrete measures for the reconstruction of Haiti. At the eighteenth meeting, held in Caracas in 2012, the draft of the Basic Document that the Brazilian PT proposed mentioned the need to review the case of Haiti. Yet the National Bureau of the party did not even refer to the Haitian crisis in its pronouncement. Finally, the Plan of Action section of the Basic Document of the forum's nineteenth meeting, held in July 2013, proclaimed

> our firm solidarity with the struggle of the sister people of Haiti to overcome the long-standing conditions of poverty and marginalization, and its support for the full democratization of Haitian society, without foreign meddling and with respect for its national sovereignty, developing efforts to support the forces of the left in Haiti.[13]

These apparent contradictions and superficial references to Haiti illustrate how those responsible for the forum have remained, in essence, silent or noncommittal about the Haitian situation. Indeed, no reference to Haitian issues appears in the forum's 2013 Final Declaration.

Since 1990, the Latin American left has presented its reading and interpretation of Haiti and its political crises through the São Paulo Forum. Noted scholars and analysts from the region have contributed support and supplemental interpretations of the forum's pronouncements. Throughout the most recent crisis—with rare exceptions such as those of the recently deceased Uruguayan Eduardo Galeano and the Argentine Juan Gelman—the declarations and analyses by intellectuals on the left have defended just one perspective: Aristide is at fault for all of Haiti's sins. Swearing their love and admiration for the Haitian people, including in their analyses overviews of Haitian history, the authors of forum declarations and intellectuals from throughout the region invariably have arrived at the same conclusion; they have placed the blame for Haiti's crisis on Aristide who, in fact, has been its principal victim.

Conclusion

As the case of Haiti illustrates, even the progressive movements of Latin America have stopped defending nonintervention as a sacrosanct principle. Some interventions, it seems, are acceptable while others are not; there are interventions of the left and the right; there are good wars and bad wars. By 2011, some voices of the Latin American left, including that of the influential Brazilian liberation theologian Carlos Alberto Libânio Christo, known as Frei Betto, was openly challenging this thinking. In a public letter to the secretaries-general of the UN and the OAS, he called for a radical change in strategy and the end of the military occupation of Haiti.[14]

With rare exceptions from small parties of the extreme left and from independent figures, groups in opposition to the current governments of Latin America have not criticized the military presence in Haiti. In Brazil, the only noteworthy opponent was former president Fernando Henrique Cardoso, who declared in January 2006 that he was "not able to see clearly wherein lies the national interest in the matter" (Chade 2006). According to Cardoso, the Lula administration had moved too hastily in making the decision to send troops to Haiti. He was "concerned about Brazil's participation in Haiti, mainly in view of the scope and duration of the mission. The situation is ever more complex, and the worst is that there is no date for the return of the Brazilian soldiers" (ibid.).

The congenital contradiction between the nature of the challenge and the instruments for addressing it reached its high point with the 2010 earthquake, the subsequent cholera epidemic, and recurrent political instability. These events, which are not examples of conflict, are incompatible with Chapter VII of the UN Charter, which permits the Security Council to determine the existence of any threat to the peace, breach of the peace, or act of aggression and to take requisite military and nonmilitary action to restore international peace and security. This is the basis for peacekeeping operations such as MINUSTAH. Despite the apparent incompatibility with the foundational rules of peacekeeping operations as the situation in Haiti evolved, and with the approval of the vast majority of the Latin American left, MINUSTAH became strengthened over time and Haiti became a preferential client of the UN Security Council. Will the voices expressing dissent from within the Haitian, Brazilian, and Latin American left be heard in this tangled milieu of institutions and politicized affiliations? Given current trends, it is difficult to imagine that this will occur any time in the near future.

Notes

1. Eighteen Latin American and Caribbean states (Argentina, Bolivia, Brazil, Chile, Colombia, Costa Rica, the Dominican Republic, Ecuador, El Salvador, Guatemala, Honduras, Mexico, Nicaragua, Panama, Paraguay, Peru, Uruguay, and Venezuela) currently participate in the Permanent Mechanism for Consultation and Political Coordination of Latin America and the Caribbean, known as the Rio Group.

2. Statement made by André Singer at a Radiobrás press conference, March 4, 2004.

3. Although the Brazilian military was hesitant at the outset, it was convinced to participate so long as all the equipment, communication and transport systems, and material to be used would be national. It is the first time in history that a large military force was sent abroad in these conditions. The operation became a challenge for strategists in terms of the preparation of the soldiers and the communications and transportation capabilities. It was also a test of the reliability of the Brazilian arms industry.

4. President Lula's discourse brought him closer to the discourse of African presidents such as Alpha Oumar Konaré, former president of Mali and of the Commission of the African Union. Referring to the duty of cooperation in relation to the Darfur episode, he stated: "We are in favor of Africa assuming its duty of non-indifference [which translates into] a solidarity-based intervention" (Seitenfus et al. 2007).

5. Note that Pierre-Charles kept the same acronym as he left Organisation Politique Lavalas (OPL) and formed Òganizasyon Pèp Kap Litè (OPL), or, in French, Organisation du People en Lutte (OPL).

6. Editors' note: Citations for direct quotations from documents sourced from the São Paulo Forum and referred to throughout this section of the chapter cannot be provided due to the fact that between the time author Ricardo Seitenfus made his presentation on this topic at the Haiti conference on May 2, 2014, and the time he completed the draft of this chapter, all documents pertaining to Haiti had been removed from the forum's website. Because of the critical importance of this documentation to Seitenfus's analysis, those quotations are maintained within the chapter without citation. Any questions pertaining to this should be directed to the chapter's author.

7. Emphasis added. Note that this adoption of a radical position preceded by a few days the attacks on the opposition of December 17 of that year. These attacks resulted in irreparable harm to Aristide's respectability and definitively distanced him from the movements and parties of the Latin American left, which had come to power in several countries.

8. See endnote 6.

9. Ibid.

10. Ibid.

11. Ibid.

12. Ibid.

13. Ibid.

14. 'Três prêmios Nobel e centenas de organizações exigem a retirada das tropas do Haiti," PSTU, October 5, 2011. Accessed Jun 19, 2016, www.pstu.org.br/node/16857.

References

Amorim, Celso. 2005. "Política externa do governo Lula, os dois primeiros anos." *Análise de Conjuntura OPSA* 4 (March). Accessed May 1, 2016. http://www.plata-formademocratica.org/Publicacoes/22214_Cached.pdf.

———. 2013. *Breves narrativas diplomáticas*. São Paulo: Editora Benvirá.

Balaguer, José Ramon. 2013. "El Foro de Sao Paulo sobrepasó la prueba del tiempo." *Granma* (Havana), April 23.

Chade, Jamil. 2006. "Fernando Henrique questiona missão no Haiti." *Estado de São Paulo*, January 24.

Report of the Secretary-General on the United Nations Stabilization Mission in Haiti, Annex II and III, UN Security Council document S/2013/493, August 19, 2013, http://www.securitycouncilreport.org/atf/cf/%7B65BFCF9B-6D27-4E9C-8CD3-CF6E4FF96FF9%7D/s_2013_493.pdf.

Seitenfus, Ricardo. 2006. "Elementos para uma diplomacia solidária: a crise haitiana e os desafios da ordem internacional." *Carta Internacional* 1 (1): 5–12.

———. 2014a. *Haiti: Dilemas e fracassos internacionais*. Ijuí, Brazil: Editora Unijuí.

———. 2014b. A intervenção militar sul-americana no Haiti: aparência e realidade. June 27. http://www.seitenfus.com.br.

Seitenfus, Ricardo, Cristine Zanella, and Pâmela Marques. 2007. "O Direito internacional repensado em tempos de ausências e emergências: A busca de uma tradução para o princípio da não-indiferença. *Revista Brasileira de Política Internacional* 50 (2): 7–24.

6

Who Owns U.S. Aid to Haiti?

Robert Maguire

Development assistance is, at least in theory, a transfer of resources from a donor to a beneficiary. Once the transfer is complete, ownership or sovereign control over the resources ideally goes from the giver to the receiver. In reality, the process is not that simple. The transfer of U.S. bilateral aid, in most cases, is a complicated, multilayered transaction that involves a variety of actors who oversee or "touch" the resources as they travel a meandering path toward their intended beneficiaries.[1] Those actors include not just the premier U.S. aid agency—the U.S. Agency for International Development (USAID)—but also the U.S. Congress and other U.S. government agencies, particularly the Department of State. The array also includes contractors and their subcontractors—all usually American—who manage the resources and implement the programs USAID has designed. On the Haitian side of the equation, actors include subcontractors from private sector, civil society, technical, and community-based organizations. Those actors have less frequently included the Haitian government, which received only 1 percent of the $2.43 billion of aid disbursed in the year after the earthquake (Katz 2013).

Critics have argued that the complexity and multiple "touches" of the aid flow result in a severe diminution of the resources that ultimately reach those most in need. Many have argued that an astonishingly high percentage of the resources entering the meandering path are captured by international or local elites along the way, pointing out that as much as 93 percent of aid resources remain in American hands (Johnston and Main 2013). In this regard, then, U.S. aid to Haiti is rarely owned by Haitians. Criticism of the fact that outsiders own most of the aid allocated to Haiti might have been muted if the billions of U.S. bilateral assistance spent in recent decades had resulted in improvements in the social and economic status of Haiti's impoverished citizens. The overall result of this complex transfer process, however, has been the failure of U.S. bilateral aid to make a significant and lasting impact on improving the conditions of Haiti's most needy, resource-starved people (Buss 2008).

From the beginning of the Obama administration in 2009, U.S. government officials have pointed out the overall need to improve aid effectiveness and increase its ownership by recipient countries. This chapter examines these concerns and the steps taken to address them in relation to aid delivery to Haiti. In spite of the acknowledged failure of the multilayered approach to dispensing aid, the resulting quest for improved approaches, and a subsequent measure of change, obstacles from within and beyond Haiti inhibit the ability to achieve goals related to increased local ownership. As a result, such failures hinder the effective use of aid as a tool for alleviating poverty and improving the lives of the majority of Haitians.

Seeking Reform

As the Obama administration took office, it was aware of the deficient aid track record in Haiti and elsewhere. By mid-2009, the administration had developed a global aid reform agenda centered on the idea that national governments should be lead actors in their nations' development and that U.S. assistance should be more effectively aligned with the development goals of these nations, supporting locally identified needs and priorities. The agenda also recognized that U.S. support should reinforce local capacity to oversee program implementation and sustainability (White House Office of the Press Secretary 2010).

Haiti played an oversized role in identifying the need to improve the effectiveness of U.S. aid worldwide. Three months into his first term, Obama directed the Department of State to conduct an interagency review of U.S. bilateral aid to Haiti. The administration's immediate objective was to identify root causes of the less-than-desired results in sustained attempts to alleviate poverty and promote economic growth in its Caribbean neighbor following the allocation of roughly $3.5 billion in U.S. foreign aid over the previous twenty-nine years.[2] Secretary of State Hillary Clinton embraced the mandate and initiated the interagency review, challenging U.S. officials to both identify root causes of weak performance and come up with strategies for correcting those issues.

Clinton presided over an International Donors' Conference on Haiti in April 2009 that sought to mobilize resources so the country could bounce back from multiple political, economic, and environmental crises in 2008 that threatened both the country's well-being and the stability of the government of President René Préval (Clinton 2014).[3] At the conference, UN Secretary General Ban Ki-moon introduced former U.S. president Bill Clinton as the UN special envoy to Haiti. In 2008, Ban had invited economist Paul Collier to visit Haiti and draft a report identifying strategies for its economic development (Perito 2009). The report focused heavily on apparel manufacture and garnered Collier an influential role in guiding international actions toward Haiti (Collier 2009). Collier's imprint on U.S. strategic thinking on Haiti was reinforced when Secretary Clinton hired his research partner to work in her office suite as a senior advisor (Katz 2015).

The State Department review identified three key explanations for the deficient track record, all related to the issue of aid ownership. First, U.S. assistance, which was executed through an assortment of mostly U.S.-based NGOs and for-profit contractors (FPCs), suffered from a fragmented approach, a broad focus, and limited coordination.[4] Indicative of this was the fact that by early 2009, U.S. bilateral aid in Haiti had been "committed to more than 30 multimillion dollar contracts that largely operate[d] in isolation of each other and other donor programs" (U.S. Department of State 2009). This strategy resulted in an aid portfolio that was "a mile wide, an inch deep, and sprinkled with pixie dust."[5]

Second, success and sustainability were hindered by an incongruity between U.S. plans emphasizing humanitarian relief and short-term stability operations and the Préval government's longer-term economic development strategies emphasizing poverty alleviation and economic growth (Government of Haiti 2007). The United States supported short-term stability operations that included a variety of costly "quick-impact projects" aimed at short-term job creation in order to stabilize an environment fraught with gang violence fueled by drugs and politics. One such project was a $20 million stabilization initiative that emphasized small, labor-intensive infrastructure improvement projects in Cite Soleil, Haiti's largest *bidonville*, or urban slum.[6] This project and similar projects did little to address the root causes of poverty or induce sustained employment or economic growth.

Third, heavy reliance on U.S.-based contractors to execute the foreign aid program had resulted in projects "not designed to be transitioned to the [government of Haiti] and . . . therefore not sustainable" (U.S. Department of State 2009). Typically, USAID devised projects with little or no input from Haitian authorities and then sought contractors to implement them. Few, if any, project resources were budgeted toward building the implementation and administrative capacity of the government of Haiti.[7] A typical outcome of this approach was the awarding of contract after contract to the same U.S. organizations and companies, sustaining their presence in Haiti but doing little to promote consistent progress in removing the social and economic obstacles to development.

Addressing these weaknesses became the focus of a revised U.S. aid strategy in Haiti that was scheduled for release in mid-January 2010, around the first anniversary of Obama's inauguration. The January 12th earthquake, however, quashed those plans, forcing U.S. officials to rework their ideas in a suddenly altered context.

Addressing Poor Performance

In January 2011, a newly established Office of the Haiti Special Coordinator in the U.S. State Department unveiled a five-year framework for U.S. assistance to Haiti.[8] The framework evolved with the participation of the new head of USAID, Rajiv Shah. Almost immediately after Shah was sworn in on December 31, 2009, he was thrust into intense engagement with post-earthquake Haiti. At a major policy address a week after the release of the framework, Shah cited Haiti when he identified the need for sweeping changes in the way USAID went about its business. He criticized the "modern development enterprise," which was brimming with "high-priced consultants" who were adept at finding "another flight to another conference or another training," adding that USAID would be "no longer satisfied with writing big checks to big contractors and calling it development" (Shah 2011). He also declared that business as usual would no longer rule the day, stressing that USAID had "no interest in our own growth and our own perpetuity. We must seek to do our work in a way that allows us to be replaced over time by efficient local governments, by thriving civil societies and by a vibrant private sector" (ibid.).

Under congressional and presidential pressure to respond quickly to Haiti's post-earthquake needs, both the State Department and USAID were cautious about modifying business as usual. The framework was presented as "a living document" that "while setting strategic parameters must be agile in responding to the continually changing landscape in which it operates" (U.S. Department of State 2011). Notably, that changing landscape included Washington, DC, where NGOs and for-profit firms, including those already holding USAID Haiti contracts and thus best positioned to respond to exhortations for quick action, were maneuvering for access to U.S. post-quake Haiti funding that at the time exceeded $1 billion (Johnston and Main 2013).

The strategic framework identified five core principles designed to address "pixie dust" and related weaknesses that had been identified prior to the earthquake. The first principle touched directly on the issue of aid ownership:

- Assistance will be country led and will build country capacity.
- Assistance will underpin a comprehensive, integrated plan.
- Assistance will leverage and coordinate resources with other partners.
- Assistance will use multilateral mechanisms wherever possible.
- The U.S. government commitment will be sustained and accountable.[9]

In support of these principles the framework identified four development pillars that would narrow the U.S. programmatic focus: infrastructure and energy, food and economic security, health and other basic services, and governance and rule of law. Notably absent was education, a sector that had previously received significant U.S. aid dollars. Its omission immediately drew a chorus of disapproval from a U.S. contracting community accustomed to receiving US-AID funding for education projects in Haiti. State Department officials pointed to their goal of narrowing the programmatic focus, adding that other donors such as the Inter-American Development Bank would maintain or augment attention to education, underscoring this as a step toward improved donor coordination. The critics were hardly mollified, especially given their dependence on U.S. bilateral funding for their work in Haiti. Confronting this discontent, the State Department recast "health and other basic services" as a "health and education" pillar even as U.S. support for education initiatives in Haiti diminished.[10] This episode provided an early indication that aid contractors accustomed to vying for U.S. bilateral aid funds would push back on reform measures they viewed as contrary to their interests.

U.S. officials also viewed their new strategy as a way of improving alignment with government of Haiti priorities based on territorial, economic, social, and institutional "action areas" set forth in Préval's post-earthquake plan for national recovery and reconstruction (Government of Haiti 2010). This alignment is portrayed in Figure 6.1.

The framework also narrowed the geographic scope of U.S. aid interventions to three "development corridors" located in and around the cities of Port-au-Prince, St. Marc, and Cap-Haïtien, as shown in figure 6.2. State Department officials argued that each corridor, each of which was a location where the U.S. government was already active with major initiatives, afforded an opportunity for U.S. aid resources to be invested in support of a comprehensive vision of development within a defined geographic space.[11]

Even before the earthquake, the Préval government had prioritized a strategy of regional growth poles as a means of decentralizing development beyond Port-au-Prince and surroundings. The pre-quake need to decentralize investment, development assistance, social and public services, job opportunities, and infrastructure development away from Haiti's primary city became even more compelling after the natural disaster (Maguire 2010).[12] U.S. officials viewed their development corridor strategy as support for the Haitian government's decentralization priority and growth pole strategy, hence further enhancing alignment with the long-term goals of the government of Haiti.[13]

The geographic corridor foci alarmed some U.S. constituencies, including Haitian Americans whose area of origin was not included in the corridors.[14] State Department officials pointed out that while geographic focus had become an important component of more effective engagement, U.S. aid would continue to touch other parts of the country. In particular, they pointed toward health-related initiatives not confined to the corridors, particularly those

GOH-USG Strategic Alignment

GOH ACTION AREAS (PSDH)   ### USG STRATEGY PILLARS

1. Territorial Rebuilding   ⟺   A. Infrastructure and Energy

2. Economic Rebuilding   ⟺   B. Food and Economic Security

3. Social Rebuilding   ⟺   C. Health and Education

4. Institutional Rebuilding   ⟺   D. Governance & Rule of Law

All USG Strategy Pillars are aligned with GOH Action Areas. Note that environment and watersheds (Territorial Rebuilding) is captured under Pillar B; Housing (Social Rebuilding) is captured under Pillar A; and Vocational Training (Social Rebuilding) is captured under Pillar B.

Updated June 3, 2013

4

Figure 6.1. Government of Haiti–U.S. government strategic alignment. Source: Office of the Coordinator for Haiti, U.S. Department of State.

Three Development Corridors

Figure 6.2. Haiti's development corridors. Source: Office of the Coordinator for Haiti, U.S. Department of State.

linked to HIV/AIDS prevention and treatment and to cholera prevention and response.[15] Officials also stressed that as an element of improved coordination, other donors would assume greater responsibility in other parts of the country. As U.S. officials sought improved aid effectiveness by limiting the sectors supported and narrowing geographic focus, the pushback they received underscored the fact that U.S. groups engaged with Haiti and with aid programs there would contest reforms they perceived as against their interests.

Heightened Haitian Ownership?

As the strategic framework became operational, indications of a transition toward greater Haitian aid ownership emerged, particularly in the context of an agricultural development project called Feed the Future North, which is part of USAID's global Feed the Future initiative. This case provides important insights into a new approach by U.S. officials designed to overcome the U.S.

government's heavy reliance on NGOs and international entities as "owners" of U.S. aid funds.

Feed the Future was created in 2010 in response to the 2008 global economic crisis that resulted in rising food prices in developing economies, particularly those such as Haiti that were heavily dependent on imported food (The Economist 2008). Active in nineteen countries worldwide, Feed the Future aims to improve domestic food security and incomes through interventions in agricultural production, marketing, and research while also improving nutrition (Feed the Future 2012). In Haiti, watershed rehabilitation is an integral component of Feed the Future. Feed the Future North, which had an $87.8 million budget in 2013, was developed squarely within the parameters of the administration's global aid effectiveness reform program and is connected to the U.S. government's Haiti framework's food and economic security goal, which includes improving income through the post-quake creation of up to 700,000 jobs in agriculture and animal husbandry in Haiti (U.S. Department of State 2011). Given Feed the Future North's integral role in meeting this goal, U.S. officials were anxious to get the project up and running as quickly as possible after USAID's request for proposals in early 2011 to fulfill the Feed the Future North contract.

The process of awarding the contract for Feed the Future North proved to be a long one that lasted more than two years. This stemmed largely from request-for-proposals requirements specifying that contractors had to begin a transition to management by Haitian organizations from the project's outset. That specification was reinforced by successive benchmarks; if the contractor did not meet these, it would incur financial penalties. As such, the Feed the Future North project design included a path for the contractor that was awarded the grant to work itself out of a job by incrementally strengthening local actors as a means of ultimately achieving ownership by a Haitian entity, thereby improving prospects for sustainability after the project was completed.

Noticeably, in this case the U.S. government's broader goal of transition toward stronger local ownership appeared to exclude the Haitian government. The Haitian actors U.S. officials projected as the ones who would incrementally move toward ownership of Feed the Future North were nongovernmental, although they did identify local public officials and technicians from the agriculture ministry as potential partners. As usual, project funds would be disbursed directly to a U.S.-based contractor that would then engage in collaborative relations with local organizations and officials and manage disbursements to an in-country project apparatus that includes subcontractors.[16]

This approach reflects an apparent belief that the government of Haiti lacks the capacity to effectively absorb and manage this scale of funding and therefore to "own" the project. The practice of bypassing the Haitian government in favor of mostly U.S. nongovernmental actors had taken hold by the 1980s, when the United States sought to avoid direct funding to the "kleptocratic" Duvalier dictatorship. Over time, the practice of skirting the government of Haiti became so entrenched that even when post-Duvalier democratically elected governments pressed for direct U.S. support of their reform initiatives they found little success (Maguire 2009). The pattern of channeling aid funds through externally based contractors was so firmly established that in the 1990s, Haitians began referring to their country as a "Republic of NGOs." Bypassing the state had the circular effect of weakening public sector capacities and keeping those sectors weak while instilling and reinforcing donor dependence on external actors (Kristoff and Panarelli 2010).

Although Feed the Future North continued the approach of bypassing the Haitian government, its program of transitional benchmarking accompanied by financial penalties for noncompliance presented new challenges to aspiring contractors, compelling them to search for solutions that would address these unusual USAID mandates. U.S. entities not accustomed to the idea of working themselves out of a job challenged both the language and intent of the Feed the Future North request for proposals, both directly and through influential associations inside the Beltway. Two such firms, Inter-Action, an umbrella organization for NGOs, and the Coalition for International Development Companies, a lobbying group, represented the interests of Beltway institutions. The fact that USAID was compelled to address these challenges and clarify its intent caused delays in the request-for-proposals process and in announcing the award.

In April 2013, the Feed the Future North contract was awarded to Development Alternatives, Inc. (DAI), a U.S.-based entity, with the transitional ownership mandates remaining in place. When the contract was announced, USAID proclaimed that Feed the Future North would "adhere to and mainstream a number of core principles" guiding both the Haiti strategy and the administration's global aid effectiveness reforms, including the goal that Feed the Future North "will be country-led [and will] build capacity of Haitian institutions" (United States Agency for International Development and United States Department of State 2013).

The early emergence of Haiti in the forefront of the Obama administration's efforts to improve U.S. aid effectiveness worldwide and the significant scale of U.S. post-quake funding there have led to close scrutiny of U.S. aid efforts in Haiti. In several reports on post-quake funding, the U.S. Government Accountability Office has pointed to significant shortcomings and mixed results (U.S. Government Accountability Office 2015). A prominent aid watchdog organization pointed out that the Obama administration's stated intentions of increasing local capacity have come up woefully short in post-quake Haiti: 99.3 percent of the U.S. government's disbursements had bypassed local organizations and gone directly to U.S. or international entities in the three years after the earthquake. In addition, 56.3 percent of those entities are firms located in the Washington, DC, Beltway (Johnston and Main 2013).

Without doubt, congressional and presidential pressure to respond quickly to Haiti's post-quake needs has contributed to the continued allocation of large sums to Beltway organizations, a practice identified in 2009 as an obstacle to effective aid. The $87.8 million allocation to DAI, a firm located inside the Beltway, appears to contradict Shah's statement that USAID would no longer write big checks to big contractors and call it development. The enforced transitional approach toward local leadership/ownership, however, appears to support his assertion that USAID and its contractors would be replaced "over time by efficient local governments, thriving civil societies, and by a vibrant private sector" (Shah 2011). The USAID administrator put a number to these expectations in September 2012, expressing his determination to have 30 percent of U.S. aid allocated to programs managed by Haitian entities by 2015, up from less than 9 percent before the earthquake (Whitefield 2012). If the ownership transition strategy enacted by DAI succeeds, that will certainly help Shah achieve that measure.[17]

Moving forward, Feed the Future North will be watched closely not only by U.S. officials but also by organizations such as OXFAM that advocate greater local ownership of development assistance (Cohen 2013). DAI's competitors also will be watching closely, particularly if the USAID mandate for transitional strategies becomes a new norm for winning a contract. As early as the first year of operation of Feed the Future North, skepticism in the aid industry arose about a key element of DAI's strategy and an apparently important factor in its successful proposal: it hired former agriculture ministry officials as second-tier, in-country project staff while maintaining a foreign national as the project's chief of party. This arrangement elicited a cynical reaction from one Beltway-based NGO official, who dismissed the tactic as "how the 'game' of country-led development is now being played," suggesting that DAI's approach was little more than a façade of change.[18] After its first year of field-based operations, Feed the Future North was already facing a variety of challenges. These included several changes of key personnel (including its chief of party), delays due to "unrealistic procurement time frames . . . for an activity of this size," and "the difficulty of finding staff with necessary experience who were willing to move to northern Haiti to manage the activity" (U.S. Government Accountability Office 2015). Just how a U.S.-based for-profit company such as DAI will manage USAID's envisaged incremental change in project management and development assistance ownership is still, clearly, a question.

Haitian Government Ownership

The U.S. post-earthquake development strategy envisaged a continually changing political landscape in Haiti. That landscape changed dramatically when Michel Martelly replaced René Préval as president in May 2011. He brought a new retinue to government posts that included individuals with familial or personal ties to the Duvalier dictatorship and its successor military governments (Daniel 2011). As Martelly took over, questions arose about the continued alignment of U.S. aid reform pillars and the priorities of the government of Haiti and the prospect for greater Haitian influence over, if not ownership of, U.S. bilateral aid. While the Feed the Future North approach offers a path toward ownership of aid resources by Haitian non-governmental entities, prospects for a parallel transitional path toward Haitian government ownership appear more limited.

During his 2010 campaign, candidate Martelly attracted U.S. attention as a man of action who would move Haiti quickly toward achieving post-earthquake reconstruction and development. His platform promised that the "four Es" of education, environment, employment, and *etat de droit* (rule of law) would guide his administration. He added energy to his platform after he was elected. During a pre-inaugural visit to Washington he assured officials that he would work closely with them to pick up the pace of post-earthquake recovery and development. Haiti, he told them, would be "open for business."[19] This was music to the ears of those promoting foreign direct investment, particularly those in the garment sector that Collier had promoted.

U.S. officials believed that Martelly's "Es" would align with their aid reform pillars. As his government transitioned into office, U.S. officials gave the new president detailed briefings on their strategic framework. Martelly endorsed the U.S. approach and placed his government in alignment with it. Initially, enactment of this continued U.S.-Haiti alignment was demonstrated principally by a variety of ribbon cuttings for activities that had begun under Préval, including the high-profile, $300 million Caracol Industrial Park on the northern coast. U.S. officials, including Bill Clinton, in his capacity as UN Special Envoy for Haiti, promised up to 60,000 new jobs (Clinton Foundation Editorial Team 2012). As Martelly cut Caracol's ribbon in October 2012 at a ceremony that both Bill and Hillary Clinton attended, the Haitian government's continued alignment with U.S. strategic goals appeared firm (Daniel 2012).[20]

Over its first two years, Martelly's government settled on a number of programmatic priorities. Prominent among them were augmenting education revenue through new fees for international telephone calls and money transfers; promoting upscale tourism; launching a variety of social programs aimed at alleviating poverty through the distribution of cash, food, and other goods; and creating a new mechanism for coordinating foreign aid in the Haitian government and challenging international partners, most prominently the United States, to support it.

In July 2012, Martelly released a strategic development plan for Haiti that largely extended the action plan the government had created in March 2010. Complementing the strategic development plan was the government's creation of the aid-coordinating mechanism, the Framework for Coordination of External Aid for the Development of Haiti (Cadre de coordination de l'aide externe au développement d'Haïti; CAED). The government of Haiti views CAED as a successor to the defunct and largely ineffective Interim Haiti Recovery Commission that was established in April 2010 as a mixed Haitian-international body to coordinate and oversee post-quake recovery efforts until a Haitian-owned development agency would replace it. CAED, which was launched in November 2012, is a Haitian public entity headed by President Martelly and his prime minister that operates under the auspices of the Ministry of Planning and External Cooperation. It was established as a mechanism of "permanent and regular dialogue between the Haitian Government and its partners" that will "giv[e] back to Haiti its sovereignty in the management of aid and especially of priorities" and allow "the Government of Haiti [to take] the unique leadership in the matter of international aid" (Haiti Libre 2012). As such, the government of Haiti views CAED as a mechanism through which international resources can be channeled, in the process increasing its ownership of foreign aid (Government of Haiti 2012b).

However, the United States has appeared reluctant to channel aid resources through CAED. Officials have attended meetings of the organization in Port-au-Prince to listen to the Haitian government's presentations and engage in dialogue, but they are noncommittal about placing resources at its disposal. This position may be attributed largely to the continuing reluctance of both the U.S. Congress and the Obama administration to channel bilateral aid directly to the Haitian government, particularly in light of issues that have cast a shadow over the Martelly administration and its ability to judiciously manage aid funds. These include growing concerns over "severe corruption in all branches of government" (U.S. Department of State 2012), the Martelly government's inability to organize parliamentary and local elections that were due to take place late in 2011,[21] and a growing track record of problematic management of bilateral resources the Venezuelan government made available directly to Haiti's president through PetroCaribe.

Through the PetroCaribe agreement, "60 percent of the oil bill [for up to 14,000 barrels/day of Venezuelan-supplied oil] is financed with terms including 1 percent interest, 25-year maturity and 2-year[s'] grace" before repayment begins (International Monetary Fund 2014, 36). The Haitian government's sale of Venezuelan oil products in its domestic market creates resources estimated at around $400 million annually. These resources are not accounted for in the national budget (Charles 2013). In addition to subsidizing the cost of electricity and paying for infrastructure projects, Martelly's government has allotted PetroCaribe funds to a social welfare program called Ede Pep (Help the People), which consists of a variety of initiatives that mostly distribute food and other commodities to the poor but that also includes some direct cash transfers (Associated Press 2012). The government argues that Ede Pep programs, which have names such as Ti Maman Cheri (Dear Little Mother), are key to its efforts to alleviate poverty. Critics of the government believe differently, characterizing them as political patronage and labeling them "slogan programs of the president" (Haïti en Marche 2012).

It is difficult to understand how PetroCaribe loan funds allocated to social welfare distributions and electricity subsidies will be paid back. Those concerns have been heightened by the fact that Haiti's debt to Venezuela, which was $1.522 billion in September 2013 (Belt 2013), has continued to grow.[22] In the wake of actions by multilateral banks and bilateral funders (including Venezuela) to erase the country's debt after the 2010 earthquake, Haiti's sudden, growing, and noteworthy indebtedness to its South American neighbor is problematic.[23] Trust in the ability of Martelly's government to manage resources, through CAED or other mechanisms, is severely weakened as a result of its apparent mismanagement of the Venezuelan PetroCaribe funds. The diminution and potential cessation of PetroCaribe funds available to Haiti because of uncertain socioeconomic and political issues in Venezuela (Bryan 2014; Schipani and Rathbone 2015) is particularly problematic for Martelly's government. These funds have played an important role in providing resources for the social programs the government promises to Haiti's poorest citizens (Belt 2013), and, in a far less noble light, in allegedly providing resources to government supporters through graft and corruption schemes.

Even if direct government of Haiti ownership of U.S. aid resources appears unlikely, recent complementary U.S. support for Martelly's social welfare programs presents the prospect of collaboration between the governments of the United States and Haiti over how U.S. bilateral aid is used. In 2013, USAID created Kore Lavi (Supporting Life), "a food security program" that "directly supports the Government of Haiti to establish a voucher-based safety-net system to increase poor households' access to food" (Embassy of the United States, Port-au-Prince, Haiti 2013). While Martelly's social programs have concentrated largely on distribution of "solidarity food baskets," imported commodities, hot meals, and cash vouchers, the four-year U.S. program provides monthly vouchers worth approximately $50 to up to 250,000 families with the stipulation that they be spent on locally produced food (The Economist 2013).[24] Like the Feed the Future North project, however, Kore Lavi is managed by a U.S. contractor, not the Haitian government.

Kore Lavi is being watched closely by advocates of aid reform. An earlier pilot program managed by a U.S.-based NGO that provided vouchers to 18,000 families was criticized by a Haitian farmers' network as a "terrible threat" to Haitian agricultural production because vouchers were used mostly to purchase imported foodstuffs. On the other hand, a Haitian merchant praised the program because it doubled his sales of rice imported from the United States (Haiti Grassroots Watch 2013). To achieve its goal of voucher expenditure on locally produced food and thereby strengthen Haitian agricultural production and food sovereignty, Kore Lavi will have to reverse this trend. To the extent that it is congruent with U.S. strategic framework principles, Kore Lavi does demonstrate U.S. support of national strategies. Ownership of the project's resources, however, remains firmly in the hands of a U.S. contractor, in this instance CARE. Whether Kore Lavi includes an ownership transition plan parallel with that of Feed the Future North is not clear from available documents or press releases.

More broadly, U.S. support of social welfare (or "presidential slogan") programs contradicts the Obama administration's 2009 finding that an emphasis on humanitarian relief and short-term stability operations constitute part of the deficient track record of U.S. aid in Haiti. Martelly's government seems to have eschewed long-term results in favor of a return to showcase projects that focus on quick and short-term resource-distribution projects that seek to maintain social stability. These social welfare and humanitarian programs have little, if any, impact on sustainable economic growth or job creation and are increasing Haiti's dependence on imported food, fueling corruption and clientelism, and failing to sustainably and irreversibly improve the social and economic status of Haiti's impoverished citizens.

Conclusion

Since 2009, the Obama administration has been grappling with ways to improve aid effectiveness in Haiti as part of its global development assistance reform agenda. A key component of that agenda is greater support for national governments as lead actors in their country's development, including more effective alignment of U.S. assistance with national goals. Another important element is an alteration of aid ownership patterns through the provision of increased support directly to local sectors and organizations and a corresponding decrease in the role played by externally based NGOs and for-profit contractors. What drives this impetus for change, particularly in the case of Haiti, is the historic failure of the multilayered approach of disbursing aid principally through U.S.-based contractors to bring about significant and lasting change in the lives of the most needy people.

Four conclusions emanate from this chapter's analysis of the ownership of U.S. development assistance in Haiti. First, the quest for improved aid effectiveness has achieved some measure of change that includes enhanced alignment of U.S. and national goals and strategies. Steps aimed at increasing local access to and control over aid resources have also been taken. Second, change is not quick and does not follow a straight line. Rather, it is incremental and not necessarily irreversible. Third, key U.S.-based organizations and interest groups push back against efforts to make change and Haiti's complex political landscape creates challenges. Finally, and especially in the case of post-quake Haiti, pressure to move quickly and achieve immediate results reinforces the pattern of disbursing aid directly to U.S. organizations.

With regard to who ultimately "owns" U.S. aid to Haiti, the most essential indicator is the extent to which those resources are transferred to the control of Haitians. In spite of various changes, the vast majority of aid ultimately remains in the control of non-Haitian entities. The prospects of shifting toward increased Haitian government ownership of aid resources appear to be especially dim. Current trends of apparent resource mismanagement by Haitian authorities only reinforce practices of bypassing the government to allocate resources to nongovernmental actors. While U.S. officials are willing to work with the Haitian government to set priorities and align programs, they are less willing to place resources directly under the government's control. As this suggests, for the foreseeable future, ownership of U.S. aid to Haiti will remain principally in U.S. hands.

Notes

1. The Inter-American Foundation, a small U.S. government aid agency that follows a bottom-up, direct-to-the-poor approach toward development, is an exception to this rule. See Inter-American Foundation (2016) and Breslin (1987).

2. Figures come from "U.S. Economic Assistance by Country: Haiti," accessed July 28, 2013, http://www.davemanuel.com/usaid-economic-assistance-by-country-and-program.php.

3. In early 2008, Haiti experienced unrest caused by increased food and fuel prices, and in August and September of that year it suffered the onslaught of four tropical storms within thirty days.

4. NGOs active in Haiti include such organizations as CARE, Catholic Relief Services, Global Communities (formerly CHF International), the International Organization for Migration, and the Pan American Development Foundation. For-profit firms include Chemonics and DAI, among others.

5. Comments of a U.S. Department of State official at a meeting on Haiti at the United States Institute of Peace, April 8, 2009, author's notes from the meeting.

6. The Cité Soleil initiative was funded through the U.S. Department of Defense 1207 Program. For more on the 1207 Program, see Perito (2008).

7. For example, in October 2008, at the ceremonial signing of a $22 million US-AID-funded, NGO-implemented early education and teacher training project called PHARE, the Haitian minister of education thanked the U.S. ambassador but reminded her that the government had a national education plan and that assistance to improve education in Haiti should be applied directly in support of it, which was apparently not the case in this instance. (Haïti en Marche 2008).

8. In 2015, the framework was extended for an additional three years (U.S. Government Accountability Office 2015).

9. These principles reflect enhanced U.S. alignment with core principles for aid effectiveness set forth in the 2005 Paris Declaration and reaffirmed at international aid effectiveness meetings in Acra (2008) and Busan (2011) and with OECD recommendations for greater aid effectiveness (see Maguire 2014).

10. As of September 2014, of $583 million in post-quake aid allocated by USAID for Health and Education, $49 million, or 8.4 percent, went to education (U.S. Government Accountability Office 2015).

11. Among major initiatives already active in the corridors selected were a USAID-

funded watershed rehabilitation initiative called WINNER, later renamed Feed the Future West (Port-au-Prince and St. Marc corridors), and the CARACOL industrial park (Cap Haitian corridor).

12. Over 65 percent of Haiti's economic activity and 85 percent of its fiscal revenue were concentrated in Port-au-Prince (Government of the Republic of Haiti 2010).

13. U.S. officials counter arguments that the Port-au-Prince corridor is not decentralized by pointing out that rehabilitating vulnerable watersheds near the city not only safeguards the security of the capital region and its close to 3 million inhabitants but also supports decentralization by improving agricultural productivity in rural areas in the corridor and therefore within reach of Haiti's major market for farm goods.

14. Haitian Americans, estimated to number at least 1 million, constitute one of several key U.S. groups that keep Haiti on the political agenda (see Maguire in Heine and Thompson 2011).

15. $84.4 million was spent countrywide in Haiti on HIV commodities from June 2006 to March 2013. An additional $74.3 million was allocated for expenditures up to September 2015. Ninety-five million has been provided for cholera prevention and response (U.S. Department of State 2012).

16. Subcontractors can be both non-Haitian and Haitian organizations, including NGOs, community-based organizations, and private sector entities.

17. Shah stepped down as USAID administrator in early 2015. After seven months of inaction, on December 1, 2015, the U.S. Senate confirmed Gayle Smith as USAID administrator. Key Republicans including Ted Cruz held up the nomination and voted against Smith. The gap in time between Shah's departure and Smith's confirmation likely means that Shah's reform efforts lost momentum.

18. Off-the-record interview in Washington, DC, August 2013.

19. This is a phrase Martelly repeated like a mantra in public and private meetings during his Washington visit. He later used it in his inaugural address (CNN Wire Staff 2011).

20. The U.S. contribution to the construction of the Caracol industrial park was $124 million, its largest single expenditure in the post-quake period. The Inter-American Development Bank earmarked $100 million and SAE-A Trading, a South Korean textile manufacturer, pledged $78 million to cover its equipment and operations (Watkins 2013). As of May 2015, some 5,400 jobs at Caracol had been created (Katz 2015).

21. As of January 2015, the terms of most Haitian parliamentarians had expired and Martelly had begun to rule by decree. Intense domestic and international pressure resulted in an electoral schedule that includes both parliamentary and local elections and culminates with presidential elections toward the end of 2015 (Maguire 2015). Following disputed and incomplete presidential elections in December 2015 that were tainted by widespread fraud, a provisional government succeeded Michel Martelly when his term ended on February 7, 2016. That government's mandate is to reform the election process so that credible presidential elections can be held sometime in 2016.

22. Interview with an IMF official, October 2014.

23. Venezuela canceled Haiti's pre-earthquake debt of $395 million in 2010.

24. As of September 2013, the Martelly government claimed that it had provided cash transfers, food kits, hot meals, and other forms of economic support to more than 1 million Haitians, paying for these "social programs" from PetroCaribe funds (Belt 2013).

References

Associated Press. 2012. "Haiti Begins Cash Transfer Program." Accessed May 29. http://bigstory.ap.org/content/haiti-begins-cash-transfer-social-program.

Belt, Rachel. 2013. "PetroCaribe Helps Fight Poverty, Build Roads, Social Housing in Haiti." *Caribbean News Now*. Accessed September 9. http://www.caribbeannews-now.com/headline-PetroCaribe-helps-fight-poverty,-build-roads,-social-housing-in-Haiti-17581.html.

Breslin, Patrick. 1987. *Development and Dignity: Grassroots Development and the Inter-American Foundation*. Washington DC: Inter-American Foundation.

Bryan, Anthony. 2014. "Venezuela's PetroCaribe to End." Petroleumworld.com, October 20. Accessed October 20, 2014. http://www.petroleumworld.com/story14101801.htm.

Buss, Terry F. 2008. *Haiti in the Balance: Why Foreign Aid Has Failed and What We Can Do About It*. Washington, DC: Brookings Institution Press.

Charles, Jacqueline. 2013. "Venezuelan Oil Program Uncertainty Fuels Caribbean Concern." *Miami Herald*. Accessed April 4, 2014. http://www.miamiherald.com/2013/04/04/3323947/venezuelan-oil-program-uncertainty.html.

Clinton, Hillary. 2014. *Hard Choices*. New York: Simon and Schuster.

Clinton Foundation Editorial Team. 2012 "President Clinton Announces Opening of Caracol Northern Industrial Park in Haiti." Clinton Foundation, October 25, 2012. Accessed May 31, 2016. https://www.clintonfoundation.org/main/clinton-foun-dation-blog.html/2012/10/25/president-clinton-announces-opening-of-caracol-northern-industrial-park-in-haiti.

Cohen, Marc J. 2013. "Diri Nasyonal ou Diri Miami? Food, Agriculture and US-Haiti Relations." *Food Security* 5 (4): 597–606.

Collier, Paul. 2009. "Haiti: From Natural Catastrophe to Economic Security, A Report for the United Nations." Accessed October 28, 2016, http://www.focal.ca/pdf/haiti collier.pdf.

CNN Wire Staff. 2011. "Former Pop Star Sworn in as Haiti's New President." CNN, May 15. Accessed May 31, 2016. http://www.cnn.com/2011/WORLD/americas/05/14/haiti.inauguration/.

Daniel, Trenton. 2012. "Clintons Land in Haiti to Showcase Industrial Park." *Washington Times*. Accessed October 22, 2012. http://www.washingtontimes.com/news/2012/oct/22/clintons-land-haiti-showcase-industrial-park/.

———. 2011. "Haiti Gov't Links to Old Regime Prompt Scrutiny." CNSnew.com. Accessed October 13, 2011. http://cnsnews.com/news/article/haiti-govt-links-old-regime-prompt-scrutiny-0.

The Economist. 2008. "The Silent Tsunami: The Food Crisis and How to Solve It." *The Economist*, April 19. http://www.economist.com/node/11050146.

———. 2013. "Feeding Haiti: A New Menu." *The Economist*, June 22. Accessed June 22, 2013. http://www.economist.com/news/americas/21579875-government-tries-load-up-plates-poorest-people-americas-new-menu/.

Embassy of the United States, Port-au-Prince, Haiti. 2013. "USAID Launches New Program to Help Prevent Hunger and Malnutrition in Haiti." Press release, October 1. Accessed October 30, 2013. http://haiti.usembassy.gov/pr-usaid-kore-lavi-oct-1-2013.html.

Feed the Future. 2012. "Feed the Future Overview." Accessed October 30, 2013. https://feedthefuture.gov/sites/default/files/resource/files/factsheet_feedthefuture_overview_april2015.pdf.

Government of the Republic of Haiti. 2007. *Pour réussir le saut qualitatif: Document de stratégie nationale pour la croissance et la réduction de la pauvreté*. Accessed November 2007. http://www.mpce.gouv.ht/dsncrpfinal.pdf.

———. 2010. *Action Plan for National Recovery and Development of Haiti*. Accessed March 2010. https://www.kirkensnodhjelp.no/contentassets/ee77fa84ec654f-b2a01ac3ea8f72bd98/haiti_action_plan_eng.pdf.

———. 2012a. *Cadre de Coordination de l'Aide Externe au Developpement d'Haiti (CAED)*. Accessed September 2012. https://www.humanitarianresponse.info/system/files/documents/files/STC-PresentationPWCadreCoordinationAideExterne final9.11.120k).pdf.

———. 2012b. *Plan stratégique de développement D'Haïti: Pays émergent en 2030*. Accessed July 2012. http://www.undp.org/content/dam/haiti/docs/Gouvernance %20d%C3%A9mocratique%20et%20etat%20de%20droit/UNDP_HT_PLAN %20STRAT%C3%89GIQUE%20de%20developpement%20Haiti_tome1.pdf.

Haïti en Marche. 2008. "L'Ambassadeur des Etats-Unis inaugure le projet Phare." *Haïti en Marche*, October 8–14, 18.

———. 2012. "Politique: Premières convocations de Lamothe." *Haïti en Marche*, 20 June.

Haiti Grassroots Watch. 2013. "USAID Funded Food Voucher Program Hurt Farmers, Favored U.S. Exports." Haiti Grassroots Watch, October 9. Accessed October 12, 2013. http://www.globalresearch.ca/haiti-usaid-funded-food-voucher-program-hurt-farmers-favored-u-s-exports/5353964.

Haiti Libre. 2012. "Haiti—Reconstruction: Haiti Regains Its Sovereignty in the Management of Aid." Haitilibre.com, November 27, 2012. http://www.haitilibre.com/en/news-7258-haiti-reconstruction-haiti-regains-its-sovereignty-in-the-management-of-aid.html.

Inter-American Foundation. 2016. "About the IAF: At a Glance." Accessed June 19, 2016. http://www.iaf.gov/about-the-iaf/at-a-glance-3798.

International Monetary Fund. 2014. "Haiti: Seventh Review Under the Extended Credit Facility." IMF Country Report 14/105. April. Accessed May 1, 2014. http://www. imf.org/external/pubs/ft/scr/2014/cr14105.pdf.

Johnston, Jake, and Alexander Main. 2013. "Breaking Open the Black Box: Increasing Aid Transparency and Accountability in Haiti." Center for Economic and Policy Research. Accessed April 2013. http://cepr.net/documents/publications/haiti-aid-accountability-2013-04.pdf.

Katz, Jonathan. 2013. *The Big Truck That Went By: How the World Came to Save Haiti and Left Behind a Disaster.* New York: Palgrave Macmillan.

———. 2015. "The King and Queen of Haiti." *Politico Magazine,* May 4. Accessed May 4, 2015. http://www.politico.com/magazine/story/2015/05/clinton-foundation-haiti-117368_full.html?print#.VW8hq1K3aSr.

Kristoff, Madeline, and Liz Panarelli. 2010. "Haiti: A Republic of NGOs?" United States Institute of Peace, April 26. Accessed April 2010. http://www.usip.org/publications/haiti-republic-of-ngos.

Maguire, Robert. 2009. "Haiti after the Donors' Conference: A Way Forward." United States Institute of Peace Special Report 232. Accessed July 20, 2013. http://www.usip.org/sites/default/files/resources/haiti_after_donors_conference.pdf.

———. 2010. "Dr. Robert Maguire Presents Senate Testimony: Reconstructing to Rebalance Haiti after the Earthquake." February 4. Accessed July 20, 2013. http://www.trinitydc.edu/media/2010/02/05/maguire-senate-testimony-haiti/.

———. 2011. "US Policy towards Haiti under the administrations of George W. Bush and Barack Obama." In *Fixing Haiti: MINUSTAH and Beyond,* edited by Jorge Heine and Andrew S. Thompson, 229–246. Tokyo: United Nations University Press.

———. 2014. "Priorities, Alignment and Leadership: Improving United States' Aid Effectiveness in Haiti." *Cahiers des Amériques Latines* 75 (1): 59–78. Accessed May 31, 2016. http://cal.revues.org/3117.

———2015. "Back to the Future?" *Americas Quarterly* 9 (2): 28–32.

Perito, Robert. 2008. "Integrated Security Assistance: The 2107 Program." July 1. United States Institute of Peace, Special Report 207. Accessed May 31, 2016. http://www.usip.org/sites/default/files/sr207.pdf.

———. 2009. "Haiti: Is Economic Security Possible if Diplomats and Donors Do Their Part?" USI Peace Briefing, May. Accessed May 2009. www.usip.org/sites/default/files/resources/Haiti_Perito.pdf.

Schipani, Andres, and John Paul Rathbone. 2015. "Oil Price Rout Forces Venezuela to Rethink Petro-Diplomacy." *Financial Times,* January 14. Accessed January 15, 2015. http://www.jsg.utexas.edu/lacp/2015/01/oil-price-rout-forces-venezuela-to-rethink-petro-diplomacy/.

Shah, Rajiv. 2011. "The Modern Development Enterprise." Remarks at the Center for Global Development, January 19, Washington, DC. Video accessed January 28, 2011. http://www.usaid.gov/press/speeches/2011/sp110119.html.

United States Agency for International Development and United States Department of

State. 2013. "Feed the Future North." Accessed October 30, 2013. http://www.usaid.gov/news-information/fact-sheets/feed-future-north.

U.S. Government Accountability Office. 2015. "Haiti Reconstruction: USAID Has Achieved Mixed Results and Should Enhance Sustainability Planning." Accessed June 2015. http://www.gao.gov/products/GAO-13-558.

U.S. Department of State. 2009. "Haiti Policy and Foreign Assistance Review." Power-Point presentation, United States Institute of Peace, Washington, DC, September 9.

———. 2011. *Post-Earthquake USG Haiti Strategy: Toward Renewal and Economic Opportunity.* January 3. Accessed January 10, 2011. http://www.state.gov/documents/organization/156448.pdf.

———. 2012. "Country Report on Human Rights Practices 2012: Haiti." Accessed May 31, 2016. http://www.state.gov/j/drl/rls/hrrpt/humanrightsreport/index.htm?year=2015&dlid=253021#wrapper.

Watkins, Tate. 2013. "How Haiti's Future Depends on America's Markets." *The Atlantic*, May 8. Accessed May 31, 2016. http://www.theatlantic.com/international/archive/2013/05/how-haitis-future-depends-on-american-markets/275682/.

White House Office of the Press Secretary. 2010. "Fact Sheet: U.S. Global Development Policy." Accessed September 22, 2011. http://www.whitehouse.gov/the-press-office/2010/09/22/fact-sheet-us-global-development-policy.

Whitefield, Mimi. 2012. "USAID Administrator's Goal: Shift More Aid to Haitian Groups." *Miami Herald*, September 22. Accessed September 22, 2012. http://www.miamiherald.com/news/local/community/article1942917.html.

7

Who Owns the Religion of Haiti?

Karen Richman

In 1804, the slaves of Saint-Domingue stunned the world economic order by liberating their labor from French colonial planters and their souls from the French Catholic Church. In the aftermath of independence, their descendants exploited the emergent nation-state's external isolation and internal political disarray to defy efforts to reinstitute the draconian plantation order and its severe limitations on workers' economic freedom. They established a holistic system of small, independent farms; an efficient female-run internal market structure; a social structure based on bilateral descent groups; and a fluid, de-centralized, syncretic system of vernacular European and African cosmological beliefs and ritual practices. This relatively autonomous religious system soon became the target of predatory world religions and complicit, despotic national leaders. Since 1860, the Vatican and the French Catholic Church have waged crusades to conquer the cultural life of the nation and retake control of Haitian Catholicism. In the mid-twentieth century, Protestant missionaries from the United States embarked on their own campaigns to accumulate converts in the Haitian countryside. Since then, the two religions have been locked in an epic "war of position" (Gramsci 1971) to possess the religious territory of Haiti and reestablish separate boundaries. When the apocalyptic earthquake of January 12, 2010, laid bare the relative strength of each competitor's spiritual and mate-rial weapons, it appeared that Protestant evangelicals had temporarily acquired the upper hand.

In this chapter, I use historical sources and ethnographic evidence that I have collected over the past three decades in Léogâne (Richman 2005) to demonstrate how this futile religious war has been waged in pursuit of control over elusive boundaries and dubious fidelity to doctrine in a persistently fluid and plural religious landscape. I argue that Haitians' pragmatic, instrumental approach to alleviating suffering and dodging misfortune has long guided individual religious choices between Catholicism and Protestantism, inevitably degrading the triumph of either crusade into Pyrrhic victory.

The Establishment of Religion in Haiti

Roman Catholicism was the official religion of the colony of Saint-Domingue, which was established in 1697, and after Haiti achieved independence, it was declared the state religion. The Catholic Church was indigenized after independence in 1804, when French colonists and their priests fled the country. Haitians controlled their own church during the six decades of political isolation that served as punishment for Haitian slaves' successful challenge to colonialism and slavery. In 1860, however, as Haiti's Francophile, mulatto elite was inviting recolonization by France and Germany and, ultimately, the United States, authority over the church was returned to the Vatican. That authority remained unchallenged for a century. As President Fabre Geffrard, Haiti's tenth president, signed an 1860 concordat with the Vatican, he declared, "Let us hasten to remove from our land these last vestiges of barbarism and slavery, superstition and its scandalous practices" (Nicholls 1979, 84). As a result of the accord, French priests regained control not only of the church but also of the principal schools, which were run by religious orders.

The rise of the United States as the new regional colonial power in the early twentieth century and the U.S. occupation of Haiti from 1915 to 1934 limited the authority of the French Catholic Church in Haiti. When the U.S. administrators and soldiers finally departed, the Catholic Church stepped into the power void. In 1941, it launched an all-out crusade against "superstition" in Haiti. *La campagne anti-superstitieuse* (the anti-superstition campaign) formally began with a pastoral letter published on January 26, 1942, in the Catholic daily *La Phalange* decrying "the irreconcilable opposition" between Christianity and "the collection of religious beliefs and practices which came from Africa" (quoted in Nicholls 1979, 182). Many of the elements of this "collection" actually came from Europe, but identifying them all as African served the Church's purpose better (Rey and Richman 2010). The Catholic Church's decision to launch the campaign received enthusiastic endorsement from the new pro-American president and former ambassador to the United States, Èlie Lescot. President Lescot's support for the anti-superstition campaign was inseparable from his "mulatrification" project, a clumsy effort to return political and economic hegemony to the mulatto elite and their U.S. allies (Nicholls 1979, 183; Ramsey 2002). Lescot took office one week after the publication of the pastoral letter that decried superstition and vowed a return to Catholic government (Plummer 1992, 148). When the "spiritual blitzkrieg" (a term *La Phalange* used) began harassing Protestants too, President Lescot was forced to intervene. He attended worship at a Protestant church to demonstrate his disapproval of the attacks.

Ti Rivyè, Léogâne, the site where I have been conducting ethnographic research since 1983, was a site of the "rejection," or *larejèt,* as the hapless anti-superstition program was locally known. Eyewitness accounts by a few of the local elders reported details of the conduct of the absurd religious and political crusade. For example, Archange Calixte, who was born in 1932, recalled a confrontation between his father, a ritual leader (*gangan ason*), and the local police and parish priest. The purportedly iniquitous contents of the two shrines he oversaw were targets of the rejection. Archange and I were standing in the same courtyard where the encounter took place when he recalled what had happened there six decades before:

> I remember during "the rejection," a priest from [the town of] Léogâne came into the compound along with two policemen. I remember it well. They had been destroying the spirits' things [in the area]. They called for my father. They said to my father, "Go into the house, get the things, bring them to us." My father said, "There is nothing I'm going to bring to you. If you want to take them, go inside and take them. I am not bringing anything to you." After that, they went across the street to the other yard at Mizdor's house [of worship] and they said the same thing. "Go into the temple and bring the things to us." He said, "I'm not going to do it. If there is something you are looking for, go inside and take what you need." They didn't do anything. As they were leaving, they said to him, "Bring the things to town for us. Come to town with the things." He said, "I'm not hauling anything to town. I don't have anything to sell." We fell out laughing. I remember that well. I was young. Everyone fell out laughing.

The cowardice underlying the authorities' blustering, inept performance of anti-superstition regulations endures in Archange's memory. The priest and the police "team" were not only incapable of carrying out their mission, they also failed to intimidate the confident ritual leader to do their work for them. The ritual leader seized control of the situation and ridiculed the bumbling crusaders. The novelists Philippe Thoby-Marcelin and Pierre Marcelin (1970) featured similarly absurd skirmishes in their novel about the anti-superstition campaign, *All Men Are Mad*. Ironically, contemporaneous North American literary critics dismissed the novel as wildly unbelievable exaggeration (Daut and Richman 2008).

Nationalism, the Vodou State, and Protestant Evangelism

As in the case of the 1860 Concordat ceding control of Haiti's state church to the Vatican, the resurgence eighty-one years later in 1941 of the Catholic Church's colonialist policies again provoked a nationalist response. And as in the late nineteenth century, the nationalist movement was allied with North American and European Protestantism. For example, Louis-Joseph Janvier, a prominent writer and diplomat, believed that Haiti should embrace the establishment of a religion that would respect the sovereignty of the state and whose clergy would defer to the state (Nicholls 1979, 118). Janvier advocated the civilizing influence of Protestantism. In his 1883 treatise on Haiti's foreign affairs, he wrote: "The Protestant is thrifty and self-reliant, he does not waste his money on carnivals and other frivolities. Protestantism permits free discussion and encourages private initiative. . . . The Protestant is almost always a more practical worker and a better citizen than the Catholic" (quoted in Nicholls 1979, 118). Janvier argued that conversion to Protestantism would provide the religious basis for capitalist economic development of the archaic peasant economy, echoing the bourgeois discourse of the seventeenth and eighteenth centuries that disparaged the indolence of European peasants and blamed the saints' days and festivals of the Catholic ritual calendar for decreasing available labor (Thompson 1967).

Yet Janvier also recommended that Haiti emulate Africa rather than Europe. He went so far as to claim that Protestantism was more suited to the African temperament than Catholicism was. He offered evidence that Protestantism could be used to introduce "primitive" populations of Africa to Western culture. However, Janvier admitted that his vision of a Protestant Haitian society was unlikely to be realized: "Protestantism will never be a danger for Haiti and Haiti would win the affection of Protestant nations" (Janvier 1883, 371). Janvier's prediction was prescient. Protestant religion eventually bolstered the Haitian secular state, in part by threatening the other Haitian state: the Catholic Church. In this discussion we will see how over the next century, Protestant evangelization increased to the point that precisely 100 years after Janvier published his 1883 tract, the pope himself was compelled to intervene to staunch the flow of Catholics into the Protestant fold.

The excesses of the U.S. occupation of 1915–1934, the Lescot presidency of 1941–1946, and the Church's anti-superstition campaigns of the 1940s provided ample reason for Janvier's nationalist followers to embrace an alternative narrative of religious authenticity and identity. The new discipline of Haitian ethnology answered the call. Studies of the peasants' religion and folklore provided the material for promotion of an authentic Haitian identity located in peasant life and rooted in African culture (Ramsey 2005). The ethnological approach was part of a counterhegemonic, nationalist discourse and recapitulated a misleading "modern" view of Haitian peasants as tradition-bound primitives (Richman 2007). Ethnologists such as Milo Rigaud and Odette Mennesson-Rigaud, writing in the 1940s and 1950s, portrayed vernacular beliefs and practices as a coherent set of essentially African legacies, ignoring the substantial European and Catholic bases of much of Haitian popular religion.

In this context, the name they chose for the religion being studied and promoted as a national heritage was significant: Vodou. It was not the indigenous name of the vernacular religion; there was no term that assimilated such diffuse, heterogeneous, localized beliefs and practices. In Creole, the term Vodou refers to a genre of ritual music and dance performed in honor of a particular category of spirit. The term derives from the Fongbe word for spirit; many slaves who came to Saint-Domingue from Dahomey spoke this language. There was (and still is) no way in Creole to say, "I do Vodou," or "I practice Vodou." The nationalistic ethnologists' use of the term to refer to the religion as a whole soon became widely accepted, though it remains foreign to many who are thought to do or practice Vodou. Similarly, their portrayal of a standardized religion based on the worship of universalistic nature spirits set a formula for subsequent knowledge of the religion which, as will be shown below, continues to play important roles in the contest over Haitians' religious sovereignty today.

Vodou thus could become a symbol of the Haitian nation and state with the election of François Duvalier to the presidency in 1957. Duvalier, who claimed Louis-Joseph Janvier as his ideological mentor, was a central member of a famed ethnological group. He wrote or co-wrote several studies of the folk religion, some of the data of which were based on his observations of rehearsed performances staged in Port-au-Prince hotels (Wilken 1992). The self-declared president for life fostered the development of a reputation not only for practicing Vodou but also for incorporating Vodou practices and the Vodou priesthood in his ruthless politics. The dictator's image as a sinister "Vodou president" only bolstered outsiders' stereotypes of the religion as exotic and mysterious (Johnson 2006).

Paradoxically, Duvalier, Haiti's first pro-Vodou, pro-peasant, black nationalist president, was at the same time the country's foremost champion of Protestantism, even though Protestants opposed Vodou far more strongly than the Catholic Church did.[1] Courlander and Bastien have observed that "the relationship between Duvalier and religion should be viewed not as one of an individual to a faith, but rather it should be approached from the standpoint of the relations between church and state" (Courlander and Bastien 1966, 56). Duvalier used Protestant evangelists to undermine the main challenge to his power, the Catholic Church. In 1966, in exchange for a promise to stop persecuting and expelling foreign Catholic priests, the Vatican capitulated to Duvalier's demand that it abrogate the 1860 Concordat and grant Haiti (or the president-for-life himself) the right to name its own priests (Abbott 1988, 381).

Fred Conway captures the paradox of the ethnologist-president's promotion of Protestantism:

> For all his identification with Vodoun, François Duvalier might well be called the "Father of Protestantism" in Haiti. Duvalier's main potential opposition in the religious sphere was a Catholic Church dominated by foreigners. In his struggle with this adversary, he enlisted both Vodoun and Protestantism in spite of the fact that the Protestants were more inimical to Vodoun than were Catholics. At a time when Duvalier was deliberately alienating foreign governments and foreign aid organizations, he welcomed Protestant missionaries, especially from the U.S. The Protestants drew people away from an allegiance to the Catholic Church without themselves presenting a monolithic front to the government. Because the missionaries were competing with each other, fiercely at times, they were not in a position to oppose the government as a group. (Conway 1978, 166–167)

Duvalier assumed that evangelical Protestants could be depended upon to avoid engagement with affairs of the state. The "second tenet of the Baptist faith," according to Edner Jeanty, a leading Haitian Baptist theologian, is that "the church and the state are separate" (Jeanty 1991, 62). Nonetheless, in the conclusion of his history of Protestant movement into the country, *Le Christianisme en Haïti*, Jeanty rejoiced over the fact that a Protestant had become acting head of state in 1990. "The Bible has entered the National Palace through the front door," he wrote (106). The theologian thus provided an illustration of Laënnec Hurbon's observation that while Haitian Protestants may profess that they reject the idea of participating in politics, they "express a willingness to mount the political stage to defend their churches' interests" (Hurbon 2001, 136).

The strategic union between Duvalier and North American Protestant missionaries was just one example of several such alliances between a repressive Latin American state (including Chile and Guatemala) and an apparently apolitical Protestant presence during the second half of the twentieth century. Perhaps Duvalier did not anticipate the extent to which his religious marriage of convenience would eventually contribute to the emasculation of the Haitian state. After he was overthrown, organizations implementing neoliberal policies routinely bypassed the allegedly corrupt and inept state to channel international development aid to seemingly moral, honest, and efficient private sector organizations (Gunewardena and Schuller 2007). The credibility of these organizations rested in large part on their discourse of Christian morality, even if they were not explicitly religious organizations (McAllister 2012, 187–215). Hence, the dictator who claimed he was the very state (Duvalier famously pronounced that he was the Haitian flag) contributed to the transfer of the nation's administrative capacity to a "republic of NGOs" (Heinl and Heinl 1997, 585).

By 1965, more than a third of the schools in Haiti were run by Protestant missionaries. A sign of the welcome Protestant missionaries enjoyed during the period was Oral Roberts' official welcome to the presidential palace in 1969 (Nicholls 1979, 412). Seventy percent of the Protestant missions in Haiti were established in the period 1950–1970, and by the latter year an estimated 20 percent of the population was Protestant (Conway 1978, 165). Starting in the 1970s, the expansion of Protestant missionization in Haiti involved the growth of Pentecostal groups, which systematically covered the geography of the country and targeted the poorest segments of the population. Echoing the findings of many observers of Pentecostal missionization in Latin America, Charles-Poisset Romain asserts that le 'take off' pentecôtiste (the Pentecostals' take-off) in Haiti was the result of their use of the Creole vernacular spoken by the masses rather than the colonial language of French that was spoken and written by the elite few (Romain 1986, 190; see also Lehmann 1996; Martin 1993; Stoll 1991). In addition, the Pentecostals harnessed their valorization of the Creole vernacular to literacy. Literacy was seen throughout the colonized world as a primary means of self-improvement, and mainline Protestants had already presented their "religion of the book" as one of "sociability and civilization" (Romain 1986, 145).

In his recounting of the history of Baptist missionization in Haiti during the mid-twentieth century, Jeanty praised North American missionaries for their skillful deployment of capitalist marketing techniques. He described the accomplishments of one proselytizer with a special knack for selling a new religion to reluctant native consumers, in the process inadvertently admitting that Christian missionization amounted to creating consumer desire for a nonessential product. Jeanty wrote that Mme. Ruben Clarke, who accompanied her husband to Pignon to spread the gospel, was *une dynamique femme capable de 'vendre un réfrigérateur même à un Eskimo'* (a dynamic woman who can even sell a refrigerator to an Eskimo) (Jeanty 1991, 91).

Conway's (1978) ethnographic research, which was conducted in the southern peninsula of Haiti in the 1970s, is an apt demonstration that Protestantism is a moral narrative of modernity (Keane 2007). Conway argues convincingly that "missionary Protestantism in Haiti gives rise less to a Protestant ethic of self-help than to the idea that the way to worldly success is identified with direct dependence on the foreign—North American—missionary" (Conway 1978, 193). He cites interviewees' statements (no doubt mediated by their perception or hope that their North American interlocutor was a missionary and thus a source of jobs or visas) that the Protestant mission churches symbolized progress and modernity. As they pointed to Protestant missions, people told Conway that "the country is becoming more and more civilized" in contrast to the backwardness blamed on peasant Vodou. Several converts said that their conversion was a contribution to development (Conway 1978, 172).

According to Conway, villagers understood that Americans needed quantities of converts and were willing to pay for them. No one benefited more than Haitian pastors from the Americans' need to build missions and count disciples. The clergy has long been one of the few jobs for men in rural areas, and the field of candidates is vast. Romain observed in the mid-1980s that "every Protestant is a pastor and a missionary at the same time" (Romain 1986, 144). The speech practice of addressing any male evangelical as *pastè* (pastor) reinforces this conflation.

Vying to Possess Vodou and Haiti: Catholics versus Protestants

In 1804, the leaders of the slave revolution in Saint-Domingue created a Catholic nation-state. For 181 years of its existence as a sovereign state, Haiti endorsed and protected this one religion despite a continued struggle for autonomy with the Vatican. Key events in this bitter history were the Concordat of 1860, which returned control of the church and thereby much of Haiti's sovereignty in state affairs to France and Rome, and the ludicrous anti-superstition campaign of

1941–1942. Another historic moment in the Vatican's intervention in Haiti occurred in 1983, when the country received its first (and so far only) papal visit. The head of the Catholic Church, John Paul II, came to Haiti to announce a new campaign to stem the advance of a religion "lacking the true message of the Gospel and with methods that do not respect real religious liberty." Surprisingly, the charlatans in the Catholic leader's sights were not practitioners of Vodou. They were Protestants.

Thus, precisely 100 years after Joseph Janvier wrote that Protestantism was unlikely to ever amount to a danger in Haiti, the Catholic Church was compelled to formally recognize the looming sectarian threat. The pope attended a conference of sixty-one Latin American bishops in Port-au-Prince, where the top item on the agenda was "preparing actions to stem the rapid growth of Protestant fundamentalist sects in the region" (Simons 1983a). Pope John Paul said that "the advance of religious groups which at times are lacking the true message of the Gospel and with methods that do not respect real religious liberty, pose serious obstacles to the mission of the Catholic Church and to other Christian confessions" (Greene 1993). Archbishop François-Wolff Ligondé, the host of the conference, announced the start of a national campaign to defend Catholicism in Haiti against "the blind proselytizing of Protestants" (Greene 1993). Two years later, the Haitian state's official recognition of Protestantism as a national religion revealed the failure of the campaign. And within two more decades, a presidential decree made Vodou the third religion of the nation-state of Haiti.

Significantly, the Haitian nationalist narrative has attributed a very different political meaning to the unprecedented visit. Rather than taking account of the pope's conspicuous counterattack on the Protestant danger in Haiti and in the Latin American region, the nationalist account emphasizes the political import of the papal intervention. It diverts attention away from the strategic alliance of the strange bedfellows, pro-Vodou Duvalier and anti-Vodou North American Protestant evangelicals. The Pope's declaration that "things must change," which actually was a call to halt "the advance of [Protestant evangelical] religious groups" (Simons 1983a) has been widely misinterpreted as a demand for political regime change and thus as the event that set in motion the popular mobilization to uproot the government of Jean-Claude Duvalier.

This version of history ignores processes that had weakened Duvalier prior to the pope's visit. These events emboldened the pope to reverse concessions the Church had made to Jean-Claude's father: He retook control of which priests were assigned to Haiti and essentially reinstated the terms of the 1860

Concordat. Resistance to the Concordat's religious colonialism, it will be recalled, is what inspired the founder of Haitian black nationalism, Louis-Joseph Janvier. His twentieth-century ethnological followers, chief among whom was François Duvalier, located the authenticity of the anticolonial nation-state in the Vodou religion and in romanticized folklore. To this day, the Haitian state ornaments official events with Vodou symbolism and folkloric performances. Ironically, children typically perform the mock Vodou rites and dances, even though children would hardly be appropriate agents for carrying out rituals or ritual dances in actual worship. But as stand-ins for the modern ideals of innocence and authenticity, the children reinforce the authenticity of the Vodou performance. At the same time, the state remains virtually silent about the Protestant turn within the nation. The Catholic Church, however, could not afford to ignore the trend.

After 1983, the year 2007 was likely the next significant strategic moment in the Catholic Church's war for control over religion in Haiti, even though that moment attracted little scholarly or media attention. In that year, Archbishop Joseph Serge Miot traveled to the countryside to reach out to professional ritual leaders (*gangan ason/manbo ason*). The head of the Haitian Catholic Church thus took the extraordinary step of signaling that the religious pluralism of Haitians could be a route to the Church's salvation from the Protestant danger. The archbishop selected Léogâne to launch what we might call the church's first "pro-superstition campaign." "Why Léogâne?" I asked Father Thomas, who is associated with the local Catholic parish and who attended the inaugural meeting.[2] "Because, as you know yourself, Karen, Léogâne is the center of Vodou in Haiti," he responded with a smile. His statement was doubly ironic. In reality, the decentralized, heterogeneous, practical system of popular belief and worship lacks a single, dominant geographical anchor. Léogâne's undeserved reputation as the premier Vodou center emerged as a product of the nationalist narrative of folk authenticity. Ethnological research conducted in Léogâne in the middle of the twentieth century played a small but significant part in the production of this special status (Richman 2007, 1–43, 2008a).

At the meeting in Léogâne, Archbishop Miot entreated the assembled Vodou leaders to remind their followers that they were "still Catholics." The archbishop thus removed the divide between Catholicism and Vodou, a separation the Church had protected for the last two centuries. The pro-superstition campaign was a complete reversal of the Church's 1941–1942 anti-Vodou crusade, whose rationale had been to uphold "the irreconcilable opposition" between Catholicism and the collection of religious beliefs and practices that are alleged to have come from Africa. It was a necessary and inevitable reconciliation given the Protestant danger. The archbishop was not able to complete the project of rapprochement with the Vodouists he began in Léogâne; he was tragically killed when the Cathedral of Port-au-Prince collapsed during the earthquake of January 12, 2010. His successors have not resumed his boundary-blurring strategy designed to save Haitian Catholicism from the Protestants by incorporating Vodou.

The Earthquake and Spiritual Reconquest

The devastating earthquake of 2010 provided impetus for renewed Protestant rhetorical offenses against Haitian devil worship. Within just twenty-four hours of the cataclysm, television evangelist Pat Robertson issued a widely circulated explanation of the apocalyptic disaster: It was divine punishment because the slaves had sworn "a pact with the devil" to free themselves and found an independent republic. He said:

> It happened a long time ago in Haiti, and people might not want to talk about it. [The slaves] were under the heel of the French. You know, Napoleon III and whatever. And they got together and swore a pact to the devil. They said, "We will serve you if you will get us free from the French." True story. And so, the devil said, "OK, it's a deal." You know, the Haitians revolted and got themselves free. But ever since, they have been cursed by one thing after the other. (CNN 2010)

At a time of incalculable Haitian suffering, Robertson's provocative remark elicited widespread indignation. As the people of Ti Rivyè were struggling to survive the aftershocks, I called several of my friends in the Ti Rivyè Diaspora. Among them was Ti Mafi, a 42-year-old woman who grew up worshipping spirits and was initiated as a servitor (*ounsi*) before leaving Haiti for Montréal. My friend offered a swift retort that exposed the imperialism of the statements of North American Protestants that they were taming the "Haitian Other." "People [in the United States] who need/want to know if the worship of the devil caused the earthquake—tell them they should buy a ticket to go to Haiti so they can ask the devil [there] if he is the one who caused the earthquake!"

Robertson's claim was neither new nor original. He was repeating a dominant narrative in Haitian evangelical discourse. That evangelical narrative is itself a form of appropriation. The story is a reformulation of the official origin myth of the nation-state, which placed the beginning of the slave revolution of 1791 at a Vodou ceremony in Bois Caïman. Like all national-origin myths, this one combined fact and legend. It was promoted during the mid-twentieth century when state-sponsored folklorists and ethnographers participated in the production of a counterhegemonic narrative of authentic folk and their Vodou (Richman 2007, 1–27). For example, in 1958, Odette Mennesson-Rigaud published a journal article that sought to demonstrate that Haitian "independence was born out of Vodou," lending substantial ethnographic support to the development of the nation-state's origin myth (Mennesson-Rigaud 1958, 43–67).

Evangelical Protestants reformulated this national narrative to claim that the nation was born out of a satanic ceremony in which the insurrectionists swore allegiance to the devil. In this narrative, Haiti's subsequent problems were punishment for the oath taken at Bois Caïman. It is not surprising, then, that Robertson understood the earthquake of January 12, 2010, as an apocalyptic punishment for the 1791 curse. His statement on January 13 condensed the evangelical version of Haiti's origin myth into two sentences: "The Haitians revolted and got themselves free. But ever since, they have been cursed by one thing after the other."

Ironically, Protestant evangelicals' representation of the devil in Haiti is alien to Haitian constructions of the devil. The Protestant use of the word devil conflates anthropomorphic spirits inherited through descent groups (*lwa*) with illicit powers (*dyab*) that are manipulated and sold by sorcerers. The Creole term *dyab*, which derives from the French *diable*, retains meanings from the old European, pre-capitalist moral economy. People confronting the collapse of their moral economy and the incursion of capitalist wage labor used their existing construct of the devil to make sense of—and critique—their "proletarianization" (Thompson 1967, 56–97). Michael Taussig (1980) has described the "proletarian devil contracts" that contemporary miners and plantation workers in the Cauca Valley, Colombia, imagined. These workers imagined the devil as wealth that reproduced itself through unnatural means by stealing life from humans and using it to vitalize money and material assets.

Haitians still imagine *dyab* as an exchange of human life for the acquisition of money for a certain period of profit, but at the end of this period, the money inexorably kills its "owner" and/or the owner's children. Representations of "pursuing" (*chache*) and purchasing (*achte*) these immoral private contracts are the opposite of the moral, social, and communal symbolism of worshipping or "serving" (*sèvi*) *lwa*. Haitian Protestants intentionally disregard this crucial distinction by branding any non-Christian worship *dyab*.

They use the terms "Satan" and "the devil" as misleadingly diffuse, catchall categories to connote and objectify the Other—the Other religion and the Others who practice it.

Elizabeth McAllister (2012) has documented how North American evangelical theologians and missionaries contributed to the production of the myth that Haitians are dominated by the devil. In addition, in the 1990s, North American evangelists introduced the aggressive symbolic methodology known as "spiritual mapping" that Haitian missionaries and pastors used to recolonize the nation "for Jesus." Wielding a rich vocabulary of military metaphors and images of organized, collective violence, Protestant Pentecostal denominations battled Catholics and Vodouists and engaged in a struggle to determine Haitian national identity (Butler 2008, 23–64). In 1997, for example, Joel Jeune, a prominent American-trained pastor, led fellow Christians, including Haitian Americans, on a widely publicized crusade to Bois Caïman, where he conducted a service to exorcize the site (McAllister 2012, 204–205). Six years later, his cousin, Pastor Chavannes Jeune, directed a year-long program to "take back Haiti from Satan." Participants included leaders from major evangelical organizations such as Promise Keepers, World Vision International, World Help, and Campus Crusade for Christ. The following year Chavannes Jeune mounted a candidacy for the presidency of Haiti (McAllister 2012).

The belief that the earthquake was the quintessential manifestation of the 1791 curse circulated between the evangelical North American core and its Haitian periphery and, as Bertin Louis has found, migrated to the periphery of the periphery: Haitian Protestants in the Bahamas (Bertin 2014). Soon after the cataclysm, members of the Haitian Protestant clergy charged that Vodou was "a demonic infestation on the land," that "death was God's response to the sinner," and that "if many survived, it was God's blessing" on those who were sinless (Desmangles 2010).

As the monuments of imperial Catholic authority in Haiti lay in ruin and the religious leadership were killed, stunned, and adrift, the more nimble entrepreneurial evangelicals quickly rushed in to assist in the rescue and recovery. The surge of North American evangelical armies flowing to Haiti after the earthquake was perhaps most striking at the Port-au-Prince airport, where seemingly endless brigades of mostly young white North American volunteers arrived. Each optimistic group was attired in brightly colored custom-made T-shirts advertising their "brand," such as www.jesusinhaiti.com, HelpHealHaiti.org, Northwest Iowa Church of God Haiti Relief Team, or St. John's Episcopal—Restore, Repair, Redeem.

The Earthquake, Conversion, and the End of Vodou?

Soon after the cataclysm, media reports emerged that vast numbers of Haitians were converting to Protestant Christianity. The dominant conjecture was that the earthquake had tested Haitians' faith in their Vodou gods because the gods had failed to prevent the disaster. Multitudes of disappointed former "Vodouists" were allegedly turning away from their traditional religion, simultaneously repelled by the gods' betrayal and drawn to the compelling messages and aid the already ubiquitous and implicitly moral Christian NGOs offered.

Several misleading assumptions underlay the claim of mass conversions to evangelical Christianity that ultimately concern notions of sovereignty and sectarianism in Haiti. First was the premise that Haitians believe in gods who are capable of preventing such natural disasters as earthquakes. Contrary to most outsiders' representations of their religion, Haitians worship spirits (*lwa*), not nature gods (Murray 1984a, 188–231; Richman 2014, 207–233). *Lwa* can be thought of as super (in the sense of all-too-human) and hypersensitive anthropomorphic beings that are inherited through family lines among landholding descent groups. They are said to be from Ginen (Africa) and to dwell there still; many bear African names.

Ritual discourse, mainly in song texts and in visual imagery on flour paintings, painted murals, and cloth banners, often compare spirits to aspects or forces of nature. Examples include comparisons of Danbala Wedo's energy with that of a water snake and Ogoun's anger with thunder. It does not follow, however, that Danbala is an actual water snake or that Ogoun in fact controls storms. The equation of Danbala Wedo and Ogoun with natural forces follows from a simplistic interpretation of symbolic representation. It is, to invoke Claude Lévi-Strauss's terminology, a reductive, "primitive" reading of analogical classification (Lévi-Strauss 1996). In addition, this reading reproduces the modern representation of the tradition-bound, scientific thought of "others" who occupy a different (read: backward) intellectual "time" and place and hold the childish belief that their fickle gods control nature (Fabian 1983). By contrast, the "great" religions of modernity have allegedly graduated from the nature-bound beliefs of their primitive antecedents.

When I informed various people who "serve their *lwa*" of the media claims that Haitians were giving up on their *lwa* because they had failed to prevent the cataclysm, they offered indignant retorts. Ti Mafi, for instance, declared, "It was God! The *lwa* had nothing to do with it. The *lwa* did not cause the earthquake." Haitians did not reject their spirits for failing to prevent a natural disaster over which they had no control. Bondye, the Supreme Being, is thought to control nature in an otiose, random, impersonal way. *Lwa* are not believed to have powers to control air, land, or water; the powers of *lwa* are far more circumscribed and are limited to involvement and interference in discrete humans' personal affairs. Their command is primarily confined to protecting or undermining the health and labor power of particular members of specific descent groups to whom they belong. The *lwa* are also distinct from ancestors, who are called *mò* and are respected in their own right and whose primary role, by virtue of their proximity to the other world, is to mediate relations between members of cognatic descent groups and their inherited *lwa*.

As Karen Brown (2001) and Gerald Murray (1984b) have shown, the *lwa* are primarily the protagonists of a "cult of affliction." These afflictions are fundamentally relational. The primary work of religious leaders such as Mama Lola (who is represented in Brown's work) is to help heal; that is, to help heal the ruptured relations whose concrete symbolic manifestation is bodily illness and misfortune. Mama Lola does not treat passive patients; instead, through pragmatic, instrumentalist discourse and performance, she empowers the afflicted to actively influence the threatening spirit. The primary purpose of rituals is to persuade spirits to "let go of" a member or members in the *lwa*'s "grasp" and to prevent recurrence of the "dis-ease" by placating the *lwa*. The spirits' ability to afflict members of descent groups, no matter where they reside, is a primary factor in the continued vitality of the religion for the many Haitian migrants living abroad. And the belief that the only appropriate site for a healing ritual is on the family land in Haiti is a powerful factor that keeps migrants tethered to their spiritual anchors in Haiti.

Conclusion: Who Owns Haitian Religion?

The founders of the independent Republic of Haiti perpetuated the colonial religion by establishing Catholicism as the official faith. In the aftermath of 1804, the ostracized country hosted an autonomous church and developed a fluid, syncretic, decentralized system of popular belief and practice. A half-century later, in 1860, and again in 1941, Catholic imperialists, abetted by Haitian heads of state, maneuvered to stamp out superstition and reclaim the nation on behalf of the Vatican and France. The "Catholic state's" hold over Haitian sovereignty did not begin to loosen until the middle of the twentieth century, when the arch-nationalist Duvalier forged a strategic pact with the Catholic Church's primary territorial rival: a growing evangelical Protestant movement. The pact between the pro-Vodou champion and the allegedly apolitical North American evangelicals set the stage for the expansion of the mission to win Haiti from Satan, which evangelicals are still conducting. They see North America and Haiti as one node in a well-coordinated global nationalist crusade.

In the 1980s, the precarious status of Haiti's religious sovereignty so preoccupied the Vatican that the pope called on the country in person. The pope's visit did little to slow the exponential increase of Protestant missions on the island and in the region, and in 1985 Protestantism became Haiti's second official state religion. While the Haitian state continues its official nationalistic celebrations of Haiti's alleged Vodou essence, the state narrative is virtually silent about the growth of Protestantism and Protestants' role in the development and expansion of "a Republic of NGOs" in a country where, as many are wont to say, *pa gen leta* (there is no state) (see Kivland, this volume).

In thinking, finally, about competition for religious dominion over Haiti in relation to broader, secular challenges to Haiti's sovereignty, it is instructive to ponder the secondary meanings of the word sovereign. One definition of sovereign is "very good or effective [as in] a sovereign remedy for all ills" (*New Oxford American Dictionary*, 3rd ed.). This sense of sovereign fits well with Haitian religious actors' preference for effectiveness over doctrine. My long-term ethnographic research has shown how ordinary agents, regardless of their religious identification, use an instrumental, pragmatic approach to religious belief and practice (Richman 2008b, 2012). As Paul Brodwin (1996) demonstrated in his study over religious contests for healing power in southern Haiti, they strategically transgress doctrinal boundaries to remedy ills. The religious system in Haiti lacks a conquerable national organization or physical structure. Its diffuse, localized, and family-based features provide a measure of immunity to the colonizing designs of religious crusaders. International campaigns in a "war of position" to stamp out superstition, to convert Haitians, and to exorcize the devil from the nation's supposed birthplace will doubtlessly continue, with or without the complicity of the Haitian state. And Haitians' fluid and sovereign spectrum of belief and practice will also persist, regardless of momentary changes in the religious allegiances and costumes of its members.

Notes

1. Duvalier was not the first to embrace this paradox. Jean Price-Mars, who in 1928 wrote the first important text on Haitian peasants' folklore and religion, *Ainsi parla*

l'oncle, was an Episcopalian who supported the expansion of his religion in Haitian society (Price-Mars 1979).

2. Author's interview with Father Thomas Streit, 2008, Notre Dame, Indiana.

References

Abbott, Elizabeth. 1988. *Haiti: The Duvaliers and Their Legacy*. New York: McGraw-Hill Books.

Bertin, Louis. 2014. *My Soul Is in Haiti: Protestantism in the Haitian Diaspora of the Bahamas*. New York: New York University Press.

Brodwin, Paul. 1996. *Medicine and Morality in Haiti*. Cambridge: Cambridge University.

Brown, Karen McCarthy. 2001. *Mama Lola: A Vodou Priestess in Brooklyn*. Berkeley: University of California Press.

Butler, Melvin. 2008. "The Weapons of Our Warfare: Music, Positionality, and Transcendence among Haitian Pentecostals." *Journal of Caribbean Studies* 36 (2): 23–64.

CNN. 2010. "Pat Robertson Says Haiti Paying for 'Pact to the Devil.'" CNN.com, January 13. Accessed April 28, 2016. http://www.cnn.com/2010/US/01/13/haiti.pat.robertson/.

Conway, Fred. 1978. "Pentecostalism in the Context of Haitian Religion and Health Practice." PhD dissertation, American University.

Courlander, Harold, and Rémy Bastien. 1966. *Religion and Politics in Haiti*. Washington: Institute for Cross-Cultural Research.

Daut, Marlene, and Karen Richman. 2008. "Are They Mad? Nation and Narration in *Tous les Hommes sont Fous*." *Small Axe* 26 (June): 133–148.

Desmangles, Leslie. 2010. "Religion in Post-Earthquake Haiti: Continuities and Discontinuities." Paper presented at 109th Annual Meeting of the American Anthropological Association, New Orleans. November 20.

Fabian, Johannes. 1983. *Time and the Other*. New York: Columbia University Press.

Gramsci, Antonio. 1971. *Selections from the Prison Notebooks of Antonio Gramsci*. Edited and translated by Quintin Hoare and Geoffrey Nowell Smith. New York: International Publishers.

Greene, Anne. 1993. *The Catholic Church in Haiti: Political and Social Change*. East Lansing: Michigan State University Press.

Gunewardena, Nandini, and Mark Schuller, eds. 2007. *Capitalizing on Catastrophe: Neoliberal Strategies in Disaster Reconstruction*. Lanham, MD: Altamira Press.

Heinl, Robert, and Nancy Heinl. 1997. *Written in Blood: The Story of the Haitian People: 1492–1995*. Lanham, MD: University Press of America.

Hurbon, Laënnec. 2001. "Current Evolution of Relations between Religion and Politics in Haiti." In *Nation Dance: Religion, Identity, and Cultural Difference in the Caribbean*, edited by Patrick Taylor, 118–125. Bloomington: Indiana University Press.

Janvier, Louis-Joseph. 1883. *La république d'Haïti et ses visiteurs, 1840–1882*. Port-au-Prince: Fardin.

Jeanty, Edner A. 1991. *Le christianisme en Haïti*. Port-au-Prince: La Presse Evangelique.

Johnson, Paul C. 2006. "Secretism and the Apotheosis of Duvalier." *Journal of the American Academy of Religion* 74, no. 2: 420–445.

Keane, Webb. 2007. *Christian Moderns: Freedom and Fetish in the Mission Encounter*. Berkeley: University of California Press.

Lehmann, David. 1996. *Struggle for the Spirit: Religious Transformation and Populist Culture in Brazil and Latin America*. Oxford: Polity Press.

Lévi-Strauss, Claude. 1996. *The Savage Mind*. Chicago: University of Chicago Press.

Martin, David. 1993. *Tongues of Fire: The Explosion of Pentecostalism in Latin America*. Oxford: Blackwell.

McAllister, Elizabeth. 2012. "From Slave Revolt to a Blood Pact with Satan: The Evangelical Rewriting of Haitian History." *Studies in Religion/Sciences Religieuses* 41: 187–215.

Mennesson-Rigaud, Odette. 1958. "Le rôle du Vaudou dans l'indépendance d'Haïti." *Présence Africaine* 18–19: 43–67.

Murray, Gerald. 1984a. "Bon-Dieu and the Rites of Passage in Rural Haiti: Structural Determinants of Postcolonial Religion." In *The Catholic Church and Religions in Latin America*, edited by Thomas C. Bruneau, Chester E. Gabriel, and Mary Mooney, 188–231. Montreal: McGill University Press.

———. 1984b. "Population Pressure, Land Tenure, and Voodoo: The Economics of Haitian Peasant Ritual." In *Beyond the Myths of Culture*, edited by E. Ross, 295–321. New York: Academic Press.

Nicholls, David. 1979. *From Dessalines to Duvalier: Race, Colour, and National Independence in Haiti*. New York: Cambridge University Press.

Plummer, Brenda. 1992. *Haiti and the United States: The Psychological Moment*. Athens: University of Georgia Press.

Price-Mars, Jean. 1979. *Ainsi parla l'oncle: Essai d'ethnographie haïtienne*. Montréal: Leméac.

Ramsey, Kate. 2002. "Without One Ritual Note: Folklore Performance and the Haitian State, 1935–1946." *Radical History Review* 84 (Fall): 7–42.

———. 2005. "Prohibition, Persecution, Performance." *Gradhiva* 1: 165–79.

Rey, Terry, and Karen Richman. 2010. "The Somatics of Syncretism in Haitian Religion: Tying Body and Soul." *Studies in Religion/Sciences Religieuses* 39 (3): 379–403.

Richman, Karen. 2005. *Migration and Vodou*. Gainesville: University Press of Florida.

———. 2007. "Peasants, Migrants and the Discovery of the Authentic Africa." *Journal of Religion in Africa* 37 (3): 1–27.

———. 2008a. "Innocent Imitations? Mimesis and Alterity in Haitian Vodou Art." *Ethnohistory* 55 (2): 203–228.

———. 2008b. "A More Powerful Sorcerer: Conversion and Capital in the Haitian Diaspora." *New West Indian Guide* 81 (1–2): 1–43.

———. 2012. "Religion at the Epicenter: Religious Agency and Affiliation in Léogâne after the Earthquake." *Studies in Religion/Sciences Religieuses* 41 (1).

———. 2014. "Possession and Attachment: Notes on Moral Ritual Communication among Haitian Descent Groups." In *Spirited Things: The Work of "Possession" in Afro-Atlantic Religions*, edited by Paul Johnson, 207–223. Chicago: University of Chicago Press.

Romain, Charles. 1986. *Le protestantisme dans la société Haïtienne*. Port-au-Prince: Henri Deschamps.

Simons, Marlise. 1983a. "Pope in Haiti, Assails Inequality, Hunger and Fear." *New York Times*, March 10.

———. 1983b. "Power of Voodoo, Preached by Sorbonne Scientist." *New York Times*, December 15.

Stoll, David. 1991. *Is Latin America Turning Protestant? The Politics of Evangelical Growth*. Berkeley: University of California.

Taussig, Michael. 1980. *The Devil and Commodity Fetishism in South America*. Chapel Hill: University of North Carolina Press.

Thoby-Marcelin, Philippe, and Pierre Marcelin. 1970. *All Men Are Mad*. Translated by Eva Thoby-Marcelin. New York: Farrar, Straus and Giroux.

Thompson, E. P. 1967. "Time, Work-Discipline, and Industrial Capitalism." *Past and Present* 38 (December): 56–97.

Wilken, Lois. 1992. "Staging Folklore in Haiti: Historical Perspectives." Paper presented at the 4th annual meeting of the Haitian Studies Association, Medford, Massachusetts, October 17.

Sovereignty and Soil

Collective and Wage Labor in Rural Haiti

Scott Freeman

Haiti's contemporary relationship to international development is tenuous at best. Between critiques of NGO-based aid (Schuller 2012) and pointed criticisms of the response to the earthquake (Katz 2013; Elliott et al. 2015), the aid industry has received a considerable thrashing from both scholars and journalists. Based largely on examinations of aid as they are implemented in and around Port-au-Prince, critiques have focused not only on where the money went but also on how urban Haiti has changed as a result. But the origins of development in Haiti lie in the countryside; hillsides and rural farmers have been the targets of aid programs since the middle of the twentieth century. Aid experts believed that the countryside was not only poor but also in some way lost in the past.

International aid experts came to save Haiti by saving its soil. Beginning with anthropologist Alfred Métraux in 1946, soil erosion in Haiti was etched into the country's profile as another area to be developed. Until that time, imagining Haiti as undeveloped was relatively unheard of. The black republic had long been portrayed as backward, its residents the "poor black cousins" of world powers such as the United States (Renda 2001). Yet seeing Haitians as undeveloped was something new, a product of post–World War II thinking that discursively divided the globe into developed and undeveloped regions (Escobar 1995). Haiti, like many other countries across the world, was described as stranded in time. According to development planners, technical expertise and education would bring an undeveloped Haiti up to the current practices of industrialized countries.

From the first aid intervention in Haiti in 1949, a significant part of that education and technical expertise was directed at Haiti's soils. As in aid interventions elsewhere across the globe, poverty was "ecologized"; that is, it was visible not only in the material conditions of the people but also in the environment of a targeted area (Mosse 2005). Haiti was seen as both economically and environmentally poor, afflicted by impoverished soils, demographic pressure, and deficient farming practices. In part, this perspective lent itself to understanding Haiti's environmental issues as self-produced. Growing populations and poor farming practices were seen as the issues to control in order to protect the hillsides. Because of the strong assumed link between farming practices and environmental degradation, the control and development of Haiti's soil was simultaneously an effort to control and develop Haitian farmers.

As foreign soil experts and their environmental conservation programs descended on the country, they soon saw the possibility of using Haitian labor groups as a ready-made form of community participation. Seeking local adoption of the imported methods of soil conservation, experts looked for a way to tie economic incentives to the imported practices. In this case, the strategy was digging canals along the contours of hillsides. The hope was that by using wage labor to implement this strategy, farmers would be incentivized to quickly spread the technique to their individual plots. Yet for over sixty years, farmers have largely refused to adopt this practice in the absence of aid-based wage labor. Rotating agricultural groups in the Damòn valley of Haiti see their group-based work as fundamentally separate from such NGO-funded activities.[1] Aid organization documents have depicted these views as the expression of an intensely self-interested rural populace. But farmers' groups should be understood as engaging in and preserving a set of traditions that are deeply rooted in a vision of the collective.

This chapter advances the discussion of sovereignty by analyzing the ways collective agricultural labor practices are part of post-independence practices of unity and are expressions of collectivism in the face of the individualized wage labor that foreign capital and aid institutions impose. First, I detail how environmental aid projects have attempted to use Haiti's collective labor groups as a site for incentivizing individualized wage labor. I then discuss how Haitian collective work groups operate in a very different way, by continuing to work for group rather than individual benefits. Finally, I demonstrate that such groups see aid-based wage labor as fundamentally opposed to Haitian rotating labor arrangements. I argue that we should understand Haiti's group labor and non-adoption of soil conservation as part of ongoing practices of labor solidarity.

Environmental Degradation and Land Use Practices

Environmental degradation in Haiti occurs as a by-product of economic exploitation of natural resources. This process began early in the colonial period, when French plantation owners cleared forests to establish and subsequently fuel sugarcane plantations. In 1690, there were no sugar plantations in Saint-Domingue. By 1705, there were 120, and by 1789 (the eve of the Haitian revolution), there were well over 1,000 sugarcane plantations in the colony (Fick 2000). Blatant extraction of forest resources by foreign owners appeared again in the twentieth century, exacerbated by the U.S. occupation of 1915–1934. The occupying Americans cleared forests to build an extensive network of roads that facilitated access to more remote areas of the countryside, which were then also cleared (Mouhot 2013). Added to this flagrant resource extraction is the fact that the majority of the contemporary Haitian populace depends on biomass (both wood and charcoal) for cooking. While the impact of charcoal production is often highlighted as a main cause of deforestation, the impact of this industry on forest cover is still debated (Shannon et al. 2003).[2]

The intensive pressure farming puts on hillside plots also significantly increases the rate of soil erosion. As hillsides are intensely cultivated, exposed, and tilled, soil becomes vulnerable to degradation during heavy rains. It would be a mistake to simply blame farmers for such practices. The broader context of economic accumulation and extraction should be taken into account in any understanding of the processes that propel soil degradation. Farmers in Haiti are not subsistence farmers. In order to pay for necessary commodities, they sell much of their agricultural production. The movement of goods from the countryside to urban centers in inequitable trade relationships continually extracts resources from the countryside. The systematic marginalization of the rural poor in Haiti (Trouillot 1990) has meant that farmers turn to their small hillside plots as their primary source of capital and accordingly demand much of the land. As economic necessity dominates the agriculturalists, farmers are obliged to make decisions based on how they cope with stressors (Blaikie and Brookfield 1987). Overworked hillside plots result in degraded soil that is increasingly vulnerable to erosion.

The role of farmers as land managers is a small part of the larger issue. Larger political and economic processes play an important role in stressing hillside plots and contributing to anthropogenic soil erosion (Blaikie and Brookfield 1987). As a result of these processes, soil, arguably the most valuable natural resource of the Haitian countryside, descends downhill and escapes into the Caribbean.

Contour Canals

The UNESCO development mission of 1946 was the first to declare Haiti's soil degradation a crisis. That mission and many that followed did not address the broader relations between farmers and the economic system in which they operate. Rather, environmental aid interventions have focused far more myopically on the relationship between farmers and the land. This perspective has led to the promotion of short-term and often ineffective soil conservation measures.

Around the globe, soil conservation interventions of the twentieth century were defined in terms of the technical knowledge of state- and agency-led interventions (White and Jickling 1995). The 1930s dustbowl crisis in the United States raised fears about the potential dangers of unfettered soil degradation around the world (Pretty and Shah 1997). In response, colonial governments in Africa and South Asia looked to soil conservation strategies that developed in the post-dustbowl United States. But rather than thinking systematically about the larger economic policies and practices that were the underlying cause of the environmental disaster in the United States, those who promoted these interventions often misdiagnosed the problem and focused on farmers. In another example, white settlers in Kenya blamed indigenous Africans for the erosion of soil despite evidence that externally introduced cereal monoculture was the reason for soil exhaustion and declines in soil fertility (Anderson 1984). Such ideas spread quickly, and farmers were often forced to adopt soil conservation measures that ignored the root causes of degradation. In response, farmers often only partially implement the coercively imposed strategies. The result has been ineffective projects and inattention to the causes of soil erosion. The history of soil conservation is all too often a history of skeptical smallholding farmers being advised, paid, and forced to adopt new soil conservation measures (Pretty and Shah 1997).

Contour canals have been a key component of soil conservation interventions since the mid-twentieth century. These consist of series of ditches lined with trees that are dug along the contours of a hillside. Widely used internationally, the canals are accompanied by a mound (or *bund*) on their downhill wall. Trees planted in that *bund* are designed to reinforce the canal as it catches and slows descending rain and water. Such canals have been praised internationally and have been implemented as part of broader conservation interventions (Tiffen, Mortimore, and Gichuki 1994). Contour canals were constructed in Haiti as part of foreign agricultural or environmental aid initiatives. They have

Figure 8.1. Contour canals dug on a hillside in southwest Haiti. Photo by Scott Freeman, 2012.

been implemented over the past sixty years as a quick and easy fix to the long-term and complex problem of sliding soils. The intervention requires little planning and can be implemented within a short time, provided the workers to do the heavy labor of digging are available.

Contour canals were introduced in Haiti through development interventions in the early 1950s. But even at that early point of implementation, they received negative reviews. As early as 1952, anthropologists and social scientists assessing the efficacy of contour canals recognized that farmers were not adopting them on their own. Farmers dug the canals when they were paid by a development agency, but when the project ended they would stop doing the maintenance the large hillside ditches require. Thus, the canals provided little benefit. Explanations for non-adoption of these strategies were largely economic: There wasn't an immediate payoff from the canals (Erasmus 1952; White and Jickling 1995). Theories about the benefits of soil conservation and the potential for higher crop yields did not appear until years later. Critics of the existing policies argued that if individual farmers were to construct these canals, they would need immediate economic incentives (Murray 1979). This would supposedly buy time for farmers to see the long-term benefits of such practices and adopt them as their own, independent of external funding. But time and again, even when farmers have received wages as incentives, they have not adopted canals in their own farming practices (White and Jickling 1995). After more than sixty years of contour canal projects, farmers and their labor groups still do not replicate contour canals of their own accord. Though various types of aid continue to support the construction of canals, they are built only when farmers and laborers are paid to do so by project funding.[3]

By the late 1970s, aid organizations that initiated the construction of contour canals began using Haitian group labor in the countryside in an effort to implement more participatory aid interventions. USAID projects up to that point had been critiqued as top-down schemes devised by technical planners who were often divorced from realities on the ground. By the 1970s, USAID in Haiti was widely criticized for propagating politically motivated "top-down development" because the institution's large programs had often benefited politically connected and well-off urban residents rather than small rural farmers (Girault 1978). As part of its response to this criticism, USAID researchers identified Haiti's collective labor groups as a way to harness "participative" group labor to the goals of development aid (Murray 1979). Aid planners revered Haiti's existing cooperative labor groups as ideal models for community participation in project-based development. Haiti was not the only place where such strategies were implemented in international aid projects; project managers in other parts of the world also looked toward participatory development models as a solution to the problem of unsuccessful projects (Cooke and Kothari 2001). By the 1980s, group labor in the countryside was both an instrument of and a target of the agro-environmental strategy in Haiti.

As aid institutions proposed group-based wage labor as the most feasible incentive for building soil conservation structures, debates raged about whether it was ethical to introduce wage labor practices to residents of Haiti's hillsides. On one side of the argument, some scholars and aid practitioners voiced fears that the practice would contaminate local types of labor exchange and reciprocation. They argued that the existing cooperative labor systems worked in fundamentally different ways than wage labor and that cooperative forms of labor would be co-opted by a type of poorly conceived development planning (Smith 2001). Other scholars and aid planners saw this argument as spurious, arguing that these groups were already practicing wage labor by renting themselves out to other landowners (Murray 1978). And indeed they did (and continue to do so). During my field work in 2012, I observed that Haitian cooperative labor groups regularly rented themselves out to other farmers, particularly at harvest time or when weeding was necessary. To understand these practices as simply wage labor, however, is problematic. In practice, labor in the countryside is not reducible to a simple exchange of wages. Such analyses impose a vision of western capitalism and individualism on practices that have an entirely different set of values.

Histories of Collective Labor

Group labor is well recognized in the anthropological literature as a ubiquitous aspect of rural Haitian agriculture (Smith 2001; Trouillot 1990; Métraux 1951; Herskovits 1952). Rotational labor groups practice cooperative labor, drawing on forms of labor organization from West and Central Africa. In Haiti, these groups are called (most famously) the *konbit* or *eskwad* or *ekip*. While the names may differ by region, the nature of their activities is fundamentally the same. For each day of work, which may include weeding, harvesting, or planting, the group works a different member's land. The group may work together once or twice a week, rotating to a different member's plot for each day of work. This rotating labor is referred to broadly as *youn ede lòt* (one helps another). No payment is exchanged; the rotation of the labor group ensures that all benefit equally. In the absence of tractors and other farming machinery, help from groups is an essential component of Haitian agriculture. Throughout Haiti, plots of land are rarely worked by solitary individuals (Murray 1978). The spirit of such collective labor is embodied in Haitian proverbs such as *Men anpil, chay pa lou* (With many hands, the burden is not heavy) and *Yon sèl dwèt pa manje kalalou* (One finger alone cannot eat stewed okra) (Smith 2001).

While cooperative labor is fundamentally based on shared and rotational work, cash is exchanged when groups are hired by nonmember landowners who need large groups for planting, harvesting, or weeding.[4] Because the small labor groups of *ekip* and *eskwad* are more likely to rent labor to those outside the group, anthropological research that informed the design of aid projects in the 1980s pointed to this as evidence that wage labor was already part of village life. Thus, using wage labor in aid projects, it was argued, would not upset existing rural labor practices. One anthropologist estimated that an *ekip* or *eskwad* "may spend about half its time working for wages" (Murray 1978, 6, emphasis in original). This report cautioned development planners not to look for "romantic ideals" of countryside labor untainted by cash exchanges. Though Murray cautioned that remuneration through hourly wages were rarely successful components of aid projects, he (1979) advocated the use of some type of monetized incentive to introduce farmers to new practices.

Today, group agricultural labor is often exchanged for predetermined amounts of cash. Those amounts are often based on the number of individuals that compose the group, though occasionally the price is calculated by quantity of land to be worked. As money changes hands, the labor potential of the group is sold for the going rate in the countryside.[5] But as I learned from farmers, any analytical construct that reduces these rates to purely individual wages misreads the practice of group labor.

One farmer explained to me precisely how this works on an early summer morning in the lower Damòn valley in the south of Haiti in 2012. That morning, I accompanied a landowner named Bekèl as he supervised an *eskwad* that was harvesting peanuts on his land. We took a donkey and two sheep to pasture on our way to meet the *eskwad*. Damòn is a very hilly region, so we followed the streams of the valley instead of scaling the large hills. When we arrived at the base of the hillside where Bekèl had planted peanuts, the *eskwad* was already there. The group was composed of two men, three women, and a female cook. Bekèl explained that the money he would pay the group does not go to each individual but would be held in common as a collective payment that would be conserved until December: "The *eskwad* joins their money together and in December buys an animal to kill." That animal is butchered and the meat is divided for the celebration of Haitian Independence Day (January 1), a day highlighted by a symbolically significant meal of pumpkin soup and meat. Following the purchase of the animal, any remaining funds left over are divided among the group members. Again and again, *ekip* and *eskwad* members in the Damòn region told me that the money they receive is not used until December. Hence, payments by landowners such as Bekèl yielded no immediate economic returns. The payout for such work might be months away.

Bekèl stated quite clearly that members of an *eskwad* are present "not because you are hungry . . . but rather because you want to buy an animal to have a part of the meat in December." This underscores the fact that hillside labor is often not wage based but instead is part of a work tradition based on a collective celebration. As one farmer put it, he and his fellow group members work in this way not for immediate remuneration but for "a goodwill that will help you in the future" (*bon volontè kap ede w devan*). This tradition, I was told, was upheld because those enslaved in colonial Saint-Domingue were not permitted to eat pumpkin soup. Jennie Smith (2001) has documented that meat was also denied to those who were enslaved and was reserved for slave owners on that day. Thus, the soup and the meat are symbolic of the privileges of freedom denied under slavery.

The determination of Haitian collective work groups to overlook immediate needs in order to meet a future collective goal is remarkable considering the pressures of costly school fees, the high cost of food and other household necessities, and unpredictable events such as crop loss due to draughts and hurricanes. By undertaking ongoing group work, collective labor groups ensure that meat, a precious and symbolically important commodity, is added to soup for each member on the anniversary of independence. These ongoing practices are powerful assertions of the unity, freedom, and humanity of contemporary rural Haitians.

"We do not do that type of work"

The structure and practices of Haiti's rural groups play an essential role in determining what type of labor they take on. Despite the continual enticements of wage labor, farmers do not construct contour canals as part of their cooperative work group efforts. They repeatedly told me that contour canals were a good thing and that they could in fact help address soil degradation.[6] But despite that, no farmer would pay another farmer for such work. As one male farmer told me, it was simply "not like that" (*se pa sa*). I was often told that "we do not do that type of work."

Through extensive interviews in Damòn about soil conservation and labor, it became apparent that Haitian farmers saw a qualitative difference between the work of project-based labor and group work done in the fields. The rate aid agencies paid for digging canals was far greater than any price an individual in the countryside could find for individual or task labor. In 2012, while development project-based labor paid a standard 200 goud per day,[7] the going local rate for an individual who hired him or herself out to a fellow farmer was about 100 goud per day, according to Lebèl, the president of a farmers' association in Damòn. For peanut harvesting, the price was far less, 25 or 50 goud, as Bekèl, Lebèl, and others I interviewed confirmed. In comparison to local rates, the 200 goud paid for digging contour canals is a sizable amount of money. Such large monetary differences contribute to the understanding in the countryside that project-based labor is conceptually distinct from agricultural labor in the countryside.

My interviews with rural Haitians about soil conservation and labor revealed that the quantitative difference in compensation contributes to a conception that there is a qualitative difference between NGO labor and rotational labor. One day I asked Nelson and his father, both members of a farmers' association, to help me understand why individuals refused to adopt the practice of constructing contour canals. Both said that they had seen many soil conservation projects come and go. Nelson's father spoke about how even though people understood soil conservation to be important, they still wanted something that would benefit them: "When soil conservation is mentioned, people know that [external] money is coming." He added that "people won't form groups to do this work." I asked Franswa's daughter, another rural farmer, if it would be possible for a landowner to pay for soil conservation. She responded: "*Se pa yon met pou peye. Se pa sa*" (It is not for a landowner to pay. It is not like that).

Whereas group labor is most often structured around collective participation and delayed benefit, project labor is structured around individualism and immediacy. While project-based labor groups appear to work as a collective "team," they receive only individual benefits immediately following their work. While it is true that much project-based labor is done by locally based organizations such as community or neighborhood associations, women's groups, and the like, these groups are not compensated as a group, as is typical in the most common labor arrangements in Haiti.

Implicit in project labor is the assumption that the unit of labor is the individual. This assumption is based on the ideas of industrialized labor and the insertion of foreign capital. With foreign capital comes the idea of an industrialized workday that regulates both time and space. While there have been various fluctuations in and contestations of the minimum wage in Haiti (Schuller 2008), in 2012, aid agencies seemed to rely on the national minimum wage rate of 200 goud per day as they calculated a project wage. Formal labor arrangements in Haiti, especially those based on trade agreements, have long taken advantage of an impoverished Haiti to pay low wages in the assembly and textile sectors (Farmer 2004). The type of funding that comes into the countryside with aid projects is thus organized into daily "wages" that are regularized by international labor accords. Such agreements, however, do not recognize the organization and practices of the countryside, practices that may not always be simply divisible into individuals and hours.

While monetized compensation for labor does exist in the countryside, it is done primarily through the work of individuals, not groups. But even for an individual, it would be a distortion to understand rural labor exchanges simply as wage labor: "Agrarian wage labor should be studied as one transaction within a system of agrarian labor transactions, and not simply as an exchange of labor for cash" (Pierre 2009, 151). Work performed by individuals for a specific task might also be exchanged for other types of labor, and sellers of labor might also be buyers of labor, challenging the dyadic patron-client model of rural work (Pierre 2009).

In rural Haiti, the often urgent need for cash is such that an offer of simple wage labor by project funding is nearly a coercive incentive to implement contour canals. In the receipt of wages, farmers, a knowledgeable and valuable part of agricultural production, are reduced to simple workers devoid of adequate technical knowledge and experience. They become merely "beneficiaries," or recipients of aid. Development-funded group labor appears to conform to the norms of the countryside but in fact fails to understand far more complex relationships.

Conclusion

An anthropologist who contracts with USAID and the World Bank described the countryside by stating that farmers are intensely self-interested and that their self-interest is tempered only by special ties and obligations. He argued that there is little evidence of any community solidarity in Haiti (Smucker 1983). Another social analysis done by USAID regarding its agroforestry intervention claims that "for good historical reasons, Haitian rural society has always been highly individualized" (Lowenthal 1990, 11). However, Jennie Smith (2001) argues that the work of the *eskwad* and *ekip* are not only acts of teamwork in the field, they are a profound assertion of dignity, independence, and interdependence in the face of constant struggle. My research carried out in Damòn demonstrates that group labor in the fields of Haiti is not simply a means to an individual end but is an ongoing practice of collectivism built on core values of independence and freedom.[8]

As aid projects contemplate the Haitian countryside, the desire to propagate short-sighted interventions and maintain a perspective of Western capitalism eclipses the powerful modes of solidarity practiced in the countryside. Ethnographic research on aid and the Haitian countryside can help present practices in appropriate historical and cultural context. Historians Laurent Dubois (this volume and Dubois 2012) and Jean Casimir (2001) trace labor and land practices in post-revolution Haiti, shedding light on how specific rural practices and systems have survived since independence. After the revolution, Haiti's rural populace vehemently opposed structures that echoed the restoration or continuation of the exploitative model of the plantation. Since then, attempts by both the Haitian government and the United States to reestablish plantations have largely failed. This post-revolution arrangement of land and labor, the counter-plantation system, was an explicit rejection of the ways plantations worked and drew on forms of African agricultural organization and spirituality and on examples learned from maroon communities of runaway slaves (Dubois 2012). Such institutions embraced collective labor arrangements that are still practiced in the countryside.

Despite concerns that development work would contaminate the cooperative work groups of Haiti, the *ekip* and *eskwad* remain connected to collective ideals and their practices and work arrangements go far beyond a simple monetary reward. Outsiders seeking to "modernize" the Haitian countryside are often frustrated by what they see as cultural or administrative impediments to progress. But these frustrations often arise from misunderstanding. The work of *konbit*, *eskwad*, and *ekip* are not only acts of teamwork, they are also part of a value set that differs significantly from those that inform individualized wage labor.

Since the dawn of the development encounter in Haiti, soils have been among the most visible and contentious targets of aid funding. By looking at the history of soil conservation interventions, we can better understand not only the state of contemporary environmental development but also the broader issues of aid in Haiti. As international experts intervene to rearrange the practices of farmers, counter-plantation institutions are strong examples of ways that practices in the Haitian countryside remain Haitian. In considering who owns soils and labor practices in Haiti, we must reconsider the intimate relationship between rotational labor and independence.

Notes

1. All names of individuals and places have been changed.

2. In fact, the degree of deforestation in Haiti is a highly contested issue. Recent studies (Churches et al. 2014) have argued that Haiti has a tree cover of approximately 32 percent. This contrasts distinctly with the often cited statistics of 2–4 percent forest cover (Bannister and Nair 2003; Dolisca et al. 2007).

3. In Freeman (2014), I examine how financialized measurement systems and a deep need for project success are key aspects of the repeated construction of contour canals.

4. Not all collective work groups sell their labor. *Konbit* I observed in 2012 did not rent labor to nonmembers.

5. In Damòn in 2012, the rate paid per person for peanut harvests was between 25 and 50 goud per day of work, approximately US$.58 to $1.15 at the time.

6. Despite the marginal benefits of contour canals, rural residents often verbally expressed initial approval or interest in the canals as an intervention.

7. Approximately US$4.67 in 2012.

8. As Smith (2001) has pointed out, it is important not to overstate collective labor arrangements as either the romanticized communalism of the "noble savage" or the trope of the economically rational actor because both of these interpretations oversimplify these complex relationships. Discussions of such actions must be based on historically and ethnographically particular research.

References

Anderson, David. 1984. "Depression, Dust Bowl, Demography, and Drought: The Colonial State and Soil Conservation in East Africa during the 1930s." *African Affairs* 83 (332): 321–343.

Bannister, M. E., and P. K. R. Nair. 2003. "Agroforestry Adoption in Haiti: The Importance of Household and Farm Characteristics." *Agroforestry Systems* 57 (2): 149–157.

Blaikie, Piers, and Harold Brookfield. 1987. *Land Degradation and Society.* London: Methuen.

Casimir, Jean. 2001. *La Culture Opprimée.* Port-au-Prince: Imprimerie Lakay.

Churches, Christopher E., Peter J. Wampler, Wanxiao Sun, and Andrew J. Smith. 2014. "Evaluation of Forest Cover Estimates for Haiti Using Supervised Classification of Landsat Data." *International Journal of Applied Earth Observation and Geoinformation* 30 (August): 203–216.

Cooke, Bill, and Uma Kothari. 2001. *Participation: The New Tyranny?* London: Zed Books.

Dolisca, Frito, Joshua M. McDaniel, Lawrence D. Teeter, and Curtis M. Jolly. 2007. "Land Tenure, Population Pressure, and Deforestation in Haiti: The Case of Forêt Des Pins Reserve." *Journal of Forest Economics* 13 (4): 277–289.

Dubois, Laurent. 2012. *Haiti: The Aftershocks of History.* New York: Metropolitan Books.

Elliott, Justin, and Laura Sullivan. 2015. "How the Red Cross Raised Half a Billion Dollars for Haiti—and Built Six Homes." ProPublica, June 3. Accessed June 4, 2015. http://www.propublica.org/article/how-the-red-cross-raised-half-a-billion-dollars-for-haiti-and-built-6-homes.

Erasmus, Charles John. 1952. "Agricultural Changes in Haiti: Patterns of Resistance and Acceptance." *Human Organization* 11 (4): 20–26.

Escobar, Arturo. 1995. *Encountering Development: The Making and Unmaking of the Third World.* Princeton NJ: Princeton University Press.

Farmer, Paul. 2004. "An Anthropology of Structural Violence." *Current Anthropology* 45 (3): 305–25.

Fick, Carolyn. 2000. "Emancipation in Haiti: From Plantation Labour to Peasant Proprietorship." *Slavery and Abolition: A Journal of Slave and Post-Slave Studies* 21 (2): 11–40.

Freeman, Scott. 2014. "'Cutting Earth': Haiti, Soil Conservation, and the Tyranny of Projects." PhD diss., Columbia University.

Girault, C. 1978. "Tourism and Dependency in Haiti." *Cahiers Des Ameriques Latines, Serie Science de l'Homme* 17: 23–56.

Herskovits, Melville J. 1952. *Economic Anthropology*. New York: Knopf.

Katz, Jonathan M. 2013. *The Big Truck That Went By: How the World Came to Save Haiti and Left behind a Disaster*. New York: Palgrave Macmillan.

Lowenthal, Ira. 1990. *National Program for Agroforestry in Haiti*. Vol. 2, *Social Soundness Analysis, Agroforestry Component, Environmental Assessment, Economic and Financial Analysis*." Bethesda, MD: DESFIL. Accessed April 21, 2016. http://pdf.usaid.gov/pdf_docs/PNABI139.pdf.

Métraux, Alfred. 1951. *Making a Living in the Marbial Valley, Haïti: Report*. Paris: UNESCO.

Mosse, David. 2005. *Cultivating Development: An Ethnography of Aid Policy and Practice*. Ann Arbor: Pluto Press.

Mouhot, Jean-Francois. 2013. "Haiti's Long History of Deforestation." Presentation at the Library of Congress, Washington, DC, June 18.

Murray, Gerald. 1978. "A Proposal for the Organization of Erosion Control Projects." United States Agency for International Development.

———. 1979. *Terraces, Trees, and the Haitian Peasant: An Assessment of Twenty-Five Years of Erosion Control in Rural Haiti*. Report submitted to USAID, Port-au-Prince.

Pierre, Yves. 2009. "Wage Labour in an Agrarian Economy: The Case of the Central Plateau of Haiti." *Social and Economic Studies* 58 (3–4): 149–174.

Pretty, Jules N., and Parmesh Shah. 1997. "Making Soil and Water Conservation Sustainable: From Coercion and Control to Partnerships and Participation." *Land Degradation & Development* 8 (1): 39–58.

Renda, Mary A. 2001. *Taking Haiti: Military Occupation and the Culture of US Imperialism, 1915–1940*. Chapel Hill: University of North Carolina Press.

Schuller, Mark. 2008. "'Haiti Is Finished!': Haiti's End of History Meets the Ends of Capitalism." In *Capitalizing on Catastrophe: Neoliberal Strategies in Disaster Reconstruction*, edited by Nandini Gunewardena and Mark Schuller, 191–214. Lanham, MD: Altamira Press.

———. 2012. *Killing with Kindness: Haiti, International Aid, and NGOs*. New Brunswick, NJ: Rutgers University Press.

Shannon, Dennis, Lionel Isaac, Carine Bernard, and C. Wesley Wood. 2003. "Long Term Effects of Soil Conservation Barriers on Crop Yield on a Tropical Steepland in Haiti." USAID and Soil Management Research Team, Auburn University.

Smith, Jennie Marcelle. 2001. *When the Hands Are Many: Community Organization and Social Change in Rural Haiti*. Ithaca, NY: Cornell University Press.

Smucker, Glenn Richard. 1983. "Peasants and Development Politics: A Study in Haitian Class and Culture." PhD diss., New School for Social Research.

Tiffen, Mary, Michael Mortimore, and Francis Gichuki. 1994. *More People, Less Erosion: Environmental Recovery in Kenya.* New York: J. Wiley.

Trouillot, Michel-Rolph. 1990. *Haiti, State against Nation: The Origins and Legacy of Duvalierism.* New York: Monthly Review Press.

White, T. Anderson, and Jon L. Jickling. 1995. "Peasants, Experts, and Land Use in Haiti: Lessons from Indigenous and Project Technology." *Journal of Soil and Water Conservation* 50 (1): 7–14.

9

Street Sovereignty

Power, Violence, and Respect among Haitian *Baz*

Chelsey Kivland

People in Haiti tend to think about sovereignty differently than people in the United States. Americans generally envision sovereignty as the freedom to act uninhibitedly or the right to do what they want with what is theirs. *Don't tread on me! This is a free country! Not in my backyard!* Such claims center on the principle of liberty. At its core, liberty concerns the freedom of an individual, the right to not be governed or the right to be a power unto oneself.[1]

The notion of liberty is also significant in Haiti. But when Haitians conceptualize sovereignty, another principle takes center stage: respect (*respè*). Unlike liberty, respect is fundamentally social. It cannot even be imagined at the level of the individual. Respect involves at least two individuals, for one does not *have* respect, one gives or receives it. Customarily, Haitians envision respect as the social value shared between guests and hosts, gods and servitors, and (just) leaders and followers.[2] In her conversations with grassroots organizers in rural Haiti during the 1990s democratic movement, anthropologist Jennie Smith (2001) noticed that her interlocutors often mobilized *respè* to define a proper democracy. This, she argued, was because respect as a social value reconciled authority and community, hierarchy and equality, and thus symbolized popular sovereignty. For her interlocutors, a democratic polity was one that had a solid leader whom followers respected as the ultimate authority but who, in turn, respected their common humanity, worth, and opinions. Further, a democracy was a society in which people not only had the right to speak and be heard but also the right to water, housing, nutrition, health care, education, security, and—daring to dream—economic and political parity with their neighbors. Judged by this standard, they did not see American liberalism to be a particularly good model of democracy. In fact, they deemed it *demo-krache*, a derisive term that played on the Haitian Creole word for spit (*krache*) (Smith 2001, 5).

The significance of respect within Haitian political life cannot be underestimated. When Haitian leaders protest their relatively minor role on the post-earthquake Interim Haiti Recovery Commission,[3] when the Haitian government is forced to accept neoliberal policies favored abroad but unpopular at home,[4] when the Haitian president makes diplomatic deals with foreign contractors that circumvent the Haitian Parliament,[5] when local organizations are passed over in favor of foreign NGOs for development projects,[6] and when a poor citizen is belittled as he or she attempts to claim a service from a state office,[7] the issue is respect—or rather, its absence. The crux of the issue is not a demand to do what one wants unfettered from consideration of others but rather a desire to be recognized by others as a consequential participant in the dialogue over what should be done. As such, it is also a demand to possess the social status and political clout to be treated with dignity. As the Martinican philosopher Frantz Fanon wrote, "Dignity and sovereignty [are] the exact equivalents, and in fact, a free people living in dignity is a sovereign people" (Fanon [1965] 2004, 139).

My experience has echoed that of Smith's, although I conduct research not in the countryside but in the poor, dense, and volatile district of Bel Air in central Port-au-Prince. Here, the value of respect also permeates discussions of power and authority. This often, as Smith suggests, reconciles an authoritarian ethos with public stewardship. But I also see here that respect aligns with a militant ideology that draws upon the figure of the revolutionary soldier who triumphed over the French colonists to end slavery and establish independent Haiti in 1804.[8] Viewing the revolutionary solider as an icon of respect unveils how violence and welfare, the power to take and give life, intertwine in grounding sovereign authority and how respect, for all its advantages, necessitates a particularly militant identity. In fact, when Fanon wrote about sovereignty and dignity as equivalents he was referring to the power and status the colonized earned when they took up arms against colonial powers. Contemporary discourses of respect in urban Haiti also reflect recent efforts to fashion an oppositional masculinity in the context of transnational black politics and street culture (Kivland 2014). Young men in Bel Air greet each other by saying "respect" as they bump fists, an affirmation of a shared and equal manhood widely observed among urban black communities worldwide. Such exchanges certainly resonate with anticolonial struggles, but they are also tied to more local spheres of competition, where young men compete for the power to act as street leaders. Competition for street leadership often involves manifestations of violence, whether material, symbolic, or spiritual. However, earning respect as a local leader is not reducible to promulgating fear. The trick is to balance a reputation for violence with the provision of protection for oneself and one's community. In other words, respect invokes an ideology of defense in which force and dignity are intertwined.

In this chapter, I draw on my ethnography of the Bel Air neighborhood to address the political significance of young men's quests to earn respect and defend their zones. I focus on the informal street organizations that emerged from the local defense groups that militantly resisted political opponents in the early 1990s. These groups are known locally as *baz* (base), a moniker that invokes both their defensive orientation (military base) and their place at the center of a multiscale project of governance (political base). Today, these groups are still engaged in an effort to defend their zones (also called *baz*), but this effort now suggests not only defense against outside threats but also defense of the zone's interests by brokering state or NGO jobs, services, and projects. *Baz* play a major role in Haitian sovereignty because they act as brokers of governance and as agents of governance in their own right.

In asserting that *baz* exercise sovereignty, I extend recent anthropological efforts to reframe sovereignty from its customary definition as a juridical property of states to a definition that includes an aspirational claim to power and respect exercised by any agent, state or *baz* leader. Several scholars have recently argued that the traditional Westphalia model of state sovereignty is unable to accommodate the new forms of power exercised by nonstate actors, such as NGOs, transnational corporations, and humanitarian organizations (e.g., Comaroff and Comaroff 2006; Das and Poole 2004; Hansen and Stepputat 2005). My definition also removes sovereignty from the domain of the state, but I specifically want to draw attention to how the collapse of traditional state authority has facilitated a localization of political power and forms of belonging. In particular, I argue that the reduction of the Haitian state coupled with development policies orchestrated by diverse governing agents, has created conditions in which the *baz* is able to perform economic and political control—or what I call *street sovereignty*—over an urban district. In what follows, I detail how young men have fashioned themselves as local political leaders, paying attention to an array of political modalities that includes armed actors, music groups, political associations, and development organizations. While I emphasize the local dimensions of *baz* sovereignty, I do not mean to suggest that *baz* formations are divorced from larger spheres of power. These micropolities represent the kind of relative autonomy that is crystallized in the social bond of respect. Because *baz* are recognized as local authorities by residents and other *baz*, national and international actors must also accord them a degree of respect.

I begin my discussion by introducing the most prominent *baz* in Bel Air. I then trace this *baz's* history in the context of the contemporary political configuration of democratic politics and international development policy. Next, I illustrate how *baz* have creatively and effectively responded to this political configuration to claim new sources of power and resources. However, in the final analysis, I show how their exercise of local sovereignty reinforces neighborhood conflicts and insecurity, ultimately giving rise to desires for state sovereignty and a robust public sector.

Defending the Block

From the first time I entered Bel Air, I was told that I should meet with a man named Ti Snap and let him know what I was doing in the neighborhood. Ti Snap was the leader of Baz Grand Black, the *baz* that has managed all political affairs in the area since 2005.[9] He was variously described as chief (*chèf*), community leader (*lidè kominotè*), or street director (*dirijan lari*), but whatever the term, the message was that all neighborhood matters went through Ti Snap. Over and over again, people told me that as a *blan* (white foreigner) interested in development, I had to meet with Ti Snap.[10] It was, people said, an important sign of respect, and if I disrespected Ti Snap, he could prove an obstacle to my work. My friend Marc, an employee at the Brazilian NGO Viva Rio, finally took me to meet Ti Snap. We met at the Popular Sector, the neighborhood's local political office, which Grand Black managed. When we arrived, Ti Snap's friend came to greet us and told us we would have to wait as their "development foundation" had to attend to some project business. I was led into a dark back room and the door was shut. In the corner of the room on a cinder block were two handguns, what I later learned were Beretta 92s, presumably kept there for safekeeping. Time passed—just, I should note, as it did when I scheduled meetings with NGO directors—and I became aware that Ti Snap was sending me multiple messages about his power and influence.

When he eventually invited me into the front room, Ti Snap asked why I was there. I told him that I wanted to do research on local politics and that I wanted to teach an English class. He said the class was a nice idea and then asked if there was any money involved. "Who is sponsoring that? What organization is sponsoring this? What NGO do you have? Who is giving the money?

Is this with MINUSTAH, the peacekeepers?" I told him it was just something I wanted to do, that there was no sponsor. He let out a big laugh and called to his friend: "The *blan* comes to talk to me, and she has no money!" He turned to me and said, "Look, we do development, we fight to defend the interests of Bel Air in the area of development, so the zone can find projects and programs. If you don't do development, what can I do?" Ti Snap then told me that we would talk later because he had a meeting with the national commission for disarmament. He got into a red Isuzu Tracker and was off. After that I spent some time talking with his friend who had greeted me. His name was Manno, and he was the mayor's popular delegate (*delege popilè*), an informal post he had been given because, as he put it, "I can manage the *baz* in the ghettos." He told me that the meeting had gone well—just that if anyone took an interest in my project (by which he meant gave money) that I should come back and see Ti Snap. In what I would learn was a common sentiment, Manno told me, "Here, everything is organizations and projects. It's them who control everything. Look, we have so many organizations, you can't even count them all. You have to defend your rights. . . . Everyone has rights. That's democracy. But you can't wait for someone to give them to you. You must organize to get respect. So everyone makes an organization. Now you have a problem. You've got to fight organizations with organizations. That can create disorder if you don't have the force to keep a hard line." The term "hard line" was a direct reference to the name of another *baz* called Ling Di (Hard Line) that acted as the armed branch of Grand Black.

This interaction illustrates how *baz* leaders' visions of community leadership tied a localized brand of militant politics to the broader political goals of democracy and development. Far from seeing violent force as being in opposition to community organizing, the leaders located it at its center. In other words, for them, becoming a community leader entailed pairing a grassroots development organization with the force of a gang, or making a "grassroots gang." Why was this the case? The answer lies with the geography of an urban polity attuned to contemporary democratic politics and development policy. In this regard, three trends are noteworthy: government retrenchment, the growth of a male underclass, and the rise of community-based development.

After the end of the Duvalier dictatorship in 1986, the United States and its allies instituted a host of neoliberal market and government reforms that included a reduction in protective tariffs, privatization of public enterprises, and the streamlining of state offices.[11] These reforms yielded cuts in government jobs, services, and benefits, but they did not lead to the absence of governance. Instead, nonstate actors, such as NGOs and local organizations such as Grand

Black, have taken up the work of governance. The shift from state-based to community-based development policy has increased this trend. Over the past decades, donor governments have limited their bilateral support to the Haitian state for centralized development plans. Citing corruption, political instability, and weak public infrastructure, they have channeled the bulk of aid money— over 90 percent since 2010—to non-Haitian NGOs or private contractors.[12] At the same time that this aid flow has further weakened the state and accelerated government retrenchment, it has also supported international development plans that have favored small-scale projects in rural villages and urban ghettos.

Since the 1950s, major international development plans for Haiti have focused on shifting the economy away from domestic agricultural production and toward the revamping of an offshore garment industry.[13] This plan, which was renewed in 2009, has prompted vast rural-to-urban migration and the growth of slum areas (Manigat 1997).[14] In addition, the combination of the dismal performance of this industry and the fact that its work force is female dominated has yielded unemployment rates exceeding 80 percent among young men in slum areas. In these conditions, many men have entered the local political economy as a means of earning an income and as a source of power and respect. For example, Ti Snap established himself as chief of Bel Air after he lost his state office job and a prominent *baz* leader died. In a public spectacle, he shot and killed a former army soldier (and therefore a political enemy) and declared himself in charge of Grand Black. This leadership gave him control over the lucrative arenas of brokering politicians' access to the neighborhood; overseeing informal water, electricity, and sanitation markets; and engaging in informal policing. It also meant exercising a protection racket over any community-based aid or development projects, including that of the resident anthropologist. In order to lay claim to these resources, *baz* throughout urban Haiti have fashioned themselves as neighborhood development organizations that administer a multitude of projects for state and NGO actors, from food aid distributions and infrastructure projects to school scholarships and welfare handouts.

Baz's governing actions are often interpreted as evidence of Haiti's status as a "failed state," a state unable to properly democratize and meet the norms of governance. Such interpretations gain credibility when *baz* governance precipitates urban violence. However, rubrics of state success and failure are inadequate for explaining violence, since they do not account for how the violence is tied to contemporary forms of statehood.[15] The challenge, in other words, is to explain how processes of democratization, economic liberalization, and international development policy foster the conditions for urban insecurity and disorder. Looked at from this perspective, the governance functions *baz* perform illustrate how the state structure in Haiti has responded to neoliberal demands that government be retrenched. The Haitian state, in other words, has streamlined its budgets and activities by outsourcing the work of government to NGOs and local organizations, not unlike how the United States has increasingly consigned public services to religious charities, nonprofits, and other elements of the private sector. While these relationships are similar to clientelist models documented throughout Haitian history, they also signal something new. In an environment where state hegemony has collapsed and sovereign space hosts a hodgepodge of governing actors, *baz* leaders do more than merely grant access to resources; they also work with multiple state and nonstate actors to control and manage the most marginalized and unruly spaces of the polity. On the one hand, the restructuring of the state and development in Haiti has produced new opportunities for the urban poor to acquire wealth and political clout. But on the other hand, these new political opportunities are located outside the legal economy or formal state sector and have not provided stable, sufficient income, let alone security. Located in an informal political racket, these opportunities have involved using violence and other methods to exercise sovereign control over the block. In order to better understand *baz*'s relationship to democracy and development, it is useful to trace the particular yet exemplary trajectory of Baz Grand Black.

A Street History of *Baz*

It is tempting to understand *baz* formations as an expression of a timeless urban netherworld or even as the frontier politics of early nation building. But they actually are a crystallization of contemporary history. Their development reflects the politically fraught history of the post-1986 democratic transition and, in particular, two contradictory facets of democratization.

The term *baz* was first associated with the popular organizations that mobilized around the Catholic priest and liberation theologian Jean-Bertrand Aristide in the early 1990s. This grassroots movement arose among many diverse sectors of the population, but it was particularly strong in the ghettos surrounding Father Aristide's church, St. Jean Bosco, which borders Bel Air. Block committees and other local groups in Bel Air became particularly involved in what Aristide called Lavalas, the movement that promised a cleansing flood of popular power and redemption.[16] The neighborhood overwhelmingly supported Aristide's election in December 1990 and his short-lived presidency, securing Bel Air's long-standing position as a staunch power base for the Lavalas movement.

Today, however, the term *baz* tends to indicate the notion of a gang (the word gang now serves as the translation in national and international media and policy discourse) rather than grassroots activism. This second usage emerged when a coup toppled Aristide's regime just eight months after his inauguration. Popular organizations in Bel Air mobilized militant factions in order to assert their demands for Aristide's return and to protect themselves against a de facto regime that systematically targeted pro-Aristide strongholds until the president returned in 1994.[17] The association intensified during Aristide's second term, which began in 2001. Several *baz* were organized into politicized militant groups supportive of the government, becoming the so-called *chimè*—a term that translates as both "ghost" and "tantrum" and invokes the figure of an elusive and enraged pro-Aristide militant. After the second coup against Aristide in 2004, militants in Bel Air and other ghettos organized a movement to restore Aristide's leadership. On September 30, 2004, after a scheduled protest came under fire from the interim government's police force, the neighborhood organized a militia force and waged a violent standoff with police and peacekeepers for several months in the hope of restoring Aristide to leadership. As the fighting continued, and especially after the movement's leader was shot and killed, *baz* became increasingly involved in thievery and kidnapping. Despite this *devyasyon* (diversion) of the movement, as people in Bel Air say, many militants maintained political objectives and continued to organize demonstrations and other political activities. However, the political opposition and the international community constructed *baz* leaders and their affiliates and Bel Air residents as criminal gangs. Indeed, Justice Minister Bernard Gousse declared in May 2005 that "*Bèlè pa gen enosan!*" (No one in Bel Air is innocent!), accusing the whole zone of engaging in a brutal "terrorist" operation called Operation Baghdad, drawing on associations with the war in Iraq.[18] Targeting the protesters as gangsters rather than as militants, police and UN forces killed or imprisoned several *baz* leaders, affiliates, and residents of Port-au-Prince.[19] In light of this history, *baz* formations can be seen as illustrating a fundamental paradox of democracy: While they reflect the democratic hopes of the Haitian underclass, they are also tied to the novel forms of violence and insecurity that have arisen in the wake of the Duvalier dictatorship.

Grand Black's ascendancy to Bel Air leadership reflects this history. At the height of the post-coup violence in late 2004, Ti Snap and Samba Boukman, another political delegate of Aristide, founded the *baz* as the organizational center of the civilian army that was fighting to restore Aristide's rule.[20] Samba Boukman, who took his name from the former slave who led the first battle of the Haitian revolution, became the movement's press secretary, and Ti Snap was among the civilian army's former chiefs. But importantly, Grand Black also points to more recent shifts in the organization of urban politics. In particular, after the 2004 coup, many *baz* formations began to reposition their politics away from a national Lavalas platform and toward a more localized project that was not defined by, but could still enable entry into, national power structures. In fact, after the coup violence subsided, the leaders of Grand Black expressed an interest in working with the new government President René Préval led, which took power in 2006.[21] This desire was materialized when Samba Boukman became the head of the National Commission of Disarmament and Ti Snap was put in charge of the neighborhood's Popular Sector (Sektè Popilè).

In this way, Grand Black's militant defense of the neighborhood shifted from a project whose goal was to defend Aristide's rule to one whose aim was to defend the interests of *baz* residents by protecting the zone from potential dangers. Despite their formal participation in a local disarmament campaign, Grand Black maintained an arsenal. They also forged an affiliation with Ling Di, which was known to be involved in kidnapping, political assassination, and other crimes. Ling Di functioned as a more undercover, more criminal, and more violent wing of Grand Black. It was, in the words of Ti Snap, "the childish disorder that the grown-up political leaders control." Grand Black controlled Ling Di by forbidding them to commit crimes locally and by using them to police the neighborhood against outside criminals. Adopting a lyric from their affiliate *rara* music band, they proclaimed, "*Pa Fè Fòs!*" (Don't Attack [Here]!) (figure 9.1). The slogan's meaning was reinforced when it was spray-painted on

Figure 9.1. "Don't Attack [Here]!" Graffiti at the Locale of Baz Grand Black in Port-au-Prince, Haiti. Photo by Chelsey Kivland, 2013.

the local Catholic church, a bullet-ridden edifice where the group held press conferences, rallies, and concerts and launched major protests in the city.

Shape Shifting from Militant Politics to Development Policy

Over the past decades, *baz* formations have localized their political project in order to both reengage in national politics and relate to dominant global political trends and interventions, especially international development. In his role as head of the National Commission of Disarmament, Samba Boukman worked closely with the UN peacekeeping mission (MINUSTAH) that began in 2004 and its Brazilian NGO affiliate, Viva Rio, which launched an extensive security and development program in Bel Air in 2006. Core members of Grand Black also held high-ranking local posts in the NGO. These roles acquainted the group with NGO culture and development policy, and in 2008, Samba Boukman oversaw the founding of the Grand Black Foundation for the Development of Bel Air. This foundation has enabled Grand Black to cultivate a degree of political neutrality and gain access to the financial and material resources of international development organizations. However, the reinvention of Grand Black did not reflect a linear progression away from militant politics toward neutral development; rather it constantly negotiates between these modes of organizing.

Partha Chatterjee (2004), writing of India, has identified a tension between two kinds of organizing in fragile states—what he calls civil society and political society. Whereas civil society represents elite, legal mobilizations, political society concerns how populations that are excluded from civil society make claims on those who govern. These marginal populations form organizations dedicated to claiming the right to government services and benefits, even though they acknowledge that their activities breach norms of good civic behavior. In fact, there is often a "dark side" to their mobilizations, whereby "criminality and violence are tied to the various ways deprived population groups must struggle to make their claims to governmental care" (75). While *baz* may appear to exemplify political society, they in fact defy categorization. They engage in interactions that fall between the categories of civil society and political society—or what in this context may be more aptly defined as between civil society and popular organizations.[22] Grand Black, for example, attempts to engage in several modalities simultaneously: a militant modality as chiefs of a contested neighborhood, a black populist modality as representatives of the urban underclass, and a social modality that is situated beyond politics in a framework of civil society and development. Hence, rather than abandon militant racial politics entirely, *baz* find themselves shape shifting, transmuting into new beings while retaining vestiges of their original form, in order to address distinct political and development audiences at local, national, and international scales simultaneously. In other words, they adopt the language of development and affiliate themselves with NGO culture, but they do so within the rubric of their *baz* identity.

This, to be sure, is not an easy task, and Grand Black's history reveals an artful manipulation of multiple forms of organization. Such organizational prowess was evident in the subtle yet potent imagery displayed on their neighborhood headquarters (figure 9.2). The two-story yellow concrete building served as the group's meeting place, organizational center, and symbol of their local sovereignty. Located across the intersection from the "Don't Attack" sign, it represented the group's control of this major intersection and, in turn, the neighborhood. Most *baz* are situated at crossroads, and the most powerful *baz* command influential, neighborhood-defining intersections. In Haitian religious schemes, the crossroads (*kalfou*) is both a spirit (*lwa*) and a place of power and judgment, the site where magic is performed and fates are determined. The *rara* music groups with which *baz* are affiliated envision themselves as serving the Master of the Crossroads (*mèt kalfou*), and the *baz*'s sovereign domain radiates from their material, social, and mystical dominance of major crossroads. The inscription on the front of the building also contained potent symbols. Painted in yellow, red, green, and black was the organization's logo, a stoplight, and its name, Fondation Grand Black pour le Developpement. The English name Grand Black—rather than the Creole *gran nèg*—was a conscious appeal to transnational black solidarity. It named a commitment to elevating the status and power of the black underclass—to make them *grand blacks*[23]— vis-à-vis the light-skinned national elites and the staff of the international development agents and organizations, the so-called *blan*. The stoplight icon likewise engaged black diasporic politics within a development frame. The stoplight invoked the social order of a modern, developed world and signaled the way Grand Black controlled traffic in and out of the neighborhood. It also incorporated both sets of pan-African tricolors, pointing to black power and the global struggle to attain racial equality.[24] Together, these symbols drew on mystical and racial idioms poor black Caribbean youth have long used to claim a kind of popular power or respect that is distinct from the forms of power elite norms of respectability represent (Wilson 1973).[25] At the same time, however, these symbols' embeddedness in development language reflected an effort to position themselves as respectable members of civil society engaged in the neutral project of "developing" the neighborhood.

Grand Black's shape shifting between an oppositional political identity and an organization fulfilling a development mission was tested in 2011, when, after the devastating earthquake, Aristide returned to Haiti and President Michel Martelly was elected. Martelly, whose family was involved with the Duvalier dictatorship and who had supported the movement that ousted Aristide in

Figure 9.2. Development foundation of Baz Grand Black in Port-au-Prince, Haiti. Photo by Chelsey Kivland, 2009.

2004, was a clear political enemy of Grand Black. Following Martelly's inauguration, Grand Black initiated an anti-government movement called Geto Ini (Ghettos United), and in March 2012, unknown gunmen assassinated Samba Boukman in what was widely considered a political act. Soon afterward, Grand Black refashioned their identity yet again. They registered as a new social (as opposed to political) organization. In an attempt to appease the light-skinned president and the development *blan*, they removed any reference to racial and militant idioms from their name, calling themselves GB Productions for the Development and Advancement of Bel Air. In other words, Grand Black members attempted to maintain local sovereignty by presenting themselves as neutral leaders capable of working with any interested party. However, even here they maintained the GB as a vestige of their more militant identity, and neighbors, attuned to these subtle name games, did not miss the dual meaning of the group's new title. As more than one resident told me, "Grand Black focuses on local development to play two camps."

The adoption of development discourse went beyond facilitating increased flexibility in national politics. It also provided access to the financial and material resources of international development organizations. Grand Black's reinvention is an example of how its members seek to position themselves as the local brokers of development projects. This brokerage entails not only downplaying politics but also adopting the signs, practices, and logics of the organizational form that dominates community-based development: the NGO. *Baz* formations in urban Haiti are not invested in becoming NGOs (a term associated with foreign or elite organizations); they are interested in becoming the local, grassroots partners with NGOs that seek to implement projects in the area. Nonetheless, this entails constructing the local organization in the model of the NGO.

This is most apparent in their creative use of acronyms, a key linguistic trope of NGOs. Take, for example, MOG, another *baz* located an intersection away from Grand Black. Their acronym spells morgue in Creole—as in "If you don't respect us, we'll put you in the morgue!"—and they present an explicitly militant—even criminal—identity. When they founded a local organization in 2008, they redefined the acronym as Moral Optimists for the Grand Renaissance of Bel Air, dramatically shifting their identity. A year later, in 2009, they furthered their affiliation with NGO culture by founding a legal social organization with an eight-letter acronym: OJMOTEEB. Defined as Youth Organization of Moral Optimists for the Educational Enrichment of Bel Air, this new title incorporated the key development terms "youth" and "education" (figures

9.3 and 9.4). To concretize these new titles, *baz* formations formalize their organizations through a host of bureaucratic procedures and material accessories. They write charters and bylaws, acquire legal attestations, and furnish identity badges. The badges represent the ministries, organizations, foundations, associations, and even federations of organizations to which they belong. Successful *baz* leaders carry multiple badges, securing them in their wallets or hanging them from their cars' rearview mirrors, and they are always ready to present them to political gatekeepers and aid workers. Like the acronym, the badge represents a key NGO practice in Haiti, and possessing several of them affirms a degree of organizational capacity, an expansive social network, and an aptitude at shape shifting, signaling that the leader is someone who can make things happen with various people and in various contexts.

Because legal and registered organizations have access to a potentially lucrative, powerful, and mysterious development domain, they are often viewed as

Figure 9.3. Graffiti for Baz MOG in Port-au-Prince, Haiti. Photo by Chelsey Kivland, 2013.

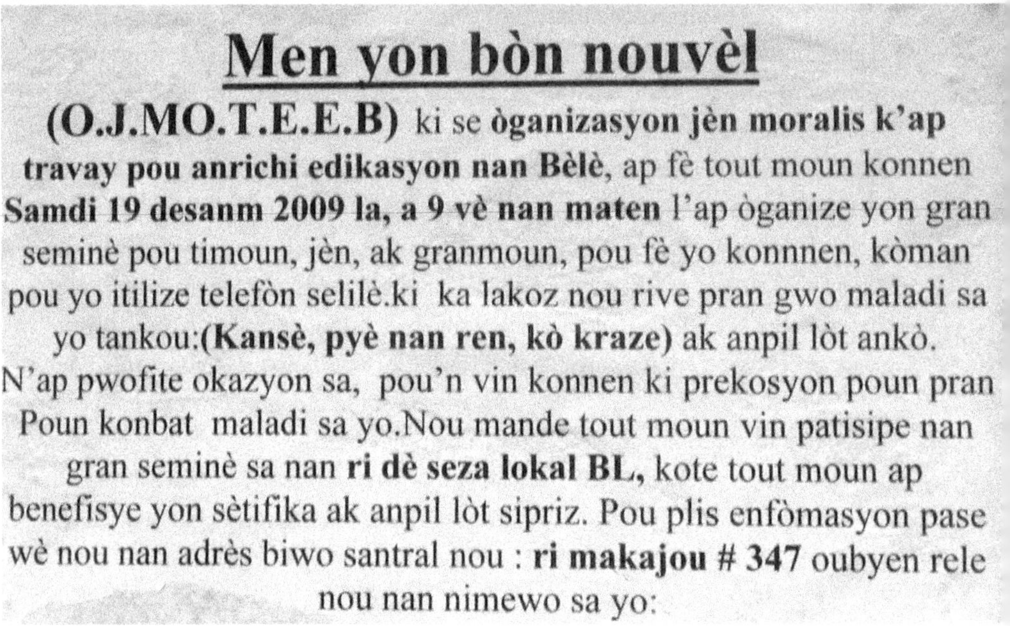

Men yon bòn nouvèl

(O.J.MO.T.E.E.B) ki se òganizasyon jèn moralis k'ap
travay pou anrichi edikasyon nan Bèlè, ap fè tout moun konnen
Samdi 19 desanm 2009 la, a 9 vè nan maten l'ap òganize yon gran
seminè pou timoun, jèn, ak granmoun, pou fè yo konnnen, kòman
pou yo itilize telefòn selilè.ki ka lakoz nou rive pran gwo maladi sa
yo tankou:(Kansè, pyè nan ren, kò kraze) ak anpil lòt ankò.
N'ap pwofite okazyon sa, pou'n vin konnen ki prekosyon poun pran
Poun konbat maladi sa yo.Nou mande tout moun vin patisipe nan
gran seminè sa nan ri dè seza lokal BL, kote tout moun ap
benefisye yon sètifika ak anpil lòt sipriz. Pou plis enfòmasyon pase
wè nou nan adrès biwo santral nou : ri makajou # 347 oubyen rele
nou nan nimewo sa yo:

Figure 9.4. Flyer advertising an OJMOTEEB development project in Port-au-Prince, Haiti. Photo by Chelsey Kivland, 2009.

magical entities. I use the term magical in the Haitian sense of sorcery—that is, to stress that shape shifting from militant *baz* to civil society organizations imputes power, prestige, and wealth to the group.[26] The notion that becoming a legally registered organization warrants such moral and material benefits is apparent in the fact that the term for local leaders is "organized people" (*moun òganize*), meaning not only those who are organized but those who are associated with one or many organizations. It is under their organizational identity that *baz* register as legal entities with state agencies and relevant NGOs, enabling them to apply for and manage projects and associated resources. In Bel Air, *baz* have negotiated U.S. Agency for International Development (USAID)-sponsored projects to pave dirt corridors and sidewalks, install solar lamps, and build an art gallery; they have worked with Viva Rio on security, water distribution, trash collection, and tree planting; they organized "cash for work" programs after the earthquake; and they have arranged their own projects in the domains of human rights, health, education, and sanitation, such as MOG's 2009 seminar, advertised in figure 9.4, on the uses and abuses of cell phones. These projects, whether initiated from beyond or within the neighborhood, were funded by an amalgamation of state ministries, aid agencies, and NGOs that directly or indirectly contracted with the local organizations.

The channeling of funds to street leaders has increased alongside the model of community-based development and its increasingly localized geography. *Baz* organizations' orientation around the neighborhood or even the block mimics the restricted target areas of small-scale, community-based projects. In claiming control of a delimited block, *baz* leaders have facilitated a point of entry, protection in an otherwise no-go zone, and, crucially, low-wage labor. The *baz* can recruit and manage workers and organize the payroll for the sponsoring organization. Through this work, state actors, NGOs, and *baz* have fortified a mutually beneficial relationship in which governance and sovereignty are shared. By working with the *baz*'s civil society branch, state and NGO sponsors can claim not only community participation but also a bona fide community partnership. In return, *baz* leaders manage the distribution of funds, resources, and labor in ways that benefit themselves and their social network, often excluding women, the elderly, or other residents unaffiliated with *baz* politics. Viva Rio's access to Bel Air, for example, was brokered in a meeting that included Samba Boukman, the head of Viva Rio, and the captain of the MINUSTAH peacekeeping operation. This meeting, in turn, facilitated the employment of core *baz* members. Consequently, many residents in Bel Air expressed ambivalence about this meeting. While they acknowledged that it coincided with a decline in violence and insecurity, they also saw it as evidence that NGOs have favored those who are engaged in violence. As they often told me, "Being honest and staying out of the game of politics does not pay off in the system of development." Despite such protestations, the high degree of local power that *baz* wield means that NGOs must respect them and work within the terms of their leadership. As a program organizer of Viva Rio elaborated in 2008:

> People complain that we work with bandits. But we have to work with them. They are the leaders for the areas. You can't say that because you don't like the way the leader became a leader, you won't work with him. You have to respect that he is the leader. Anyway, if you don't work with them you'll have problems. It's simple. We need them to do the work.

Still, residents' complaints highlight the ways these micropolities foster forms of gender and age exclusion and internecine conflicts that put the lives of *baz* leaders and neighborhood residents at risk. I now turn to sketching the entanglement of violence in *baz* politics in order to reveal the problems associated with outsourcing state duties to powerful groups at the margins of the polity.

The Dark Side of *Baz* Politics

When I asked residents about the causes of insecurity in the area, at first casually and then as part of a sixty-three–household survey, I regularly heard responses that blamed not only *baz* formations but also their entanglement with democracy and development. In citing reasons for the violence, people often referenced "elections," "NGOs," and "projects." At the root of these responses was a complaint about social divisions. One respondent, a married man and father of two, told me, "[NGOs] come to do development but they just divide people. The only real development that happens is when people in a community come together to solve a problem without stirring up money. One thing NGOs don't understand is that we need jobs but project money causes divisions." During my time in Bel Air, such divisions appeared more a normal part of doing development than cases of development gone wrong. In order to explain why this is so, it is useful to unpack the example of the post-earthquake wave of violence and insecurity that engulfed Bel Air and surrounding areas.

Immediately after the 7.0-magnitude tremors rocked Haiti, several international news reports readily predicted that criminal gangs would take over the city. These fears were unfounded. Amid the initial chaos and uncertainty of the earthquake, when Haiti appeared most vulnerable, criminal gangs did not take over the city. In fact, the rate of kidnapping and murder declined.[27] It wasn't until several months later, as aid money flowed into the capital, that the story began to change. In Bel Air, the homicide rate skyrocketed, going from 40 per 100,000 in 2010 (the year of the earthquake) to 138 in 2011 and 164 in 2012.[28] Such rates of violence had not been seen since the post-coup period of the mid-2000s, and *ensekerite* (insecurity) reemerged as Bel Air residents' dominant concern. Why was this the case? As I have suggested, the answer involved the entanglement of *baz* politics and development economies. More specifically, it involved a series of conflicts over postdisaster cash-for-work programs.

These conflicts reveal a complex story, but the general sequence of events reflects a common pattern. Basically, there were four major developments. First, in 2011, a group of youth in a nearby community broke from a more prominent *baz* there and formed a rubble removal team. The youth then established themselves as Baz 117 Aslè. Though the group had only a few members, they boasted of their network of 117 malicious (*aslè*) bandits. The group used the $300 they earned from the rubble removal project to purchase a few handguns and began a spree of muggings and robberies in the zone. People referred to 117 as a gang rather than a *baz* because instead of making a claim to local authority by protecting against outside threats, they engaged in predatory crimes in their home community.

The second major event was that a rival of Grand Black in Bel Air—a *baz* called Pale Cho (Talk Tough)—acquired control of most of the area's rubble removal brigades and a reconstruction project to pave area sidewalks. As a result, a few members of Baz Grand Black joined Baz Pale Cho in search of its newfound power and resources. In response, Ti Snap began a campaign to reclaim Grand Black's standing. The third development was that Ti Snap and Grand Black formed an alliance with Baz 117, and together they declared war against Baz Pale Cho. This war precipitated more robbery and theft as the groups struggled to acquire weapons and artillery. In effect, Baz Grand Black transformed into a gang, and residents in Bel Air protested by spray-painting all over the neighborhood "Ti Snap is chief of the 117 thieves!"

Ti Snap fled the neighborhood in early 2012, but instead of resolving the problem, the vacuum in leadership created an environment in which small armed groups, such as MOG and others called Al Qaeda and Kolon Blan, began to stake violent claims to authority.[29] Ultimately, the situation deteriorated until June 2013, when the government and Viva Rio helped restore Ti Snap and Grand Black as chiefs of Bel Air. Together, the government and the NGO channeled development funds to Grand Black for an annual street festival, a community food distribution, a major street-sweeping program, and a peace concert. Though he was relieved, Ti Snap was not exactly pleased to return to his post. He told me that he wished the state would establish a police station in the area and make him a bona fide policeman so that he could better control the disorder. As he said, "Without the state in charge, there will just be more insecurity!"

This story reveals much about street politics in urban Haiti. The moral of the story might appear to be that neighborhoods function best when strong *baz* leaders lead them. After all, the homicide rate declined to 2010 levels when Ti Snap's leadership was restored. But we should keep in mind that Ti Snap is not an elected representative of his block and that although neighborhood residents claimed that he had respect, they often qualified this as "respect by the gun." Instead, what we see here are the contradictory outcomes of outsourcing the work of development, aid, and governance to *baz* leaders. In this example, the political economy of development was mobilized in order to remedy the very violence it had helped precipitate. This illustrates that while such political economies provided young men in Bel Air with increased opportunity, it also rendered them vulnerable to attacks from rivals and reinforced the long-standing insecurities that have perpetuated the economic and political marginalization of the neighborhood.

The anthropologist James Ferguson (1994) has argued that the political economy of development resembles an "anti-politics machine," constantly whisking political realities out of sight and all the while strengthening, almost unnoticed, the state presence in the local region. Contemporary Haiti presents a related yet unique scenario. By following neoliberal dictates and outsourcing government functions to local communities, the state has become increasingly absent and defunct. Furthermore, outsourcing government functions has not eliminated but has rather relegated politics (and thus political conflict) to street sovereigns who compete to claim a piece of the dwindling public sector, often with devastating consequences. Despite *baz* attempts to craft civil society identities, they ultimately ruled locally by retaining militant identities. Put differently, although they refashioned their local orders of rule as grassroots organizations, they still recognized the politics—the competing players and interests—at stake in governance and development and, in turn, their need to enforce respect through appeals to militant forms of power. As Manno said, "You must organize to get respect. So everyone makes an organization. Now you have a problem. You've got to fight organizations with organizations." In this sense, their entanglement of militant and civil and political and development agendas points to a fundamental tension in all statecraft: that control of force is a constitutive part of political community.[30] After all, how different is *baz*'s embrace of civil society from an NGO's ties to the UN peacekeeping mission or, for that matter, a state's ties to the military? The chronic conflicts *baz* engaged in point to the fact that *baz* leaders have only ever been marginally able to fulfill the role and work of the state. Knowing this, they paradoxically long for the state to take on its sovereign duties and provide the security, income, and authority to support their work.

Conclusion

State sovereignty worldwide and especially in fragile states such as Haiti appears to be in flux today. Many in this volume have argued that the sovereignty of the Haitian state is increasingly challenged by the infiltration of a host of external actors and forces claiming to "develop" Haiti—from global capital, liberalization policies, and free-trade zones to NGOs, religious charities, and multinational governing boards such as the Interim Haiti Recovery Commission. What I have attempted to illustrate here is how this globalization of Haiti's sovereign space has occurred alongside and in relation to an inverse dynamic: the localization of sovereign power. Put differently, the collapse of Haitian state sovereignty has yielded a new form of rule and order in which local collectivities operate at the nexus of national and global power structures. In urban Haiti, *baz* formations have emerged as key players not only on the block but also in Haiti's multiscale political space; they have both assumed state functions and become key mediators for a diverse set of power brokers.

These emergent micropolities demand new ways of conceptualizing sovereignty and statehood and the relationship between them. On one level, *baz* formations suggest a need to reorient our understanding of sovereignty as the domain of the nation-state and expand our definition to include the way a community fashions itself for the execution of power and governance locally. On another level, they suggest a need to recast sovereignty as being less about an ideal state of total liberty and more about an ideal relationship of recognition and respect. *Baz* leaders did not engage in efforts to rule their territory in a way that was unconnected to external actors; they engaged with external actors. They did not wish to wield the same authority—in terms of power, resources, and responsibilities—as state or NGO actors do. Rather, they aspired to a kind of relative autonomy by which they handled the local administration of the governing resources state or NGO actors had. Indeed, their claims to power locally rested on the fact that they could command the respect by those in power as much as by local residents.

However, as I have illustrated, this system of rule ultimately failed to furnish harmonious relations of mutual respect and, in fact, promulgated insecurity. This was because those who governed—whether they were in the fragile state sector or the project-based NGO sector—could not fulfill demands for a robust public sector and because this environment of scarce resources entailed ever-more-intense competitions between local groups. In these conditions, many *baz* leaders have embraced calls for a stronger, more robust state apparatus that would be capable of furnishing state services, jobs, and benefits for them. For example, on the occasion of the truce that reestablished Grand Black as in charge of Bel Air, a leading *baz* member offered a solution to neighborhood insecurity that directly appealed to the state. With Ti Snap standing behind him, he told me, "We don't need violence anymore but peace, for all of Bel Air to become one. It's my role to speak with the youth so they don't take a bad path. This peace accord is one part. We need the Ministry of Justice, the police, everyone in the world to accompany us. . . . I want the state to accompany our work. Viva Rio does its part. Now the state must also help. For the youth to find security, pleasure, work, food, drink. That's what can bring a solution." Another leader proclaimed, "What I ask of the Haitian government, as a youth leader, what they can give the community. What we ask of the Haitian state is to offer us a police station in Bel Air, so they can have more control of the zone and the population can live better. . . . We feel we can't live. We, as leaders, ask the press and the Haitian state, let's take responsibility."

These sentiments emphasize two key points that continue to resound in urban Haiti and with which I would like to conclude this chapter. They highlight the multiple conditions that would provide a holistic restitution in residents' lives—security, work, education, nutrition—and they emphasize the need for the state to work with community leaders in furnishing this life. If we take such claims seriously, as I think we should, our task is to ask new questions and, most significantly, to attune our conceptual and critical vocabulary to how people are both empowered and exploited by contemporary localizations of governance and development. As *baz* leaders in Bel Air often defiantly but also frustratingly told me, "Here, *we* make the state!"

Notes

1. The core philosophers of liberalism—from Thomas Hobbes to John Locke to John Stuart Mills—have used a rubric of individualism (of natural rights or law) to define the principle of liberty. For them, liberty is a constitutive part of political community, but, as Alasdair MacIntyre ([1981] 2007, 195) has argued, "for liberal individualism a community is simply an arena in which individuals each pursue their own self-chosen conception of the good life, and political institutions exist to provide that degree of order which makes self-determined activity possible."

2. In a traditional Haitian greeting, a guest calls out *"onè"* (honor) when approaching a house or courtyard and the host responds with *"respè"* (respect) to welcome the guest.

3. For reporting on the Interim Haiti Recovery Commission and the minor role of Haitian leaders on it, see Sontag (2012).

4. For an analysis of how the Haitian government reluctantly accepted unpopular neoliberal reforms in the mid-1990s in order to obtain crucial aid funds, see Dupuy (2005).

5. A recent example concerns Haiti's minimum wage policy. In 2009, after Parliament passed a law raising the minimum wage by 60 percent (from 125 to 200 gourdes), President René Préval, facing pressure from the U.S. State Department and foreign apparel industry executives, vetoed the law and instituted a two-tier wage structure that maintained the low wage for export assembly workers. For more information, see Bell (2013).

6. The United Nations Office of the Special Envoy for Haiti (2012) has reported that of the $6.43 billion in aid money disbursed by donors in the period 2010–2012, over 90 percent went to foreign NGOs and private contractors and less than 1 percent to Haitian NGOs.

7. Several scholars have documented how state agents and representatives treat the rural and urban poor with a lack of respect during daily bureaucratic encounters (e.g., Smith 2001; Smucker 1982) and the predatory structure of the state apparatus. The Haitian state, as Trouillot (1990, 64) asserted, has "chosen to live at the expense of the people." See also Dupuy (1989) and Fatton (2002).

8. Several have argued that Haiti's revolution engendered a nationalist ideology centered on the army and its male soldiers (Laguerre 1993; Sheller 2012). In the 1805 Constitution of Haiti, Jean-Jacques Dessalines, revolutionary army general and first ruler of Haiti, went so far as to conceive of the nation as a fraternal army and the citizen as "a good father, a good son, a good husband, and above all, a good soldier."

9. All names are pseudonyms, except for the names of those deceased.

10. I prefer to translate *blan* as "white foreigner" rather than simply "foreigner" in order to stress that the idiom is embedded in a particular racial order wherein class, status, and citizenship are tied to racial parameters. This racial order was codified in the 1804 Declaration of Independence, where Jean-Jacques Dessalines referred to citizens as *nèg* (black) and foreigners as *blan* (white).

11. For more information on neoliberal reforms, see Dupuy (2005), Farmer (2003), Schuller (2012), and Fatton (this volume).

12. See note 6.

13. Haitian assembly of U.S. apparel has been promoted by both Haiti and the United States as development aid to Haiti since the last years of François Duvalier's rule. During Jean-Claude Duvalier's rule (1971–1986) and his "liberalization" of the economy, the offshore assembly industry expanded rapidly as investors took advantage of cheap labor, tax exemptions, few foreign exchange controls, and limited government intervention. However, with no mechanisms for domestic investment, the assembly industry provided no long-term benefits for the country (Perito and Hsu 2006; Trouillot 1990). By the mid-1980s, it had not substantially affected income distribution or the growth of other industries. In addition, the political instability of the 1990s precipitated factory closings and massive layoffs (Farmer 2003).

14. In 2009, the economist Paul Collier issued a report to the secretary-general of the United Nations that touted the garment industry as Haiti's main development possibility. U.S. president Bill Clinton subsequently used the Collier report to promote the financing of the Caracol Industrial Park, a garment assembly plant located in northern Haiti funded by the Inter-American Development Bank, the Clinton Foundation, and the governments of Haiti and the United States.

15. Among others (e.g., Bogues 2006; Burr 2005), Enrique Desmond Arias and Daniel Goldstein (2010) have argued that in Latin America, urban violence is integral to the founding of democratic states, a key component in the maintenance of economic

inequality, a feature of the administration of governance, and an instrument for making popular challenges to the political system.

16. Bel Air was central to Lavalas despite (or perhaps because of) the Duvalier family dictatorship's ties to the neighborhood, which once was home to over 500 of the regime's *tonton makout* militiamen (Laguerre 1976).

17. Eyewitness reports estimated that 1,500 people were killed during the first days of the coup (Farmer 2003). An estimated 300,000 went into hiding in Haiti or abroad (Siebentritt 1994), and 37,000 took to the high seas in a desperate attempt to reach Florida in 1991 and 1992 (Mitchell 1994). The urban and rural poor were also particularly affected by the international aid embargo enforced on the de facto regime and thousands died of hunger (Berggren et al. 1993).

18. The origin of the term Operation Baghdad is highly contested. My research suggests that it was developed by a Bel Air *baz* to connote the illegitimacy of the foreign invasion into the neighborhood and then appropriated by the leaders of the post-coup interim regime to suggest a terrorist campaign.

19. Using random surveys of 1,260 households, Kolbe and Hutson (2006) found that twenty-three households had had a member killed in the ten months following the coup d'état. The researchers then calibrated this figure with the population of Port-au-Prince to estimate that 8,000 people were killed, about half by criminal perpetrators and the other half by political perpetrators (see also Mendonça 2008).

20. Samba spelled his name this way in an intentional departure from the standard Haitian Creole spelling "Sanba."

21. A June 12, 2006, U.S. Embassy cable reported on the willingness of Samba Boukman and other militants to "give Préval a chance to deliver, rather than fight for Aristide's return." This cable was made publicly available by WikiLeaks: Ambassador Janet Sanderson, "Lavalas Reunification Meeting Fails," telegram, June 12, 2006, https:// wikileaks.org/plusd/cables/06PORTAUPRINCE1028_a.html, accessed July 1, 2014.

22. The binary between civil society and popular organizations was established in Haiti as a formal political division in 2000, after Aristide's second election to the presidency. This divide was between the Civil Society Initiative, a collection of private and nonprofit groups opposed to Aristide, and the popular organizations affiliated with urban *baz* formations that supported Aristide.

23. The phrase *grand blacks* was a conscious inversion of the colonial term for white planters, the so-called *grand blancs*.

24. The pan-African tricolors can be traced to two flags, the red, yellow, and green flag Ethiopia has used since 1897 and the red, black, and green flag the Universal Negro Improvement Association and the African Communities League adopted in 1920.

25. My understanding of the relationship between respect, violence, and masculinity in Haiti is indebted to Peter Wilson's (1973) seminal framework of respectability and reputation in Providencia and to countless subsequent reworkings of it (e.g., Sutton 1974; Thomas 2013). For a more detailed analysis of how urban discourses in Haiti elaborate this framework, see Kivland (2014).

26. In using the term magical, I am drawing on discourse surrounding *maji*, or sorcery, in Haiti. Accusations of sorcery in Haiti follow lines of inequality and disturbances in the moral order (Farmer 1992; Larose 1977; Richman 2005). I also use the term magical to stress that *baz's* shape shifting should be approached in terms of a fluid understanding of identity. Put differently, the *baz* should not be viewed as shielding a presumed "real" identity with fanciful development language but rather as showcasing how they can, and indeed must be, capable of manipulating perceptions to perform multiple identities in diverse contexts.

27. It is difficult to find reliable reporting on crime statistics in the immediate aftermath of the earthquake, but eyewitness reports confirm that kidnapping and armed robbery declined immediately after the earthquake (Wilentz 2013). However, it should be noted the some kinds of violence, such as rape and other forms of sexual assault, escalated in the months after the earthquake when over a million people were housed in encampments (MADRE et al. 2011).

28. These figures were compiled by cross-referencing data gathered by Viva Rio's Biwo Analyiz Kominotè and the Justice and Peace Commission of Haiti, both located in Port-au-Prince, Haiti.

29. The names of *baz* formations consciously draw on a militant vocabulary, and they often make reference to larger political struggles. The names Al Qaeda and Kolon Blan invoke the "war on terror" and colonial idioms of power, respectively.

30. Max Weber famously defined the state as a "human community that (successfully) claims the monopoly on the legitimate use of physical force within a given territory" ([1946] 1998, 78). More recently, several anthropologists have revitalized a conception of postcolonial sovereignty and statehood based on violence (see Das and Poole 2004; Hansen and Stepputat 2005; Mbembe 2003).

References

Arias, Enrique Desmond, and Daniel Goldstein, eds. 2010. *Violent Democracies in Latin America.* Durham, NC: Duke University Press.

Bell, Beverly. 2013. *Fault Lines.* Ithaca, NY: Cornell University Press.

Berggren, Gretchen, Sarah Castle, Lincoln Chen, Winifred Fitzgerald, Catherine Michaud, and Marko Simunovic. 1993. *Sanctions in Haiti: Crisis in Humanitarian Action.* Cambridge, MA: Harvard Center for Population and Development Studies and Harvard School of Public Health.

Bogues, Anthony. 2006. "Power, Violence, and the Shotta Don." *NACLA Report on the Americas* 39 (6):21–26, 37.

Burr, Lars. 2005. The Sovereign Outsourced: Local Justice and Violence in Port Elizabeth. In *Sovereign Bodies: Citizens. Migrants, and States in the Postcolonial World,* ed. T. Blom Hansen and F. Stepputat, 192–217. Princeton, NJ: Princeton University Press.

Chatterjee, Partha. 2004. *The Politics of the Governed: Reflections on Popular Politics in Most of the World.* New York: Columbia University Press.

Comaroff, Jean, and John L. Comaroff, eds. 2006. *Law and Disorder in the Postcolony*. Chicago: University of Chicago Press.

Das, Veena, and Deborah Poole. 2004. *Anthropology in the Margins of the State*. Santa Fe, NM: School of American Research Press.

Dupuy, Alex. 1989. *Haiti in the World Economy: Class, Race, and Underdevelopment since 1700*. Boulder, CO: Westview Press.

———. 2005. Globalization, the World Bank, and the Haitian Economy. In *Contemporary Caribbean Cultures and Societies in a Global Context*, ed. F. W. Wright and T. Martinez-Vergne, 43–70. Chapel Hill: University of North Carolina.

Fanon, Frantz. (1965) 2004. *The Wretched of the Earth*. Trans. R. Philcox. New York: Grove Press.

Farmer, Paul. 1992. *AIDS and Accusation: Haiti and the Geography of Blame*. Berkeley: University of California Press.

———. 2003. *The Uses of Haiti*. Monroe, ME: Common Courage Press.

Fatton, Robert. 2002. *Haiti's Predatory Republic: The Unending Transition to Democracy*. Boulder, CO: Lynne Rienner Publishers.

Ferguson, James G. 1994. *The Anti-Politics Machine: "Development," Depoliticization, and Bureaucratic Power in Lesotho*. Minneapolis: University of Minnesota Press.

Hansen, Thomas Blom, and Finn Stepputat, eds. 2005. *Sovereign Bodies: Citizens, Migrants, and States in the Postcolonial World*. Princeton, NJ: Princeton University Press.

Kivland, Chelsey. 2014. "Becoming a Force in the Zone: Hedonopolitics, Masculinity, and the Quest for Respect on Haiti's Streets." *Cultural Anthropology* 29 (4):672–698.

Kolbe, Athena, and Royce A. Hutson. 2006. "Human Rights Abuse and Other Criminal Violations in Port-au-Prince, Haiti: A Random Survey of Households." *The Lancet* 368 (9538):864–873.

Laguerre, Michel S. 1976. "Black Ghetto as an Internal Colony: Socioeconomic Adaptation of a Haitian Urban Community." PhD diss., University of Illinois, Urbana Champaign.

———. 1993. *The Military and Society in Haiti*. Knoxville: University of Tennessee Press.

Larose, Serge. 1977. "The Meaning of Africa in Haitian Vodu." In *Symbols and Sentiments: Cross Cultural Studies in Symbolism*, edited by J. Lewis, 85–116. New York: Academic Press.

MacIntyre, Alasdair. (1981) 2007. *After Virtue: A Study in Moral Theory*. Notre Dame, IN: University of Notre Dame Press.

MADRE, KOFAVIV, FAVILEK, Women's Link Worldwide, and the International Women's Human Rights Clinic at the City of New York University School of Law. 2011. *Gender-Based Violence against Haitian Women & Girls in Internal Displacement Camps*. Submission to the United Nations Universal Periodic Review. Accessed April 26, 2016. http://ijdh.org/wordpress/wp-content/uploads/2011/03/UPR-GBV-Final-4-4-2011.pdf.

Manigat, Sabine. 1997. "Haiti: Popular Sectors and the Crisis in Port-au-Prince." In *The*

Urban Caribbean: Transition to the New Global Economy, edited by A. Portes, C. Dore-Cabral, and P. Landolt, 87–123. Baltimore, MD: Johns Hopkins Press.

Mbembe, Achille. 2003. "Necropolitics." Translated by Libby Meintjes. *Public Culture* 15 (1): 11–40.

Mendonça, Maria Luisa. 2008. "UN Troops Accused of Human Rights Violations in Haiti." http://www.cipamericas.org/archives/810.

Mitchell, Christopher. 1994. "U.S. Policy toward Haitian Boat People, 1972–1993." *Annals of the American Academy of Political and Social Science* 534: 69–80.

Perito, Robert, and Emily Hsu. 2006. *Haiti's Economic Challenge*. Washington, DC: United States Institute of Peace.

Richman, Karen E. 2005. *Migration and Vodou*. Gainesville, FL: University Press of Florida.

Schuller, Mark. 2012. *Killing with Kindness: Haiti, International Aid, and NGOs*. New Brunswick, NJ: Rutgers University Press.

Sheller, Mimi. 2012. *Citizenship from Below: Erotic Agency and Caribbean Freedom*. Durham, NC: Duke University Press.

Siebentritt, Gretta Tovar. 1994. *Fugitives from Injustice: The Crisis of Internal Displacement in Haiti*. New York: Human Rights Watch, Jesuit Refugee Service, National Coalition for Haitian Refugees.

Smith, Jennie Marcelle. 2001. *When the Hands Are Many: Community Organization and Social Change in Rural Haiti*. Ithaca, NY: Cornell University Press.

Smucker, Glenn. 1982. "Peasants and Development Politics: A Study in Haitian Class and Culture." PhD diss., New School for Social Research.

Sontag, Deborah. 2012. "Rebuilding in Haiti Lags after Billions in Post-Quake Aid." *New York Times*, December 23.

Sutton, Constance. 1974. "Cultural Duality in the Caribbean." *Caribbean Studies* 14 (2): 96–101.

Thomas, Deborah A. 2013. "Sovereignty/Intimacy: Political Openings in Contemporary Jamaica." In *Caribbean Sovereignty, Development, and Democracy in an Age of Globalization*, ed. Linden Lewis, 165–188 New York: Routledge.

Trouillot, Michel Rolph. 1990. *Haiti, State against Nation: The Origins and Legacy of Duvalierism*. New York: Monthly Review Press.

Weber, Max. (1946) 1998. "Politics as a Vocation." In *From Max Weber: Essays in Sociology*, edited by H. H. Gerth and C. W. Mills, 77–128. New York: Oxford University Press.

Wilentz, Amy. 2013. *Farewell, Fred Voodoo: A Letter from Haiti*. New York: Simon and Schuster.

Wilson, Peter J. 1973. *Crab Antics: The Social Anthropology of English-Speaking Negro Societies of the Caribbean*. New Haven, CT: Yale University Press.

10

Conclusion

Reflections on Sovereignty

Robert Maguire, Scott Freeman, and Nicholas Johnson

The goal of this volume, a fairly lofty one, is to consider how ownership and sovereignty have become essential concepts for the examination of contemporary Haiti. Since Haiti's independence in 1804, both its territory and individuals have been free, perhaps making the question of ownership anachronistic. It is just that sentiment, however, that this volume challenges. Despite the overt semblance of independence, freedom, and self-determination, the chapters of this book point to how sovereignty manifests in Haiti against a far more complex backdrop. The reality is that there are constant challenges to Haitian independence that should give us pause.

Haiti's status as the first black republic is invoked almost as much as its status as the poorest country in the Western Hemisphere. A romantic image of independence and complete freedom is deployed almost as an antidote to the depiction of Haiti as both poor and violent. Within this dueling paradigm, what we often miss is that both of these narratives are far more complex. When we refer to the independence of Haiti, we must also note responses to that independence—the racialized isolation led by France and the United States that was intended to suffocate the fledgling republic. We must recall the U.S. occupation as another racially charged action. And we must remember the myriad other moments when international actors have challenged the autonomy of Haiti. Over the ten years preceding this volume, legions of foreign political officials, soldiers, scholars, journalists, so-called experts, and aid workers reported on, worked on, and spoke for Haiti and Haitians. In posing the question of who "owns" Haiti, we follow the tradition of other scholars (see, for example, Farmer 1994) in drawing attention to the fact that Haiti has never been free of international meddling. In doing so, we must draw attention not only to these actions but also to the continual responses by Haitians designed to reclaim and assert their ideas of ownership.

During the symposium that led to this volume, participants from Haiti, the United States, Brazil, and the Caribbean—including scholars, civic activists, officials and businesspeople—spent three days discussing the question of who "owns" Haiti. The symposium considered that question in the contexts of politics, history, culture, and the economy, focusing principally on a ten-year period that began with the country's 2004 bicentennial of independence: 2004–2014.

The idea for the larger discussion arose from a reflection on statements aspiring Haitian presidential candidates made during the 2010–2011 election campaign. These individuals declared that if elected, they would expand their country's sovereign space. In the aftermath of that election—and even during it—violations of sovereignty continued. Thus, it seems fitting, and arguably necessary, that a symposium focusing on Haitian "ownership" ought to take place in Washington, DC, close to the institutions and individuals that are widely viewed as the primary drivers of those violations.

At the 2014 symposium, speaker after speaker—and in this volume, author after author—documented both infractions of and aspirations to "ownership" and Haitian strategies and actions for deflecting them. Given the contentious and multidimensional nature of Haiti's sovereignty, it is important to consider how sovereignty has been forged, maintained, modified, or extended by different groups at different times and in different ways. As authors underscore throughout this volume, scholars and practitioners must broaden their consideration of both infractions on sovereignty and efforts to safeguard it and think beyond simple analyses that reify the boundaries of the nation-state. Indeed, neither infractions on Haitian sovereignty nor Haitian responses to them have been monolithic. On one hand, for example, the authors of this volume have demonstrated the varied ways that economic and development policies have been imposed in ways that exclude Haitian participation. On the other, they have shown how rural and urban forms of solidarity are practiced and how spiritual traditions continue despite unending efforts to convert Haitians to other religions. It seems that for every assertion of external ownership there are responses by Haitians that resist or cunningly accommodate external efforts to control.

This concluding chapter, which draws principally from a conversation among the symposium's speakers and panelists, does not seek a definitive answer to the complicated question of who owns Haiti. Rather, it offers a synthesis of participants' reflections on contemporary ownership and sovereignty, which frequently juxtaposed questions, concerns, and ideas. These reflections include not just ideas evident in the chapters of the volume but also insights into a larger set of concerns and possibilities that will no doubt course through Haiti's third century of independence.

Onè—Respè: Honor—Respect

Among many Haitians, especially in the countryside, the practice of calling out "Honor" (*Onè*) upon entering a front yard, a veranda, or a home earns a response of "Respect" (*Respè*) from its occupant. This common practice is imbued with a sense of mutual recognition, unity, and acknowledgement of the autonomy of the other. Borrowing from this tradition, each symposium session began with the call and response of *onè—respè*.

We do not refer to this basic greeting in order to paint an idyllic or inherently politicized vision of a countryside where all are united and social differentiation does not occur. Rather, we present it as a Haitian sense of how mutual recognition can be a primary point of reference. As seen, for example, in Chelsey Kivland's chapter in this volume, among members of urban *baz* organizations, *respè* is invoked in complex ways that touch upon military violence and power, mutual recognition and fear, competition and force. The idea of respect is thus not always embedded in peaceful simplicity. But these complex personal affirmations of respect that occur in Haiti, in both rural and urban areas, seem to be a foundational part of acknowledging the dignity in one another.

While respect is part of a common personal greeting throughout Haiti, symposium participants acknowledged a conspicuous absence of respect in the dealings of international actors in Haiti. This volume raises questions about how institutional actions embody the idea of respect. How does a respect for Haitian institutions or individuals permeate (or not) the actions and ideologies of external and internal institutions? What sort of respect occurs or is absent in the daily actions of *l'international* who dominate the direction of aid and, very often, Haiti's domestic affairs? Is there a fundamental acknowledgement of the humanity and self-determination of Haitians, or are relationships founded on paternalistic notions of who knows best? Implicit in these questions is the concept that the legacy of colonialism is not yet over. It does not go unnoticed in Haiti that international entities present there—including the U.S. Agency for International Development, the United Nations, and the U.S. Department of State—have acted with questionable levels of respect.

This analysis, of course, cannot shy away from an examination of Haitian political institutions and actors. As discussed in this volume, many of the machinations of the international community have brought Haitian leaders into power—with or without popular support from Haitian voters. As exemplified by, but not limited to, the regime of Michel Martelly, elite politicians have continually sought self-benefit through power. The political polarization between the executive and legislative branches since the 2010–2011 election emerged in large part as the result of lack of mutual respect and competing interests that seek personal benefit. Domestic political actors face the same critiques we might wage against foreign individuals and institutions: The interests of the elite are prioritized at the expense of those of the poor majority. Yes, symposium participants acknowledged, Haiti is fraught with weak government, inequality, injustice, social and economic dichotomization, a crisis of trust, and other obstacles to its development. But if the Haitian state is a failed one, they insisted, it is because it works well only for certain segments of society.

Yet not all is doom and gloom. During this same ten-year time frame, we have examples of political rivals sitting together in constructive conversation at moments of crisis. Illustrating an acknowledgement of respect for fundamental rights of speech and assembly, we see examples of what can happen when respect is an a priori part of a relationship.[1]

This basic idea of honor and respect must become a robust guiding feature of the social, economic, and political relationships between Haitians and those who enter Haitian geographic and political space. Perhaps for our purposes the greeting *onè-respè* should be considered as a model for engagement. In that model, a solitary individual cannot complete the salutation; it is based on a call followed by a response. If we look to honor and respect as a model for institutional and individual relationships, we look to a model where two parties acknowledge dignity and autonomy in each other.

To be clear: This reflection is not intended to reify some simplistic notion that respect can cure the ills of foreign involvement in Haitian affairs through introducing a discursive act. It is, however, an effort to denounce the lack of respect that most often permeates these relationships.

Participation in Decision Making

While behavior that reinforces respect is important, the reality is that certain sectors of the population are routinely excluded from participation in dialogues and decisions pertaining to Haiti. Conferences, donor meetings, and planning events may invoke honor and respect, but the list of attendees may indicate otherwise. How many meetings about Haiti take place without diverse or representative groups of Haitians in the room? When do rural residents and women participate? Many planning meetings that occurred in the aftermath of the 2010 earthquake took place in English, facilitating international actors and excluding Haitian ones (Farmer 2011). Since the vast majority of Haitians speak only Creole, conversations in French, English, or Spanish isolate and exclude.

Similarly, the location of these conversations is of utmost importance. Many key conversations occur outside Haiti—in hearing rooms, conference rooms, and offices of institutions located in New York and Washington, DC. The complications and costs of international travel create barriers for participation by certain individuals but facilitate the engagement of others. The voices of Haitian women and the *pep* (ordinary people) become conspicuously absent when such meetings are held at the convenience of foreign consultants or functionaries. A paradigm shift away from the exclusivity of elites and from the continuation of a business-as-usual approach to who participates and decides is of utmost necessity.

A well-known Haitian proverb proclaims that "when you cannot bring the cow to the pasture, you can take the pasture to the cow." International actors and their Haitian counterparts need to do a better job at bringing their hearings, meetings, consultations, and conferences to localities that will facilitate more inclusive participation in decision making. Expanding the range of participation of Haitians in decision-making processes relevant to their lives and the future of their country will help assure a better Haiti. But while fewer obstacles exist when meetings take place in Haiti, geographic proximity does not guarantee equal access or voice to all. Participation has long been desired and invoked in development work, but all too often it takes the form of "box checking," not legitimate integration into decision making (see Cooke and Kothari 2001; Anderson, Brown, and Jean 2012). Thus, incorporating broader sections of Haiti into decision making is not a simple task, and unfortunately, can all too easily become a way that voices are further co-opted by others. In thinking through participation, we need to question how participation is invoked and practiced, making it, too, a target of our analysis of ownership.

Foreign scholars and researchers are also part of the problems related to participation. The processes of gathering knowledge and conducting research have long been processes of extraction, whereby knowledge and information is taken from marginalized groups for the benefit of those who are better off (Smith 1999). This issue is particularly pressing as increasing numbers of partnerships form between foreign universities and Haitian counterparts. The lives and livelihoods of foreign researchers and practitioners revolve around the publication (and veritable "ownership") of information on Haiti. Studies done in Haiti may benefit Haitians in the broadest sense of scientific pursuit, but all too often the format and availability of the publications such studies generate do not reach the populations who participated in the original study (Sheller 2013).

This absence of participation fuels distrust in a society that has long been polarized in terms of race, geography, and socioeconomic status. As participants noted, these stark divisions have resulted in nearly two countries that exist within the same space. The absence of inclusivity can result in the imposition or adoption of reforms and activities from elsewhere that do not respond broadly to the priorities or needs of the majority. Reform initiatives in the areas of rule of law, administration of justice, public administration, and education are among those ideas that have been largely imported into Haiti without the benefit of inclusive engagement.

Lack of access to information and exclusion from discussions and decision making were key themes for the symposium, as for this volume. For each assertion of ownership by one group, the possibility of loss exists for another. This is particularly clear when thinking about participation. As language, location, and more overt strategies limit the contribution of particular sectors of the population, we seem to be talking less and less about participation and more and more about its obverse: exclusion.

Identifying Needs

How needs are defined is related to the question of exclusion. As anthropologist James Ferguson (1990) famously observed, a great deal of the work of development and political institutions is devoted to defining development problems. How a problem is defined has a profound bearing on what solutions are proposed. Particularly when it comes to international aid, defining a problem from the outside can easily be aligned with foreign interests, fostering solutions that are divorced from supposed beneficiaries and are "owned" instead by planners and so-called experts.

Participants in the symposium questioned the concept of "need" in the context of project planning and design, challenging the intentions of large aid institutions. Do forms of assistance to rural Haitians such as vouchers for food purchase help Haitian farmers or do they ultimately benefit the United States through practices of "boomerang aid," whereby food imports sourced from the

United States are woven into aid programs? More broadly, do these programs do more to benefit external actors than Haitians? Participants raised concerns about how foreign aid targets agriculture, particularly its focus on export crops. This policy emphasis, which includes crops such as mangoes and bananas, would not improve the country's ability to directly feed itself, a key Haitian priority. Accordingly, such policy interests propelled participants to question the design of such programs: Do Haitian farmers want a focus on export crops? What are the historical successes of such models? Given the questionable benefits to ordinary Haitians of large monocropping initiatives in Haiti's past, from eighteenth-century sugarcane plantations to twentieth-century sisal, rubber, and banana farms, such recommendations put at risk both food security and food sovereignty. More broadly, do projects designed without input and participation from farmers result in strategies that address the core needs of Haiti and its people? Arguably, the answer is no. A more productive approach to identifying development problems and plans would be for outsiders to ask "What do you do and how can we help you do it better?" than to take it upon themselves to identify needs and plan accordingly.

As the presence and work of U.S.-based NGOs and for-profit contractors (FPCs) in Haiti is fundamentally couched in a conversation of "need," the topic of "the Republic of NGOs" captured the attention of participants. Widely perceived by Haitians as a tool to facilitate U.S. objectives for Haiti, NGOs and FPCs often have led to frustration among Haitians. Half-completed or unsustained projects that define needs without Haitian participation seem to be a common experience in Haiti. While a diversity of NGO and for-profit actors exists, it is their fundamental structure that is of concern: They are accountable to the needs of external funders and planners rather than those of Haitians.

This accountability to foreign donors is of particular concern in light of the fact that tax-exempt arrangements with NGOs cause the government of Haiti to lose a great deal of potential revenue. While arguments might be launched about the nonprofit intentions of NGOs, the questionable benefits they usually provide create a great deal of skepticism about who really benefits from such ventures. Removing these tax exemptions would increase the revenue of the Haitian government by about 4 percent of GDP. However, it would likely be politically impractical, if not impossible, for the government of Haiti to take on such an economic reform. U.S.-based NGOs would likely rally lobbyists to the U.S. Congress at the first sign of such measures. This of course raises again the question of who gets to make decisions regarding Haiti. The interests of non-Haitian groups often take a primary role in what otherwise would be a government decision.

Ironically, tax relief for international NGOs helps perpetuate a highly regressive taxation system in Haiti that places the heaviest burden on the poorest people in Haiti's cities, towns, and countryside. Such a system extracts wealth from small farmers. Because these small-holding agricultural producers are actually net consumers, their economic status is increasingly and continually marginalized by a taxation system that favors foreign interests and domestic elites by creating so-called favorable business climates. Exasperated symposium participants concluded this discussion by reasserting that Haiti's sovereignty can be expanded only when the identification of needs and the imposition of ideas from the outside morphs into respect for what Haitians know and do and when outsiders respond in ways that reinforce that knowledge and experience.

The Idea of Haiti

The amorphous "idea of Haiti" meanders in and out of our conversations and chapters. It was seen by those engaged with the country's history, society, culture, and arts as particularly critical in a discussion of who owns Haiti. The idea of Haiti arises from the country's unique historical experience and manifests itself in institutions and expressions that grew out of that experience. It is nestled in multiple facets of Haiti's social organization and cultural expression and in the pride of being Haitian. It fortifies a deep desire for dignity, respect, and dominion. It is a concept, albeit nebulous, that is fluid in its meaning and diverse in its expression. It is something that should belong to all Haitians.

But all too often, the idea of Haiti seems to be deployed far outside Haiti. It is invoked as mission groups and service trips use Haiti as an exotic destination for bringing salvation and development. It is deployed as aid workers who live and work in Haiti wear a badge of pride, expressed through the ever-common expat greeting of "How long have you been here?" The idea of Haiti is invoked in marketing campaigns: It becomes a name on Instagram hashtags for posts about service trips and a quintessential "do-good" fashion statement. The roots of these ideas may originate in an exotic, simplified, and erroneous idea of Vodou or a media-fueled image of Haiti as dangerous and poor. Yet these ideas, which are continually deployed both within and outside Haiti, are ironically the very things that have marginalized it as a pariah black republic. These concepts both produce and benefit from a romanticized idea of Haiti and contribute to its marginalization.

In the final analysis, it is the continually unfolding story of Haiti that can allow Haitians to confront and dismiss misplaced perceptions. Self-determination compels a rejection of the labels of Haiti as a "failed state" and "the poorest country in the hemisphere." Self-confidence fuels resistance to the entreaties of *l'international*. The everyday moments when Haitian sovereignty is exerted, in community organization, spiritual practice, and rural labor, can—and should—be the conceptual framework on which Haiti's future is constructed. These ideas and the achievements they represent provide an already existing Haitian road map for the future. They support conceptions of democracy that are built upon participation and dignity.

How can Haiti be "failed" when the country and its people have constantly found ways of asserting themselves and protecting their space despite serial intrusions by powerful external forces and entities that would impose ineffective, inappropriate, or self-serving policies and practices? How can Haiti be "the poorest" when throughout its history its people have produced rich and ongoing efforts to protect their space against strong odds and powerful intrusions and then have found ways of moving forward?

Arguments that blame Haitians for the present condition of Haiti should look to this volume as part of the large body of work pointing to the problematic role of the international community in Haiti's affairs. Those who wish to help Haiti develop further ownership must be prepared to welcome and listen to diverse sectors of the population in deliberations and decision making and be prepared to work as partners, not as those who would impose their will or seek to own Haiti or a part of it. Yet while we implore all actors to reflect on and listen to a diversity of Haitian perspectives, we recognize that these exchanges are steeped in unequal power relationships and that there has been an overwhelming tendency of those in more powerful positions to ignore potentially liberating conversations. Our hope is that this volume will create a space for more constructive, considerate, and mutually liberating conversations to take hold.

Thinking through both assertions and infractions of sovereignty should force all those engaged with Haiti to reflect seriously on their roles. How do their actions as Diaspora, *blan* (white or foreigner), or even Haitian counterparts or partners of those who seek a piece of Haiti facilitate or reject various ideas of sovereignty? Do they seek to prescribe solutions *for* Haitians, or do they seek to support Haitians' quest for a better future? In closing, we ask that these questions be considered in ongoing movements of support and solidarity, ones that are based fundamentally on *onè* and *respè*.

Notes

1. Such a moment took place toward the end of 2014, when diverse political actors worked together to create a nonpartisan presidential commission that helped defuse a crisis related to the Supreme Court and the election council (see Charles 2015).

References

Anderson, Mary B., Dayna Brown, and Isabella Jean. 2012. *Time to Listen: Hearing People on the Receiving End of International Aid*. Cambridge, MA: CDA Collaborative Learning Projects.

Charles, Jacqueline. 2015. "Haiti Supreme Court Chief Resigns: New Electoral Council to Come." *Miami Herald*, January 7.

Cooke, Bill, and Uma Kothari. 2001. *Participation: The New Tyranny?* Zed Books. New York, NY.

Farmer, Paul. 1994. *The Uses of Haiti*. Monroe, ME: Common Courage Press.

———. 2011. *Haiti after the Earthquake*. New York, NY: PublicAffairs.

Ferguson, James. 1990. *The Anti-Politics Machine: Development, Depoliticization, and Bureaucratic Power in Lesotho*. Minneapolis: University of Minnesota Press.

Sheller, Mimi. 2013. The Islanding Effect: Post-Disaster Mobility Systems and Humanitarian Logistics in Haiti. *Cultural Geographies* 20 (2): 185–204.

Smith, Linda Tuhiwai. 1999. *Decolonizing Methodologies: Research and Indigenous Peoples*. London: Zed Books.

Contributors

Laurent Dubois is a professor of romance studies and history and the director of the Forum for Scholars and Publics at Duke University. From 2010 to 2013, he was the co-director of the Haiti Laboratory of the Franklin Humanities Institute. He is the author of six books. *Avengers of the New World: The Story of the Haitian Revolution* was selected as a best book of the year by the Los Angeles Times and has been published in translation in Haiti under the title *Les Vengeurs du Nouveau Monde* by Éditions de l'Universite d'État d'Haïti. His *Haiti: The Aftershocks of History* was selected as a New York Times Notable Book of the Year. His most recent book is *The Banjo: America's African Instrument*.

Robert Fatton Jr. is the Julia A. Cooper Professor of Government and Foreign Affairs in the Department of Politics at the University of Virginia. His books include *Black Consciousness in South Africa*; *The Making of a Liberal Democracy: Senegal's Passive Revolution, 1975–1985*; *Predatory Rule: State and Civil Society in Africa*; *Haiti's Predatory Republic: The Unending Transition to Democracy*; *The Roots of Haitian Despotism*; and *Haiti: Trapped in the Outer Periphery*. He is also co-editor, with R. K. Ramazani, of *The Future of Liberal Democracy: Thomas Jefferson and the Contemporary World*; and *Religion, State, and Society*.

Scott Freeman, an environmental anthropologist, focuses on environmental development initiatives in both Haiti and the Dominican Republic. He is currently a professorial lecturer at the School of International Service at American University, and he recently completed his PhD at Columbia University. His work has appeared in *Anthropology News* and the *International Encyclopedia of the Social & Behavioral Sciences*. He is writing a book on the intersection of the development "project" and soil conservation and agricultural practices in Haiti.

Nicholas Johnson is an undergraduate student in the Elliott School of International Affairs at George Washington University, where he studies international development and economics. He has worked for the Focus On Haiti Initiative at the Elliott School since 2013, where he coordinated the symposium "Who 'Owns' Haiti? Sovereignty in a Fragile State: 2004–2014" in 2014 and the symposium "Voices of Haiti's Voiceless: Post-Earthquake Aspirations & Achievements" in 2015. He received undergraduate research fellowship awards from the Elliott School in 2014 and 2015 to study rural development strategies in Marmelade, Haiti, and the role of information communication technologies in international development.

Chelsey Kivland, a cultural anthropologist, focuses on street politics, everyday insecurity, and social performance in contemporary urban Haiti. A recent PhD from the University of Chicago, she is assistant professor in the Department of Anthropology at Dartmouth College. She has published articles in *Cultural Anthropology, PoLAR: Political and Legal Anthropology Review*, and *Journal of Haitian Studies*. She is preparing a book titled *Street Sovereigns: Young Men in Search of the State in Urban Haiti*, which traces how local forms of governance interact with a range of state and NGO actors and the conflicts those interactions produce.

Robert Maguire is professor of international development studies and former director of the Latin American and Hemispheric Studies Program at the Elliott School of International Affairs at George Washington University. He has worked for years on issues of bottom-up development in post-plantation societies in the Americas, including Louisiana, where he conducted PhD research, and in Haiti and the English-speaking Caribbean. He is recognized as a leading U.S. expert on Haiti, having been engaged with that country since 1974. His book *Bottom-Up Development in Haiti* was published in 1981 and has been translated into both Spanish and Creole. He is currently focused on issues of U.S.-Haiti policy, politics, post-disaster development, and effective poverty alleviation.

Francois Pierre-Louis Jr. is associate professor of political science at Queens College, CUNY. His research interests include immigration, transnationalism, and Haitian and Caribbean politics. He served in the private cabinet of President Jean-Bertrand Aristide in 1991 and on the senior staff of Prime Minister Jacques-Édouard Alexis in 2007–2008. He is the author of *Haitians in New York*

City: Transnationalism and Hometown Association. His articles have appeared in *US Catholic, Wadabagei,* the *Journal of Haitian Studies, Education and Urban Society,* and the *Journal of Black Studies.* He served as a senior advisor for the Haiti-CUNY Program to the chancellor of the City University of New York from 2011 to 2015.

Karen Richman is a cultural anthropologist whose research focuses on the intersections of migration and religion. She is the author of *Migration and Vodou* and numerous articles and book chapters on Haitian and Mexican transnational societies. Her article "Innocent Imitations? Mimesis and Alterity in Haitian Vodou Art" won the Robert F. Heizer Award in 2009 for the best article in ethnohistory. She is the director of undergraduate studies in the Institute for Latino Studies, concurrent faculty in Anthropology and Romance Languages and Literatures, and a fellow of the Kellogg Institute for International Studies and of the Eck Institute for Global Health at University of Notre Dame.

Ricardo Seitenfus is the former special representative of the OAS in Haiti and is a professor at Universidade Federal de Santa Maria, Brazil. He has written eleven books and numerous articles and chapters on international relations and Brazil in the international community. He holds a PhD in international relations from the University of Geneva. His most recent book is *L'échec de l'aide internationale à Haïti: Dilemmes et égarements.*

Amy Wilentz is the author of *Farewell, Fred Voodoo: A Letter from Haiti; The Rainy Season: Haiti since Duvalier; Martyrs' Crossing;* and *I Feel Earthquakes More Often Than They Happen: Coming to California in the Age of Schwarzenegger.* She is the winner of the Whiting Award, the PEN/Martha Albrand Award for First Nonfiction, and the American Academy of Arts and Letters Rosenthal Foundation Award. In 2014, she won the National Book Critics Circle Award for *Farewell, Fred Voodoo.* Wilentz is a longtime contributing editor at *The Nation* and has written for the *New York Times,* the *Los Angeles Times, The Huffington Post,* and many other publications. She teaches in the literary journalism program at the University of California, Irvine.

Index

Page numbers in *italics* refer to figures (*f*) and tables (*t*).

Lightning Source UK Ltd.
Milton Keynes UK
UKHW04f1437080818
326950UK00001B/88/P